REALIZING OUR INTENTIONS

REALIZING OUR INTENTIONS

A Guide for Churches and Colleges with Distinctive Missions

ALBERT J. MEYER

Abilene Christian University Press
Abilene, Texas

REALIZING OUR INTENTIONS

A Guide for Churches and Colleges with Distinctive Missions

ACU
PRESS

LIBRARY OF CONGRESS CATALOGING-IN-PUBLICATION DATA
Meyer, Albert J., 1929-
 Realizing our intentions : a guide for churches and colleges with distinctive missions / Albert J.
Meyer.
     p. cm.
 Includes bibliographical references.
 ISBN 978-0-89112-537-2 (trade) -- ISBN 978-0-89112-539-6 (paper-over-board)
 1. Church and college--United States. 2. Church colleges--United States--Administration. I. Title.
LC383.M46 2009
070.92--dc22
 [B]
                                        2009034959

Cover design by Rick Gibson
Interior text design by Sandy Armstrong

For information contact:
Abilene Christian University Press
1626 Campus Court
Abilene, Texas 79699-9138

1-877-816-4455 toll free
www.abilenechristianuniversitypress.com

09 10 11 12 13 14 / 7 6 5 4 3 2 1

CONTENTS

Acknowledgments 7

Introduction... 9

PART I: THE LARGER SCENE

1   Longer-Term Trends 17

2   Recent Developments... 27

3   Secularization 35

4   Organizational Dynamics.. 47

5   Generalizations from Experience...................................... 57

6   The Recent Past and the Present Situation 65

PART II: WHO MIGHT WANT SCHOOLS THAT ARE DIFFERENT?

7   Curriculum: A Different "What" 83

8   Instruction: A Different "How" 97

9   Why Might Some Churches Want Schools That Are Different? 103

10 Intentional "Secularization"...117

PART III: CURRENT ISSUES

11 Diversity, Pluralism, and Community 125

12 Academic Freedom 141

PART IV: HEALTHY LONG-TERM CHURCH-SCHOOL RELATIONSHIPS

13 Faculty Teams for Distinctive Missions...........................149

14 A Student Peer Environment That Furthers the Mission....................173

15 Missions That Guide Decision-Making...........................185

16 Trustees That Hold in Trust the Long-Term Future 201

17 Presidents Who Implement the Long-Term Mission 233

18 Churches That Want Schools with a Difference 243

19 Intervening in the System...269

Epilogue: What Are the Prospects? 279

References 281

ACKNOWLEDGMENTS

For stimulating conversations on colleges and universities with distinctive missions, I have been indebted over the years to my co-workers on the staff and the board of the Mennonite Board of Education—especially Donald Kraybill, Daniel Hertzler, Wilbert Shank, Elvin Kraybill, Betty Livengood, Orville Yoder, Loren Swartzendruber, Alice Roth, Donald Garber, Timothy Burkholder, and Thomas Stuckey. Board and faculty members at Bethel College in Kansas, where I began to reflect on some of the issues discussed in this book in my first years in academic administration, have warmly welcomed me back to the campus for conversations on the issues on many occasions since.

Ernest L. Boyer, at that time president of the Carnegie Foundation for the Advancement of Teaching, and Robert Wuthnow, director of Princeton University's Center for the Study of American Religion, invited me in the mid-1990s to spend over a year with a stimulating seminar circle of friends in Princeton. I acknowledge my indebtedness to David Riesman of Harvard for a conversation with him in Massachusetts on his work and an early draft of this book and his encouragement in the work on the present project. I am indebted to my brother, John W. Meyer, who, with Brian Rowan, wrote the seminal work in neo-institutional theory in 1977 and who was, at the time of my sabbatical in the 1980s in Berkeley, chair of sociology at Stanford University. Sociologists John Schmalzbauer and Patricia Wittberg have also read drafts and given very helpful suggestions. Richard Hughes and associates of the circle of denominational Executives for Church-Related Higher Education have been long-time friends and colleagues.

For help in editing the manuscript, I am grateful to Leonard Allen and Heidi Nobles of the Abilene Christian University Press, and to Ervin Beck and Anne Meyer Byler.

Our five children and their good spouses, all of whom have had undergraduate and graduate educational experiences, have contributed to lively discussions in the family. I am indebted most of all to my wife, Mary Ellen, whose love and encouragement have been unwavering.

Introduction

In 1835, Alexis de Tocqueville chronicled the contributions to American public life made by many different kinds of churches and voluntary associations. Since then, many observers have seen the diversity of colleges and universities on the American scene as one of their strengths. Private church-related and non-church-related institutions and public colleges and universities have all made important contributions to American higher education and to American life. Strong independent institutions started new educational programs before the public was ready to support them. Public institutions had governmental resources not available to private institutions for meeting some societal needs—they contributed, for example, to innovative farming practices with needed agricultural experimental and extension programs.

Historically, most American colleges and universities were private institutions started by churches that represented different points of view. But today more than seven out of eight American students are attending colleges and universities with no church relationships. Churches are much less involved in American higher education today than they were earlier. In commenting on developments in church sponsorship of higher education in his précis for a conference on "The Future of Religious Colleges" held at Harvard University on October 6–7, 2000, Paul Dovre said:

> . . . Religiously affiliated colleges and universities experienced significant change during the second half of this century. These changes are exemplified by the laicization of governance in Roman Catholic institutions, the benign neglect of Presbyterian sponsorship and the diminution of financial support on the part of Lutheran church bodies. And in their new found circumstances most church related colleges became more religiously diverse in the composition of their faculty, staff and student body and more secular in character and content.[1]

In recent decades, private institutions have become more like public ones, and public ones have increasingly sought support from non-governmental sources and become more like private ones. There are also considerably fewer women's colleges, all-male colleges, and African American colleges.[2] While the population of students in individual colleges is increasingly diverse, the population ecology of educational institutions—to borrow a term from the biologists—is generally characterized by decreasing diversity.[3] Wade Cole of Stanford documents the "increasing 'isomorphism' or ritualized homogeneity of formal curricula at all levels of schooling . . . ."[4] Institutions are becoming more alike.

Forty years ago, Warren Bryan Martin of Berkeley started to write a book on diversity in American higher education. He surveyed the field and consulted widely. When he finished, he found that he could not really title his Jossey-Bass book *Diversity*. Instead, he called it *Conformity*.[5]

North Americans are facing major public policy challenges. The financial crisis includes a gap between rich and poor. Some jobs and whole industries have been moving to overseas locations. Homelessness and senseless crime are evident in a wealthy nation. Some national leaders and other observers claim that a self-centered individualism has contributed to stresses in family and community life. Various religious and political groups propose different ways of dealing with these problems. Important questions must be explored: What is the role of government in addressing pressing social problems? The private sector? How much diversity should be encouraged and how much can be sustained as the American society seeks innovative solutions? On questions like these, colleges and universities with distinctive missions have important contributions to make to American higher education and American life, and they should not compromise the elements that make their contributions special and needed.

Although most non-public colleges and universities in the past were church institutions, other subgroups within the larger American society have also established higher education institutions. Muslim and Far Eastern religious groups, which currently have a few institutions, have become more significant in recent decades. Most of the examples in this book will come from the church sector, the largest sector for which we can study historical trends, but certain dynamics are characteristic of institutions with special missions generally, whether or not they are church-related. Some of the proposals for change made here can be useful for rabbinical schools, Muslim, African American, and women's colleges. Some of the suggestions on faculty team development and board functioning can also help schools whose sole goal is traditional academic excellence.

In citing cases, especially of situations in which the actors might, in hindsight, have wanted to act differently, I have tried to preserve the anonymity of the schools or groups in question. To do so, I have changed some details. And for brevity, in some instances, I have combined the features of several similar cases and presented them as a single case. The goal is not to embarrass or draw attention to individual colleges or constituents. Instead, I want to focus on repeated patterns and systemic behaviors that need examination and possible change.[6]

The liberal arts college and the research university are well-established institutions of the American society. Sustaining distinctive colleges that do not, over the long term, want to join what David Riesman has called the "snake-like procession"[7] following Harvard is not easy. It requires an understanding of the forces acting upon institutions and of the ways institutions work, an understanding that many American churches have not readily apprehended in the past. Colleges follow prevailing institutional patterns not only because of the putative self-interest of their faculties. Students, parents, donors, and other societal constituents all have understandings and expectations, and an attempt to have a college that is different has to involve the understandings and expectations of many or all of these groups.

Colleges and universities do not need to be the unwilling victims of external forces that push them toward conformity. With adequate information and commitment, they can break from the ways of their institutional peers. Leading colleges and universities that are different is not easy, but higher education institutions can be different if they face realistically the forces that push toward conformity.

The focus in what follows is not on schools that have distanced themselves from their founders (or on groups that have distanced themselves from the schools they have founded) in cases where eventual distancing was the intent of the schools and the founding groups from the outset. The focus is on understanding the dynamics of unintended distancing and dissociation, and then on asking how schools and groups that want to stay together and collaborate in achieving distinctive missions can realize their intentions.

An extensive literature deals with the way schools have distanced themselves from their founders. My conclusions also come from personal consultative visits and visits for the North Central Association Committee on Liberal Arts Education to sixty or seventy colleges and universities over several decades. After several years in study and work abroad and in college academic administration, I was, for twenty-eight years, able to observe and gain experience as chief executive for the Mennonite Board of Education, the body responsible for appointing and orienting institutional board members and providing denominational board oversight for Mennonite Church colleges and universities. Prior to a sabbatical leave for organizational theory studies at Berkeley,[8] I served for two years as chair of the Executives for Church-Related Higher Education, the group of denominational leaders working with most of the Catholic and Protestant church-related colleges and universities in the United States, and I continue to represent the Mennonite Church USA in that group.

This study seeks to go beyond the available histories and other resources and give very practical proposals for those who would like to develop or maintain healthy church-school relationships in the future.

This book is written from a "post-Establishment" perspective. The days of the white Anglo-Saxon Protestant establishment and hegemony are over. We need to remember that African Americans and women were not allowed to vote in the early days of this country. Roman Catholics and Jews and members of many other groups were seen as marginal and unqualified for many leadership positions in the American society. The United States was 185 years old before it elected its first Catholic president. Only in the year 2000 did the United States nominate its first Jew to the vice-presidency. Its first African American was elected to the presidency in 2008. Partly under the influence of some church groups themselves,the larger American society has moved from an assumption of white, Anglo-Saxon, Protestant, male dominance and establishment to a widely held conviction that we are living in a pluralistic society and that discrimination on racial, gender, and religious grounds is unacceptable.[9]

I identify with the descendents of what some historians have called the first Free Churches of modern times, the sixteenth-century Anabaptists, who said that people should be counted as church members when they are able to make free commitments of their own (rather than to be counted without their consent when they are born into given geographical regions). They said that churches that invoke the name of Jesus Christ should begin by modeling Christlike corporate and individual behaviors rather than using the power of the state to try to force other people to behave the way the churches want them to behave.[10] The subtitle of this book might have been, "Church-College Relations in a Post-Establishment Era."

These observations are relevant, not only for the "what" and "how" of pedagogy, but also for an understanding of relationships between churches and schools. Years ago, establishment churches could assume that their religious perspectives would be included in public school curricula. These churches did not need schools of their own with distinctive religious missions. The religious missions they favored were supported by the larger society through the state. Whether some churches and other societal sub-groups now want to sponsor schools with special missions will depend on whether the mandating subgroups have special missions they want to carry out in school settings with interested young people and future leaders, missions that will not otherwise be carried out by the state.

In summary, this book says:

1. Over the years, colleges and universities have been becoming more alike. In particular, some churches are giving lower priority to higher education. We observe a drift toward a "secularized conformity."
2. Colleges and universities with distinctive missions can and should make a special contribution to American higher education.
3. Specific policies and practices can enable groups and educational institutions with special missions to make the contributions they want to make in the longer-term future.

In approaching books with specific proposals, some readers turn first to the last chapters. Readers of this book who want to begin with specific steps that boards, faculties, and churches can implement should turn immediately to Part IV. Part I is written to help board members, busy administrators, and friends of higher education who ordinarily do not have time to follow the regular issues of *The Chronicle of Higher Education*, *Change*, *The Journal of Higher Education*, and similar journals to understand and reflect on contemporary educational and societal trends that bear on the prospects for distinctive church institutions and the need for future initiatives. Part II discusses reasons some groups want schools that are different. And Part III deals with current issues that interested stakeholders need to address as they implement the changes and actions outlined in Part IV.

Introduction Endnotes

1   Paul J. Dovre, Program on Education Policy and Governance, J. F. Kennedy School of Government, Harvard University, 79 J. F. Kennedy Street, Taubman 308, Cambridge, MA 02138. Dovre is president emeritus of Concordia College. Dovre adds that "this [religiously-affiliated] group of colleges has demonstrated remarkable resilience and constitutes a small but dynamic sector in the mosaic of American higher education."

2   There were about three hundred women's colleges in 1960; there were seventy-three in 2001, and about fifty in 2009. (Private communications, Jadwiga Sebrechts, president, Women's College Coalition, March 29, 2001, and Susan E. Lennon, executive director, Women's College Coalition, March 17, 2009, and *The Chronicle of Higher Education*, March 25, 2005.)

    There were almost 250 all-male colleges in the mid-1960s; four remain. (Peter Applebome, "The Final Four," Education Life Supplement, *The New York Times*, April 23, 2006).

3   Raymond F. Zammuto, "Are the Liberal Arts an Endangered Species?" *Journal of Higher Education* 2 (1984): 184–211. Ecologists have for years emphasized the importance of biological diversity. The Nature Conservancy, a large nonprofit organization, says it is "dedicated to preserving the diversity of life on Earth."

4   Wade M. Cole, "Accrediting Culture: An Analysis of Tribal and Historically Black College Curricula," *Sociology of Education* 79, no. 4 (2006): 355–88.

5   Warren Bryan Martin, *Conformity: Standards and Change in Higher Education*, ed. Joseph Axelrod and Mervin B. Freedman, The Jossey-Bass Series in Higher Education (San Francisco: Jossey-Bass, 1969).

6   When I have mentioned some cases in oral presentations, listeners have thought they could identify the institutions in question, and then we discovered that they were thinking of institutions half a continent from the ones to which I was referring. This book is about some widely-observed practices and patterns in American colleges and universities.

7   David Riesman, "The Academic Procession," in Riesman, *Constraint and Variety in American Education* (Lincoln: University of Nebraska Press, 1956), 25–65.

8   The seminal work in the neo-institutional theory of organizations referred to earlier was done in the Bay Area. (John W. Meyer and Brian Rowan, "Institutionalized Organizations: Formal Structure as Myth and Ceremony," *American Journal of Sociology* 2 [1977]: 340–63.)

9   Many countries still have state churches. England and Norway do, and Sweden did until 2000.

10 See the references to the works of historians George H. Williams of Harvard and Roland H. Bainton of Yale in Donald F. Durnbaugh, *The Believers' Church: The History and Character of Radical Protestantism* (New York: Macmillan, 1968). Durnbaugh notes that Max Weber coined the term "Believers' Church" to refer to the Free Church concept in *The Protestant Ethic and the Spirit of Capitalism*, trans. T. Parsons (New York: Charles Scribner's Sons, 1958).

PART I

---⊗⊗⊗---

THE LARGER SCENE

1

LONGER-TERM TRENDS

Chapters 1 and 2 of Part I deal with significant trends in higher education and the larger society and the environments within which private
schools and churches live and work today. Chapters 3 and 4 examine basic
concepts important for understanding the relationships and dynamics of
change between schools and their mandating societies. Chapter 5 reviews
learnings from past experience. Chapter 6 lists challenges and opportunities
that churches and colleges face at this time and sets the stage for the specific
actions proposed in Part IV.

Expansion and Change

Enrollments at American colleges and universities have increased dramati-
cally in the past century, and especially following World War II. Only two
percent of American eighteen- to twenty-four-year-olds were in higher education institutions a century ago. By the end of the past century, that two
percent had increased to fifty-eight percent.[1] Skill expectations for jobs have
risen, and enrollments in higher education have increased.

The growth in the United States is actually a part of a worldwide expansion in higher education enrollments. For years, America was a world leader
in the proportion of its adult population with college degrees; but now a
larger proportion of twenty-five- to thirty-four-year-olds in eight other
countries have graduated from college. Participation in higher education has
been growing at high rates in virtually every country in the world.[2]

A shift in the center of gravity from the church sector to the public sector accompanied the expansion of American higher education in the past century. At one time, all of the colleges and universities in America were private institutions founded by churches. (Indeed, centuries earlier, the first universities of the whole Western world were founded by churches and church leaders in Europe.) By the end of the last century, fewer than one-fourth of the higher education institutions in America had a church relationship of any kind, and fewer than one-eighth of the college and university students in America were attending church-affiliated institutions.[3] Many American church schools have been closed, especially in the last century. Others have become independent or public institutions.[4]

Academically, a century ago, no land grant colleges or other state institutions were in a league with Harvard and other leading private institutions. The emergence of Berkeleys and Michigans with reputational rankings among the best institutions in the United States is a relatively recent phenomenon.

Richard Hofstadter has said that a "drift toward secularism" is "the oldest and the longest sustained" of the themes that command the attention of the historian of American higher education.[5] A few years ago a religion columnist of the *New York Times* wrote, "The steady secularization of American higher education over the last hundred years has often been viewed as a virtually irresistible trend."[6] Overall, it is a story of dissociation, of increasing distance between higher education institutions and the churches that gave them birth and early sustenance.

End of an Age

Not only the schools have changed; the larger society has also changed.

Episcopalian Loren Mead[7] says that the church has existed in two eras in the past two millennia: the Apostolic Age of the first three centuries, and the Age of Christendom, which began when the new faith became the official faith of the Roman Empire and which has continued until recently. Mead's essential message is that the age of Christendom is now "breaking apart."[8] Some dissident groups challenged the Age of Christendom before and during the Reformation 480 years ago. The Anabaptists, the so-called Radical Reformers of the Reformation, and the Quakers and other Free Church reformers of more recent centuries challenged the established churches of their times. Now, almost seventeen centuries after Constantine, it is evident that the Age of Christendom is coming to an end—"breaking apart," as Loren Mead puts it.

What was Christendom? What is coming to an end? Christendom was that era, since the time of the Roman Emperor Constantine in the Fourth Century, when a great part of the Christian church allied itself with governments and, more generally, with the cultural establishments the governments represented. Churches used state forces to keep whole populations in line.

The consequences of the end of Christendom for changes in higher education in the past century have been dramatic. Many state universities were religious and, indeed, explicitly Protestant until only relatively recently. Almost all of the major state universities had chapel services at the beginning of the past century, and attendance was required of all students in about half of them.[9] "In the 1920s [Colorado] . . . government officials directed . . . George Norlin [the University of Colorado president] to fire all Catholic and Jewish faculty."[10] George Marsden, formerly of Duke and currently historian at the University of Notre Dame, says that "American universities . . . were defined in the late nineteenth century as part of an effort to build a unified culture that would support an advanced capitalist economy."[11]

In the Christendom era, many American Protestant leaders assumed that they could count on the Christian larger society to provide for the Christian education of oncoming generations. But now many American Christian leaders are joining with the heirs of those who objected to the Christendom church-state establishment of earlier times. They say that churches today should be communities of commitment, that people should have freedom to make authentic decisions about joining or not joining such communities, and that it is wrong for Christian subgroups to use the power of the state to try to enforce Christian worship and Christian behaviors on others. Although the changes in our time certainly have some unfortunate concomitants and pose new challenges, some leaders join Loren Mead in welcoming the end of the age of Christendom. They want schools of their own to educate students interested in their vision in today's world.

"Societal Religion"

Partly under the influence of some church groups, American society has moved in recent decades from an acceptance of white, Anglo-Saxon, male dominance to a widely held foundational—and almost religious—conviction that discrimination on racial and gender grounds is unacceptable. Problems remain, but by now many kinds of overt discrimination have been outlawed by the U.S. Supreme Court and the U.S. system of justice. On the global scene, international bodies have adopted human rights expectations for countries that want to be a part of the world community of nations.

Oberlin College was originally an institution of what is now the United Church of Christ. It pioneered in the education of women and minority students—ahead of its time, it was coeducational and admitted African Americans on an equal footing with whites. It became a station on the Underground Railroad by which slaves could escape to freedom in Canada. Oberlin was a distinctive church-related school founded in a time when African Americans and women could not be voting citizens. Now African Americans and women can vote.

As some church-affiliated colleges and universities have become more like other institutions of the larger society, the larger society has also changed—it has adopted some values and expectations formerly seen as religiously based. In the new social context, some churches continue to see themselves as countercultural, holding beliefs and practices that are not widely held in the larger society." (This will be discussed in Part II.) But some churches that saw themselves as prophetic at one time now find that their ideas are widely accepted. The society has adopted some of their values as a part of its "civil religion." These churches can now retire with honor from the educational scene. Their old missions have been accomplished. They now no longer need schools of their own to test and communicate their values. Public institutions have adopted these values and can carry the freight.

But some churches and colleges continue to object to components of the "civil religion" of the American society at large. Americans say they want people to be free to be themselves. But for many this freedom has meant an expressive individualism in which they want to be free to do whatever they want to do whenever they want to do it. In this situation, some of the rich have used their freedom to get richer, and the gap between the haves and the have-nots has increased. Parents have been told they should be free to be themselves, but this "freedom" has sometimes been bad for their children. Internationally, we have said ethnic groups should be free, but then we have not known what to say when small tribes around the world have wanted to split themselves into tiny nations that are hardly viable, and many larger ones want to have equal opportunity to have nuclear bombs in order to maintain their independence and enhance their roles in the world.

Churches and church schools, in particular, need to ask about their missions in a new context, in the face of new challenges. Some will say "mission accomplished," find that they no longer want to have church schools, and turn to other tasks. Others will want to focus their missions even more sharply as they distinguish themselves from some aspects of the societal religion of the cultures in which they find themselves.

Professionalization of the Faculty

The professionalization of the faculty by discipline is probably the most significant change in North American higher education in the past century. It is the so-called "Academic Revolution" described in the 1968 classic with this title by Christopher Jencks and David Riesman of Harvard.[12]

One hundred fifty years ago, a leading Ivy League university would have had a "professor of natural philosophy"—a professor who studied the world of nature. Now there are instead professors of anatomy, physiology, botany, molecular biology, zoology, astronomy, physics, chemistry, and various kinds of engineering—representing perhaps more than twenty different fields in the natural sciences and engineering alone, each with its own professional associations, journals, and bureaucracies.

A small college I visited recently had only two programs a hundred years ago. All of the courses in each program were required. A student could choose one of the two programs, but that was the extent of the student's choice. There were no electives. In more recent times, a student at that college could choose among forty-seven majors and electives in twenty-four departments.

The quality and depth of studies in many fields have been enormously enhanced through the professionalization of academics in specialized fields of research and scholarship. But with this "revolution" came also the dominance of the research mission over the university's teaching mission and a fragmentation of the undergraduate curriculum. A major study of the undergraduate curriculum in 1977 by a Carnegie task force said that general education in American colleges and universities had become "a disaster area."[13] A 1998 Carnegie report on research universities by an eleven-member panel of educators confirmed the earlier charges.[14] The chair of the panel said, "For 30 years, universities have been saying that we've got to fix the problem of undergraduate education, and we have done a lot of interesting things. But the core has not changed."[15]

Three years later, Carnegie's Boyer Commission issued a follow up report and said that research universities had made "considerable headway" in implementing some of the 1998 recommendations.[16] With greater public awareness of the problem, several elite research universities are starting to try to give higher priority to undergraduate liberal arts education.[17]

Some church educators in liberal arts colleges believe that they can make a needed and special contribution in general education. But many faculty members who once would have seen themselves as members of interdisciplinary teams participating in institutional missions, expressed especially in general education programs, have come to identify themselves more as loyal campus representatives of their respective disciplines. With these developments, emphasizing distinctive institutional missions in liberal arts education has become a greater challenge.

Differing Church Perspectives on Dissociation

Church people have differed in their thinking on what they should be planning to do in higher education in the foreseeable future. In part, their differences have been rooted in basic differences in their understandings of the role of the church in the larger society. Those who in the past have had an Establishment Church vision of church membership as being essentially coextensive with that of the civic community, and who have felt that their views were not very different from those widely held in the larger society, have been more ready to see governments carrying the main responsibility for the education of the next generation of citizens and church members. Those with a more countercultural vision of the Christian community in the larger society have thought that they should have institutions where they could explore and test their distinctive understandings and vision with interested young people and future leaders.[18]

Churches with more distinctive beliefs and practices have found it easier to gain support from their members for church-related programs in higher education. Those churches whose understandings have been more similar to those of the larger society have understandably found it harder to call their members to support independent church-related ventures in education.

Robert Sandin's study of church-related colleges and universities in the years 1980 to 1991 showed that average enrollments at baccalaureate colleges and comprehensive universities that were more distinctively religious grew more rapidly (over twenty-four percent) than did those at mainline denominational institutions that were "nominally church-related" (ten percent) or "independent institutions with historic religious ties (three percent)."[19]

From 1990 to 1999, undergraduate enrollments increased four percent at public institutions, seventeen percent at all private institutions, seventeen percent at institutions with religious affiliations, and forty-two percent at the U.S. member institutions in the Council for Christian Colleges & Universities.[20] Enrollments increased more rapidly at private institutions that had distinctive religious identities than at those whose religious identities were less distinctive.

We have, then, two phenomena occurring simultaneously: a general drift among most institutions in the direction of a secularized conformity, as Hofstadter has identified it; and greater enrollment increases among institutions with more distinctive religious missions. Both of these phenomena are occurring at the same time through what population ecologists call "resource partitioning." When newspapers become more alike on a national scale, niches open up for more distinctive local weeklies and dailies. In the same way, as American colleges and universities become more alike on a national scale, a greater niche opens up for schools with distinctive missions.

Chapter 1 Endnotes

1   *Digest of Education Statistics 1998*, National Center for Education Statistics, U.S. Department of Education, and *The Chronicle of Higher Education,* August 27, 1999.

2   "In 1900, only about 500,000 students were enrolled in higher education institutions worldwide, representing a tiny fraction of one percent of college-age people. . . . By 2000, the number of tertiary students had grown to approximately one hundred million people, a number that represents about 20 percent of the relevant age cohort worldwide. . . . The bulk of the growth occurred after 1960, in just the last four decades." (Evan Schofer and John W. Meyer, "The Worldwide Expansion of Higher Education in the Twentieth Century," sixty-two-page unpublished manuscript, Stanford University, January 18, 2005. The data cited are from A. S. Banks, "Cross-national time-series data archive" [Binghamton, NY: Computer Systems Unlimited, 2001], and "UNESCO Online Database" [UNESCO Institute for Statistics Online Publication, 2004].) The data on college graduates are from "Education at a Glance 2008: OECD Indicators" (Paris: Organisation for Economic Co-operation and Development, September 2008).

3   A project database was prepared in 1996 by Donald Garber of the Mennonite Board of Education and the author from National Center for Education Statistics institutional survey returns. The data were corrected using information from contacts with denominational offices and, in some instances, reports from institutions. For a recent report, see Robert C. Andringa, "900 Religiously Affiliated and Accredited Institutions of Postsecondary Education in the USA," Council for Christian Colleges & Universities, December 6, 2004.

4   Of over 830 different institutions founded by Methodists alone in the United States, most were closed in the nineteenth century, and only 122 with a formal relationship with the United Methodist Church remain. (Private communication, May 20, 2009, Wanda Bigham, Board of Higher Education and Ministry, United Methodist Church, Nashville, TN.) "Fewer than one-third of the 174 Catholic colleges survive that were started in the first century [of the American experience]. . . ." (Philip Gleason, as reported by Gene Stowe in "Catholic Education Topic of Talk: Speaker Describes Changes That Led to New Obstacles," *South Bend Tribune*, sec. Nation, September 30, 2005.)

5   Richard Hofstadter, "The Development of Higher Education in America," in *The Development and Scope of Higher Education in the United States*, ed. Richard Hofstadter and C. DeWitt Hardy (New York: Columbia University Press, 1952), 3. In a review article in the *New York Times Book Review*, James M. McPherson, Princeton historian, has said, "By anyone's ranking, [C. Vann] Woodward and [Richard] Hofstadter are the two leading American historians of the second half of the 20th century" (September 19, 1999): 35.

6   Peter Steinfels, "Beliefs: Catholic Bishops and Educators Near Another Round over Effort to Resist Secularization," *New York Times,* October 16, 1999. The phenomenon is discussed in all of the histories of American higher education. Among works that have focused on the trends are George M. Marsden and Bradley Longfield, eds. *The Secularization of the Academy* (New York: Oxford University Press, 1992); George M. Marsden, *The Soul of the American University: From Protestant Establishment to Established Nonbelief* (New York: Oxford University Press, 1994); James Tunstead Burtchaell, "The Alienation of Christian Higher Education in American: Diagnosis

and Prognosis," in *Schooling Christians: "Holy Experiments" in American Education*, ed. Stanley Hauerwas and John H. Westerhoff (Grand Rapids: Wm. B. Eerdmans, 1992), 129–83; and James Tunstead Burtchaell, *The Dying of the Light: The Disengagement of Colleges and Universities from Their Christian Churches* (Grand Rapids: Wm. B. Eerdmans, 1998). See also Patricia Wittberg, *From Piety to Professionalism—And Back? Transformations of Organized Religious Virtuosity* (Lanham, MD: Lexington Books, 2006).

7   Loren Mead founded the Alban Institute, the most respected church consultation service on this continent. After twenty-plus years of leadership of the Institute, he retired and has published a distillation of his learning of a lifetime in *The Once and Future Church* and subsequent Alban works.

8   Loren B. Mead, *The Once and Future Church* (New York: The Alban Institute, 1991), 12.

9   Marsden and Longfield, eds. *The Secularization of the Academy*, 46-55.

10 Robert M. O'Neil, "The Ward Churchill Case," *Change: The Magazine of Higher Learning* 38, no.5 (2006): 37.

11 Unpublished paper for Baylor University Sesquicentennial Symposium, October 1995.

12 Christopher Jencks and David Riesman, *The Academic Revolution* (Garden City, NY: Doubleday, 1968).

13 Carnegie Foundation for the Advancement of Teaching, *Missions of the College Curriculum: A Contemporary Review with Suggestions* (San Francisco: Jossey-Bass, Inc., 1977). One editorial writer picked up the theme with this question: "What are we to make of today's jumble of bizarre courses that, without a core of fundamentals, can add up to an intellectual junk heap?" (Marvin Stone, "Common Sense in College," *U.S. News and World Report*, January 23, 1978, 84).

14 Boyer Commission on Educating Undergraduates in the Research University, "Reinventing Undergraduate Education: A Blueprint for America's Research Universities" (Carnegie Foundation for the Advancement of Teaching, 1998).

15 Robin Wilson, "Report Blasts Research Universities for Poor Teaching of Undergraduates," *The Chronicle of Higher Education*, April 24, 1998.

16 "Reinventing Undergraduate Education: Three Years after the Boyer Report," *Greater Expectations: A New Vision for Learning as a Nation Goes to College* (Washington, DC: Association of American Colleges, 2002).

17 Reforming Harvard's general education program was one of Lawrence Summers' top priorities when he assumed the Harvard presidency in 2001. In early 2006 he resigned. In a 2006 book, Derek Bok, former president of Harvard, speaks of professors' "casual treatment" of the purposes of undergraduate education (*Our Underachieving Colleges: A Candid Look at How Much Students Learn and Why They Should Be Learning More* [Princeton, NJ: Princeton University Press]). The Harvard faculty adopted a new general education curriculum in May 2007.

18 Marsden picks up this point in his review essay, saying that the crucial elements of the stories have to do with "how [a given] tradition sees itself as standing against the mainstream as part of its primary identity" (*Christian Scholars Review* 29, no. 1 [1999]).

19 The relatively small number of religiously-unaffiliated *two-year* colleges grew much faster (fifty-five percent) than did their religiously-affiliated counterparts (twenty percent). Overall, religiously-affiliated colleges and universities of all kinds grew faster (average of twelve percent) than did unaffiliated colleges and universities (eight percent) in those years. (Robert T. Sandin, *HEPS Profiles of Independent Higher Education* 2, no. 3 [1992–93], 1–18.) Offices of the Higher Education Planning Services are at 28900 Forest Lake Lane, Green Oaks, Illinois 60048. Sandin is former provost of Mercer University and author of works on independent higher education.

20 Robert C. Andringa, "The State of Christian Higher Education: Thriving" (Washington, DC: Council for Christian Colleges & Universities, 2003).

2

RECENT DEVELOPMENTS

At the beginning of the 1990s, the American public was not sure about the degree to which higher education could provide answers to current social problems. On the one hand, people sensed that much of what happens in colleges and universities is not relevant to societal needs. On the other hand, people believed that education is crucial for American economic competitiveness in providing for a competent work force.

In 2009, college graduates found themselves in the worst job market in many years. Prospective students found that a college degree is not an automatic ticket to a good job, but they also found that, in a job search, the value of a college degree was never greater.

One consequence of the recent public ambivalence about colleges and universities has been a new demand for "accountability" by educational institutions, reflected in a new interest in public audits of learning-related indicators that go beyond reputational rankings or the traditional confidential accreditation reports on institutional resources.[1]

Greater Public Interest

In the late 1990s, both of the leading American political parties were engaged in a bidding war to see who would do the most for education. Before 9/11, support was increasing. Since 9/11, public interest in higher education has continued, but budget deficits in many states and the worldwide financial crisis have created budget problems for both public and private institutions.

Accreditation used to be a voluntary system whereby colleges and universities would work together for self-improvement. Now, it is increasingly being seen by the federal government as a process through which the government decides which institutions' students are eligible for federal student aid.

In 2009, President Obama made education one of the three priorities of his administration, and he indicated interest in the private, as well as the public, sector.

Less Diversity in Funding

Public and many private institutions have become more alike in their funding sources. In the past, most independently raised dollars went to independent colleges and universities. Now public universities have enormously increased their contributions from private sources.[2] Katherine Lyall writes of a "privatization of public colleges and universities."[3] In their turn, private institutions have become increasingly dependent on attracting students who receive governmental student aid—and, sometimes, dependent on government funds available for the institutions themselves. Private colleges with distinctive missions are therefore finding themselves competing with public institutions for funds.

Uncertain Legal Environment

In America in the past three decades, the constitutional basis for the civil rights of individuals has been developed without a commensurate development of the constitutional rights of voluntary associations, including churches and church-related institutions.[4] Some faculty prospects have argued that they have a right to teach in any college or university for which they have the formal qualifications for teaching in their respective disciplines. Less attention has been given to the question of whether a church or other private association has a right to have a school with teachers committed to the school's distinctive mission.[5]

In its earliest usage in medieval European universities, "academic freedom" referred to the freedom of the university as a university from outside interference. Today it has come to be used almost exclusively to refer to the freedom of individual faculty members vis-à-vis that of the university.

In a paper on American constitutional democracy, Yale philosopher Nicholas Wolterstorff has distinguished between a Jeffersonian "wall of separation" view on the one hand, and an "impartiality" view—that the government should treat all religions and comprehensive perspectives impartially—on the other. Wolterstorff notes that the First Amendment "is ambiguous as between the impartiality and the separation positions"; he favors and argues for the former.[6] There is ambiguity; the question continues to be debated in public forums.[7]

In 1971, in the well-known Tilton v. Richardson case,[8] the U.S. Supreme Court said that church colleges or universities could receive government funds if they were not "pervasively sectarian" or "pervasively religious." But it was not clear how the decision about whether a given institution was "pervasively religious" or not was to be made. Conclusions on the constitutionality of state aid programs in the United States have been even more complicated. There are differences among the fifty states.

Passage of the GI Bill was one of most important events in post-World War II higher education in the United States GIs could take financial aid to any accredited college in the country, since the aid was regarded as aid to the student, not aid to the institution. Then came the 1984 ruling in the Grove City College case,[9] in which the U.S. Supreme Court said, among other things, that government grants and loans were aid to the institution. To those who favored "GI Bill" kinds of aid, this seemed like saying that food stamps are aid to grocery stores, not to the recipients, or that Medicare payments are aid to hospitals and doctors, not aid to citizens needing medical care. Tuition payments at colleges and universities typically cover only a part of the real costs. In this sense, government payments toward tuition costs are not comparable to food stamps, and they cover a smaller part of the full costs than do Medicare payments. In this view, government student aid is focused on helping students, not institutions.

In 2001, in Columbia Union College v. Oliver,[10] the Fourth Circuit U.S. Court of Appeals reviewed more recent decisions of the U.S. Supreme Court and found that the "pervasively sectarian" test was increasingly and consistently being replaced by a "principle of neutrality, upholding aid that is offered to a broad range of groups or persons without regard to their religion."[11] It ruled that whether or not Columbia Union was "pervasively sectarian" was not a sufficient reason for denying state aid. (It also ruled that Columbia Union College was not "pervasively sectarian," in any case.)

The "principle of neutrality" was affirmed by the U.S. Supreme Court in 2002 in Zelman v. Simmons-Harris.[12]

To make the implications concrete, we can ask whether a college with a church mission can hire faculty members who support its mission without losing possibilities of getting governmental aid. Two kinds of questions arise:

1. Can the aid be considered aid to students or to the colleges they choose to attend? If the government aid is aid to students to help them go to the schools of their choice, and especially if the aid does not entirely cover the costs, leaving the college to cover the remaining cost of educating each of the additional students it receives because of the government aid, then the aid would seem to be primarily aid to the students. If a student is free to choose which school he or she wants to attend, the government should want to know if the student is qualified to attend that institution, not to know who sponsors and chooses the faculty members for the institution.[13]
2. If the government grant is viewed as aid to a college, should the state be aiding a range of colleges, including ones with special and church-related missions? Should the principle of "impartiality" or the one of "separatism" prevail?

As these considerations relate to the legal environment for institutions with distinctive missions, we can observe that, on the one hand, the rights of individuals have sometimes been given priority over the rights of institutions. When administrators have tried to hire faculty members who would help them achieve their distinctive institutional missions, they have sometimes been criticized for engaging in "discrimination."

But, on the other hand, the American public has supported institutional diversity and innovation and has supported students who wish to go to private institutions as well as those who choose to attend public institutions. The American public has supported plans like the GI Bill that let funds go to students who choose to attend any accredited private or public schools. Present federal student aid plans permit students to go to any accredited private or public institutions, but there could in the future be restrictions on the kinds of institutions to which the students could take the governmental aid.

In sum, colleges with distinctive missions live today in an uncertain legal environment.

Change in the Student Population

By the mid-1980s, each of the twenty-four largest city school systems in the United States had a "minority majority." In 2008, the U.S. Census Bureau projected that so-called minority racial and ethnic groups would make up more than fifty percent of the U.S. population by 2042. College enrollments were projected to increase by sixteen percent from 2002 to 2014, with African American, Hispanic American, and Asian American students accounting for eighty percent of that growth. Minority students were twenty-nine percent of college student bodies in 1995; they are projected to comprise thirty-seven percent of college enrollments in 2015.[14]

The fastest growth in many church groups in recent years has been in minority churches and members. Some denominations have initiated special minority education programs to meet some of the needs.

Affirmative action programs have been under fire in recent years. Americans seem to agree that schools should educate more students from traditionally underrepresented populations, but seem not to agree on how this should be done.

Chapter 11 will consider the interest of churches and other private groups in diversity.

Distance Education and Lifelong Learning

More adults making job changes in a changing employment environment and professionals keeping abreast of developments in their fields are going to school. Developments in technology and the "information highway" are opening up new educational possibilities for adult learners. Many denominations have initiated new distance education programs. There has been a dramatic increase in degree-completion programs for adults who have had some years of college and want credit for life experiences in completing degrees. The U.S. Department of Education's National Center for Education Statistics reports that sixty-six percent of the degree-granting postsecondary institutions in a 2006–07 survey offered distance-education programs. The biggest increases in such programs have been among public and large institutions.[15]

Night courses, programs for commuting students, and distance education meet some important needs. Some schools focus solely on meeting those needs. However, research findings show that distance education programs do not fill the educational functions of good residential programs in which students participate in on-campus learning communities.[16] This is especially true for groups that want their schools to educate students for living and working in community and for groups that have distinctive visions of the good society—for groups that want education that goes beyond facts and "head-knowledge." In the foreseeable future, distinctive programming for groups of these kinds will presumably continue to require having some strong residential colleges and graduate theological faculties and universities.

Developments in information technology have made feasible some kinds of cooperation among small private colleges to enable students to have the advantages of life in smaller residential learning communities with distinctive missions, and, at the same time, to provide some of the specialized offerings of larger institutions.

Chapter 2 Endnotes

1   Ben Gose, "A New Survey of 'Good Practices' Could Be an Alternative to Rankings: Colleges Seek Their Own Measures of Quality, but Will Institutions Make the Data Public?" *The Chronicle of Higher Education,* October 22, 1999.

2   John L. Pulley, "Public Universities' Ambitious Campaigns Vex Many Small Private Institutions," *The Chronicle of Higher Education*, December 3, 1999. Sara Lipka, "Privatizing Trend Among Public Universities Could Hurt Smaller Institutions, Credit-Rating Agency Says," *Today's News, The Chronicle of Higher Education*, May 4, 2005.

3   Katherine Lyall, president emerita of the University of Wisconsin system and an economist who has been a visiting scholar at the Carnegie Foundation, has been interested in the financing of public higher education. She writes, "Public support (per student) for public universities has been falling for two decades or more—and with growing fiscal pressures on states, there is no relief in sight" (*Carnegie Perspectives*, April 2005). 2, http://www.carnegiefoundation.org/perspectives/sub.asp?key=245&subkey=568. The whole January/February 2006 issue of *Change: The Magazine of Higher Education* is devoted to "The Privatization of Public Higher Education."

4   This section focuses on the U.S. situation. The Canadian and U.S. legal traditions are different. In the terms used in the paragraphs which follow, Canada could be said to have an "impartiality" approach rather than a "wall of separation" tradition. After a time when the tide was shifting to public institutions, new Canadian private degree-granting institutions are emerging and being recognized.

5   William T. Cavanaugh, "Sailing under True Colors: Academic Freedom and the Ecclesially Based University," in *Conflicting Allegiances: The Church-Based University in a Liberal Democratic Society*, ed. Michael L. Budde and John Wright (Grand Rapids: Brazos Press, 2004), 31–52.

6   Nicholas Wolterstorff, "Constitutional Democracy and Cultures of Belief," introductory panel statement at Seminar on Religion in America, Center for Human Values, Princeton University, April 12, 1996. For a fuller discussion, see Wolterstorff's chapter in *Schooling Christians: "Holy Experiments" in American Education.* eds. Stanley Hauerwas and John H. Westerhoff (Grand Rapids: Wm. B. Eerdmans, 1992), 3–28.

7   Stephen V. Monsma, *When Sacred and Secular Mix: Religious Nonprofit Organizations and Public Money*, ed. Allen D. Hertzke, Religious Forces in the Modern Political World (Lanham, MD: Rowman & Littlefield Publishers, Inc., 2000) is a book-length statement of the case for "positive neutrality," or "equal treatment." See Stephen V. Monsma and J. Christopher Soper, eds. *Equal Treatment of Religion in a Pluralistic Society* (Grand Rapids: Wm. B. Eerdmans, 1998) for a treatment of the issues from a variety of perspectives. After ten months of discussion, a diverse and non-partisan group of twenty-six national leaders issued a consensus statement on faith-based social services and discussion of issues on which they were not in agreement in April 2003, "Harnessing Civic and Faith-Based Power to Fight Poverty." The document can be found on the Search for Common Ground Web site, www.sfcg.org.

8   *Tilton v. Richardson*, 403 U.S. 672 (1971). Excerpts from the cases mentioned in this chapter can be found in Ronald B. Flowers, Melissa Rogers, and Steven K. Green, *Religious Freedom and the Supreme Court* (Waco: Baylor University Press, 2008).

9   *Grove City College v. Bell*, 465 U.S. 555 (1984).

10 *Columbia Union College v. Oliver,* 254 F.3d 496 (4th Cir. 2001).

11 Similar to Wolterstorff's principle of impartiality discussed above.

12 *Zelman v. Simmons-Harris*, 536 U.S. 639 (2002). This case involved parents of elementary and secondary children, and the Court ruled that parents could use Ohio voucher funds to send their children to either private or public schools, because the state was neutral and it was the parents who were deciding how to use the funds for their children. Allowing students to choose to which colleges and universities they would take their financial aid has, since the years of the GI Bill, typically been recognized as acceptable by the courts even when it seemed less clear in the case of children attending elementary and secondary schools. In *Colorado Christian University v. Weaver* (2008), the Tenth Circuit U.S. Court of Appeals favored the "principle of neutrality" in a higher education case.

13 See Albert J. Meyer and David H. Sikkink, "What Does It Profit A College to Add More Students? The Relationship between Enrollment Growth and Financial Strength," *Christian Higher Education* 3, no. 2 (2004): 97–113, and *Colorado Christian University v. Weaver* (2008).

14 Anthony P. Carnevale and Richard A. Fry, "Crossing the Great Divide: Can We Achieve Equity When Generation Y Goes to College?" (Princeton, NJ: Educational Testing Service, 2000): 8. Rebecca Aronauer, "College Enrollments Are Expected to Continue Rising through 2014," *Today's News, The Chronicle of Higher Education,* September 12, 2005).

15 The data are from reports of the National Center for Education Statistics, "Distance Education at Degree-Granting Postsecondary Education Institutions: 2000–2001," http://www.nces.ed.gov/pubsearch/pubsinfo.asp?pubid=2003017, and "Distance Education at Degree-Granting Postsecondary Institutions 2006–07," http://www.nces.ed.gov/pubsearch/pubsinfo.asp?pubid=2009044.

16 We refer to findings of the kind summarized in the comprehensive publications of Alexander W. Astin, *What Matters in College? Four Critical Years Revisited*, The Jossey-Bass Higher and Adult Education Series (San Francisco: Jossey-Bass, 1993); Kenneth A. Feldman and Theodore M. Newcomb, *The Impact of College on Students* (San Francisco: Jossey-Bass, 1969); Ernest T. Pascarella and Patrick T. Terenzini, *How College Affects Students: Findings and Insights from Twenty Years of Research*, ed. Kenneth A. Feldman, The Jossey-Bass Higher and Adult Education Series (San Francisco: Jossey-Bass, 1991); and Ernest T. Pascarella and Patrick T. Terenzini, *How College Affects Students: A Third Decade of Research*, Higher and Adult Education Series (San Francisco: Jossey-Bass, 2005). In "More Community Colleges Are Building Dormitories," Eric Lords said that more community college students wanted a residential experience (*The Chronicle of Higher Education,* November 12, 1999). See Sarah Carr, "As Distance Education Comes of Age, the Challenge Is Keeping the Students," *The Chronicle of Higher Education,* February 11, 2000. Distance education course completion rates are often lower than those in traditional courses, and courses involving student peer meetings are not inexpensive.

3

SECULARIZATION

Much of the recent discussion and literature about the trends in higher education I have been describing in these pages uses the word "secularization." The term has several different meanings and connotations.[1]

Several Perspectives

Social scientists have used the term secularization to refer to the decline in the social and political influence of the church as an institution in a culture and society. In a different technical sense, secularization refers to the transfer of ownership of properties and institutions (including schools) held by a church body to civil or independent ownership. In a still different technical sense, secularization refers to the lifting of monastic restrictions on a member of a religious order who becomes a member of the secular clergy or a lay person. In popular usage, secularization connotes the loss of religious and spiritual distinctiveness—the acculturation of a church or church institution to the values and practices of the larger society in which it finds itself.

These meanings are not identical. When the Martin Luther who said "Here I stand!" left the Augustinian order—"went secular"—and married in 1525, one could hardly say he was losing his spirituality and simply adopting the values and practices of the Northern Europeans of his time. He may have been going secular in a technical ecclesiastical sense, but he was certainly not going secular in the contemporary popular sense.

Even if the term secularization is used to refer to a decline in the social and political influence of a church as an institution, the term can still be viewed positively or negatively, depending on the context. In the era of Christendom, some churches held enormous political power and used it to condemn to public torture and cruel forms of execution parents whose only crime was that they did not have their babies baptized. Most of us today would say that we have benefited from a decline in those kinds of church activities and that kind of political influence—we have benefited from that kind of secularization.

A Religion-less Era?

Are we witnessing a decline in interest in religion in our time? For children of the Enlightenment, has scientific rationality displaced religious faith?

We can document a decline in religious faith and practice in North American intellectual and academic circles and in Western Europe generally. To the extent that intellectual and academic leaders are influential in Western societies, trends in their thinking deserve our attention. But we also need to observe that, in North America in general and in most of the world, expressions of religious faith have not declined significantly. Indeed, we are witnessing an explosion of new religious movements and of revivals of religious fundamentalisms, and there is no indication that these trends will change in the near future. In Peter Berger's words:

> In the course of my career as a sociologist of religion I made one big mistake. . . . The big mistake, which I share with almost everyone who worked in this area in the 1950s and '60s, was to believe that modernity necessarily leads to a decline in religion. . . . Most of the world today is as religious as it ever was and, in a good many locales, more religious than ever.[2]

Working with a Lilly Endowment grant, Conrad Cherry and his co-authors have done case studies confirming the vitality of religion on American private and public campuses.[3]

Has the "Secularization" of Colleges and Universities Been Good?

As we have seen, we can document an almost universal pattern of increasing distance between schools and the churches that gave them birth and early sustenance.[4] Secularization, in that sense, has been a dominant theme in American higher education. For over six hundred years, from the founding of the first colleges and universities in the Western world, all institutions of higher education were church institutions. In the past 150 years, and particularly the past fifty years, the church's role in higher education has decreased. Today, as we have noted, fewer than one-eighth of the students in the United States are attending institutions with any kind of church relationship.

Different observers look at this history in different ways. Some observers look at the contribution of the church to higher education in the past eight hundred years and say the church has accomplished its mission gloriously. The larger society is picking up the responsibility of educating the next generation, and the church can now turn to new areas of greater need. But other observers say that the withdrawal of the church from the educational and cultural scene portends an increasing problem for the societal role of the church in the world of the future.

Why do these observers have such different points of view as they consider the same historical and contemporary developments? Their differences arise, at least in part, from differences among them on what they view as the mission or missions of the church in higher education. In part, they arise even more fundamentally from different understandings of the role they believe the church should play in the larger society.

The situation has parallels with the different perspectives different observers had on the role of the United States and NATO in Kosovo. Different groups proposed different missions. If the mission was to stop the advance of the Serbian army in Kosovo, it was successful. If it was to create a united and multi-ethnic Kosovo, its success was less clear. If it was to avoid atrocities and human suffering, it failed. How observers view success in several of these kinds of American interventions around the world has depended on differing understandings of the missions the United States was to accomplish and of the role the United States should be playing in a new world order.[5]

When we ask about the different perspectives on the present and future involvements of a church group in higher education, we need to ask: What are the missions the church wants its colleges to assume? How do the college missions relate to the larger missions of the sponsoring church?

If a denomination launched a college intending that it should become a public institution as soon as the larger society was willing to give it needed support, then the secularization was a part of the church's intention for its college from the outset. The early colleges of the Congregational Church, for example, were intended to bring learning to the New World and help civilize the wilderness. The church intended that its colleges on the frontier would provide access to higher learning for their respective regions. (Of course the cultural dominance of white male Anglo-Saxon Protestants and their values was assumed in those days.) Encouraging the larger public to assume its responsibility for educating its citizens was a part of the church's mission from the outset. When the church turned its schools over to the larger society, the church could do so with the confidence that it had accomplished its original mission.[6]

In some situations a denomination finds itself increasingly at home in its social context. Some mainline denominations do not see themselves as having beliefs and practices very different from those of many others in the larger American context—especially at a time when the larger American public has moved closer to these churches in many ways, such as in trying to overcome racial, gender, age-related, and other forms of discrimination.

A conservative denomination may find itself at home in a larger interdenominational American Evangelicalism or Fundamentalism. It may be quite willing to see its educational institutions moving toward looser denominational relationships and appealing to broader American interdenominational constituencies. Although looser church-school relationships may not have been a part of the initial vision of either church or school, they may be an appropriate response to changes in the social context within which both school and church find themselves.

As noted earlier, pioneering in the establishment of institutions needed by the larger society has been an important contribution of the church throughout the centuries. Where secularization has been a part of the conscious and long-term intention of college and church, it should be affirmed. Indeed, in Chapter 10 I give attention to ways in which intentional secularization can be facilitated in situations where it is desired and appropriate.

But some churches have founded colleges, universities, and theological schools without intending from the outset that their schools should become independent or public institutions. Some churches have continued to see their visions of the order of God's intention as distinctive in the contexts in which they find themselves today. If such churches have distinctive visions and want to have colleges or universities as a way of relating to the oncoming generations and searching for the truth in changing times, and if the churches and colleges then drift away from each other and from their shared distinctive visions under the influence of outside pressures, that kind of secularization cannot be regarded as fulfilling the churches' missions in their relationships with their schools.

Researchers have said for decades that colleges with distinctive missions and clear niches will be more likely to survive and gain strength in the long-term future than will those trying to be all things to all people. A front-page article in a recent *Chronicle of Higher Education* says, "Small private colleges that have failed to differentiate themselves will face increasing obstacles as the student population shrinks."[7]

Consider, for example, a report of a small college closing:

> Shifting strategies, lack of a niche, and unrealistic projections doomed Bradford. . . . It tried to weld together a hodgepodge of appeals to different constituencies. . . . Bradford never clearly articulated who its student body was. . . . The college did build up special ties, but never comprehensively marketed them. . . .

A small-college consultant "recommended that Bradford define its specialties, concentrate on them, and get rid of everything else." The college failed to do that.[8]

All too often in the history of American higher education the increasing distance of a college from its sponsoring church was not intended by either college or church. The story has been a story of unintended consequences on a continental scale. Richard Hofstadter, the historian cited earlier, implied this when he referred to the secularization in the history of higher education in North America as a "drift." Indeed, as several major recent studies have emphasized, that kind of secularization has frequently been the long-term and unintended outcome of actions taken in response to immediate challenges by church and school leaders who were deeply committed to having colleges and universities as an ongoing part of the work of the church. Many of these past leaders were denominational executives and church-ordained presidents. Typically, dissociation was not a part of the conscious intention of either college or church, at least not until the distance between church and school reached a point where the trend was irreversible. And intentional secularization of all of their schools has not generally been the goal for historically distinctive groups.

The landscape is replete with instances of church-school dissociation. If that is not what we want, we can learn from the cases of unintended dissociation of church and school that dominate the scene. We can analyze the factors that need to be considered by churches and institutions that want to go against the stream in establishing and maintaining mutually beneficial church-school relationships. We can begin to project what churches and

schools that want good relationships over the long term need to do differently to realize their intentions.

Churches need to know who they are theologically, but clarity of vision
alone will not be enough if they do not understand the dynamics of extra-
congregational higher educational organizations, i.e., how church colleges
and universities work and how forces lead to changes in these institutions.

The challenge for organizational theorists as social scientists is to
explain why organizations change as they do—sometimes in directions very
different from those intended by their leaders. The challenge for administrators is to find ways of implementing intentions and goals. Both are
important.

In the very common case in which secularization is not intentional, but
rather the long-term outcome of short-term responses to external and internal forces, we must analyze the forces and propose ways in which churches
and church schools that see themselves as having distinctive missions over
the long term can realize their intentions better in the future than they have
at many times in the past.

The Place of Religion in a Democracy

In the writings of Alexis de Tocqueville,[9] in the assumptions of many white
Anglo-Saxon Protestant political and educational leaders in the American
past, and, again, in the more recent comments of writers concerned about
public life in our times, thoughtful students of American culture and political
institutions have observed that the American democracy has flourished, at
least in part, because of the foundational religious beliefs of many of its citizens and the religious sub-communities that have been important in its life.
The American democracy has depended on the influence of its churches and
its other voluntary associations, not only on the coercive power of the state.
The success of the American project has depended on having many citizens
with deeply held religious convictions that have provided a foundation for
public morality and community life. How the American society can best provide for this kind of foundation in a time of increasing pluralism is one of the
issues in contemporary American political debate.

There are some current political winds blowing in the direction of sub-
sidiarity, i.e., of a devolution of action from national agencies to more local
governmental and voluntary—and churchly—centers of initiative. At the
same time, Americans are concerned about religionists who seem to take
their convictions too seriously. They recall all too vividly what happened to

the disciples of Jim Jones and David Koresh, and the actions of some anti-abortionists who believe they have a religious calling to kill abortion doctors create similar concerns in the public arena.

A kind of common-sense, pragmatic approach says that America needs some religious zeal to motivate and activate the better impulses of its citizenry—but not too much zealotry! We want some religion, but not a religion or sectarianism that is "pervasive."[10] Faced with a naked public square on the one hand and zealotry on the other, perhaps we can try to find a common-sense middle ground somewhere on the continuum between these extremes and muddle our way through somewhere in that middle.

An alternative to this kind of "muddling through" needs further attention. As pointed out in Chapter 2, the traditional formulation of the relationship between church and state in terms of a wall of separation has served some purposes in the past, but is not adequate as we look to the future. The idea that religious convictions are private matters and should not enter into public discussion robs public discourse of insights and of an impetus for change we need in our time. The whole "wall of separation" concept on which this is based is really extra-constitutional. What we really need is fairness and impartiality in the relationships between governmental leaders and agencies, on the one hand, and different religious and nonreligious voluntary groups on the other.

Keeping religious considerations out of public life or promoting religious zealotry—or a position somewhere between the extremes—are not the only options.

Especially since religion became the official religion of the Roman Empire in the fourth century, religious zeal has often been associated with intolerance. From the forced conversions of Germans in Charlemagne's time through the long years of Christendom to the mutual genocide of Hutus and Tutsis who carried the name of Christ in Rwanda, "true believers" have injured and killed their enemies and those who would not conform to their beliefs. A sociological study of American college and university students found a correlation between the kind of religious belief and practice typically found in America, on the one hand, and intolerance and discrimination, on the other.[11]

However history offers another alternative. Some Christians have believed so passionately in allowing people space to make authentic adult decisions and in incarnating God's love for everyone in loving, rather than violent, actions—in opposition to the official positions of the religious and political authorities of their times—that they gave their lives for these beliefs. One cannot say that they did not have convictions. They had strong beliefs. But central among these beliefs was that they should seek to discern God's will also in conversation with those with whom they disagreed and that they should treat their enemies, not only with respect, but also with love.

In the Protestant Reformation, the forerunners of the Free Churches of modern times were martyred for treason, as well as heresy, because they did not join with the authorities in taking up arms against the Turks, who were at Vienna and seen as threatening "Christian" Europe. Within less than three years of the beginnings of the Anabaptist movement, which some have seen as a forerunner of the Free Churches of modern times, at his trial in 1527, Anabaptist Michael Sattler was asked whether he would fight the Turks. He said:

> It stands written: thou shalt not kill . . . We should not defend ourselves against the Turks . . . If waging war were proper, I would rather take the field against the so-called Christians who persecute, take captive, and kill true Christians . . . for the following reason: the Turk . . . knows nothing of the Christian faith. . .But you claim to be Christians, boast of Christ, and still persecute the faithful witnesses of Christ.[12]

The response of the government official at the trial: ". . . The hangman will debate with you . . ." Sattler's testimony no doubt helped to contribute to the cruelty of his torture and execution.

Michael Sattler (and his wife, who was drowned for her beliefs a few days later) had strong convictions. In addition to Anabaptists, Quakers and others with strong religious convictions have respected the religious choices of others, developed strong community life among those who voluntarily chose to join their circles, and tried to witness to the good news of God's love by showing love for others, rather than by trying to force others to accept their religious beliefs or practices.

Most mainline Protestant and Catholic groups in America have had Establishment Christendom roots. Some of today's militant Christian fundamentalism has been rooted in a kind of American Establishment culture and has aspired to gaining political influence to impose its beliefs and practices on others.[13] Historic Establishment traditions and tendencies that have continued into the present[14] do not need to determine the future. One can hold strong beliefs about not trying to kill those who disagree. Many churches in the United States have been influenced by the Free Church tradition, and most would have some formal commitment to the separation of church from too much state influence and to the separation of churches from using the methods of the state to achieve their ends. Religious conviction does not need to be correlated with coercing others to conform. In our post-Christendom time, church people should spend less time arguing about where they want to be on a horizontal left-right political continuum and more time reflecting on where they can be on a vertical Establishment-vs.-post-Establishment axis.

Summary Comments

If secularization means an end to the inappropriate use of political and cultural power by established churches to enforce attitudinal or behavioral conformity, many of us welcome it. Some of us in religious or ethnic minorities do not want to be a part of Establishment groups. Some of us had our origins in a break from monolithic state church systems. We believe it is time that our friends and fellow citizens recognize and accept the pluralism of today's world.

Some churches find that their beliefs and practices are fairly similar to those of many others in the changed and changing society within which they find themselves. They believe that their colleges and universities would receive support and do well as independent or public institutions. If secularization means that the churches involved would encourage these institutions to be autonomous or government-supported, the churches could appropriately focus their funds and attention on meeting other needs.

At the same time, if those churches that do have distinctive beliefs and practices dissociate themselves from an involvement in higher education, they might be abdicating responsibility in today's world. A secular society that does not recognize that there is metaphysics—something beyond physics—as well as physics is in trouble. The biggest problems today do not involve growing better wheat, growing better silicon, or building bigger rocket boosters. Instead, the most pressing challenges are whether pieces of the former Soviet Union or Yugoslavia or Somalia or Kosovo or Iraq can relate to one another, or whether Israelis and Palestinians can live together in the Middle East. Can we thrive if many members of our own society cannot get the kinds of jobs we will have in a high-tech world? Can we go on indefinitely with the rich getting richer and the poor poorer in our own society? In dealing with questions of these kinds, we need more than what we can learn from observation of the world as it is. We need a vision of a world that could be and ought to be. For some of us who are religious, visioning and working for a world that could be is a part of the stuff of religion.

In what follows, to avoid confusion among the various meanings of intended and unintended secularization, and to avoid negative connotations where they are not intended, I will usually refer to the phenomenon of increasing church-school distance as "dissociation," rather than as secularization.

Chapter 3 Endnotes

1   For bibliographical references on some of these meanings see Mark Chaves, "Intraorganizational Power and Internal Secularization in Protestant Denominations," *American Journal of Sociology* 99, no. 1 (1993): 1–4.

2   Peter L. Berger, "Protestantism and the Quest for Certainty," *The Christian Century* 115, no. 23 (1998): 782–91. More recently Alan Wolfe has written, "In the 1950's and 1960's, American social scientists were strongly committed to what was known as the 'secularization thesis.' The idea was put forth in one way or another by sociologists as diverse as Talcott Parsons and the young Peter L. Berger. . . . If anything, the United States has experienced a religious revival that the social scientists of the postwar years could never have predicted. . . ." ("What Scholarship Reveals About Politics and Religion," *The Chronicle Review, The Chronicle of Higher Education*, September 8, 2000.) Christian Smith says that secularization has not been an inevitable byproduct of modernization. (Christian Smith, *The SecularRevolution: Power, Interests, and Conflict in the Secularization of American Public Life* [Berkeley: University of California Press, 2003].)

3   Conrad Cherry, Amanda Porterfield, and Betty A. Deberg, *Religion on Campus* (Chapel Hill, NC: University of North Carolina Press, 2003).

4   In denominations with dual and parallel religious authority and agency structures, Chaves refers to the declining scope of religious authority vis-à-vis agency authority in the past century as "internal secularization." (Chaves, "Intraorganizational Power and Internal Secularization in Protestant Denominations," *American Journal of Sociology* 99, no. 1 [1993]: 1–48.)

5   Some of the same questions arose in connection with the intervention of the United States in Iraq. If, as announced, the mission was to remove weapons of mass destruction—the weapons were not found. If the mission was to remove Saddam Hussein from power, the mission was accomplished. If it was to create a stable democratic society, the administration's early "mission accomplished" announcement was premature.

6   After World War II, Mennonites established psychiatric centers in various parts of North America. At the outset, some saw the centers not as continuing missions of a church, but as institutions that would have become based in and supported by their local communities. In that case, secularization could appropriately have been affirmed as a part of the initial intention of those founders.

7   "13 Reasons Colleges Are in This Mess," *The Chronicle of Higher Education,* March 13, 2009. (Author not identified.)

8   Martin van der Werf, "The Death of a Small College," *The Chronicle of Higher Education,* May 12, 2000.

9   Alexis de Tocqueville, *Democracy in America*, trans. George Lawrence, ed. J.P. Mayer (New York: Doubleday, Anchor Books, 1969).

10 David Tracy, Catholic theologian at the University of Chicago, says: ". . . 'Everybody' already knows what religion is: It is a private consumer product that some people seem to need. Its former social role was poisonous. Its present privatization is harmless enough to wish it well from a civilized distance" (*The Analogical Imagination: Christian Theology and the Culture of Pluralism* [New York: Crossroads, 1981], 13).

11 Among other criteria, Goldsen et al. used attendance at religious services and belief in God as metrics for belief and practice (Rose K. Goldsen and others, *What College Students Think* [Princeton, NJ: D. Van Nostrand Company, 1960]). See Ronald J. Sider, *The Scandal of the Evangelical Conscience: Why Are Christians Living Just Like the Rest of the World?* (Grand Rapids: Baker Books, 2005), especially Chapter 1. The languages of theologians and of sociologists differ. Theologians tend to speak of norms for behaviors; sociologists tend to speak of averages of actual behaviors. There is a place for speaking of specific churches as aspiring to certain norms, but we can and must also ask whether there actually are any churches modeling such norms in a significant way.

12 John H. Yoder, *The Legacy of Michael Sattler*, ed. Cornelius J. Dyck, Classics of the Radical Reformation (Scottdale, PA: Herald Press, 1973), 72–3.

13 For work by two leaders of the religious right who have had second thoughts, see Cal Thomas and Ed Dobson, *Blinded by Might: Can the Religious Right Save America?* (Grand Rapids: Zondervan Publishing House, 1999). In commenting on the Southern Baptist Convention and its universities in the nineteenth century, Baptist sociologist Nancy Ammerman writes, "The Southern Baptist Convention was the religious establishment of the region, and these schools were an essential part of that establishment." ("Living Together, Living Apart: Particularity and Pluralism in Christian Higher Education," Baylor University Sesquicentennial Symposium, October 1995.) Randall Balmer, evangelical Christian and professor of American religious history at Barnard, says, "The religious right hankers for the kind of homogeneous theocracy that the Puritans tried to establish in seventeenth-century Massachusetts: to impose their vision of a moral order on all of society" (*Thy Kingdom Come: How the Religious Right Distorts the Faith and Threatens America: An Evangelical's Lament* [New York: Perseus Books, 2006]).

14 They have continued among groups that have called themselves Christian in Rwanda, Burundi, Serbia, and other places in the Two-Thirds World, as well as in places in the West.

4

Organizational Dynamics

If we want to understand unintended dissociation, we will have to consider the organizational dynamics of colleges and universities—the forces acting upon colleges and universities and the ways they change over time.

Institutions

To learn from the best current understandings of researchers who spend their time studying the ways organizations change over time, we need to be clear on terms. Organizational theorists think in terms of what they call "institutions." They view an institution as a set of roles and expectations held by a society.[1] People in the American society have a general consensus on what a second-grade teacher or a principal—or an elementary school as a whole—is expected to be and do. The American elementary school is an institution of the larger American society. The roles and expectations are understood, not just by staff people within the elementary school, but also by pupils, parents, and Americans generally. Organizational theorists would not use the term institution to refer to a particular elementary school. To them, a given school is an educational "organization."

Other examples of institutions, in the language of organizational theorists, would be "the U.S. presidency," "the Jewish Passover," and "the community hospital." When social scientists talk about "the state," they are not talking about a given government, but about government as an institution in today's societies and world system. When John Henry Newman wrote *The*

Idea of the University in the nineteenth century, he was not talking about a particular university but about the university as an institution of his time.

A problem can arise from differences in our use of words. In everyday usage, we refer to Oberlin College or Harvard University as higher education institutions. In technical contexts, sociologists and organizational theorists call Oberlin or Harvard educational organizations. They speak of "the liberal arts college" and "the research university" as institutions of the American society. To organizational theorists, a specific college like Oberlin is an educational organization that exists within an institutional field.

In focusing on schools, we need to think in terms of what sociologists would call institutions, but it would be awkward and unusual to have to refer to specific schools always as organizations and never as higher education institutions. For these reasons and for brevity, in what follows I will be free to follow popular usages. I will at times refer to given colleges or universities as higher education institutions. To refer to what sociologists call institutions, I will use "cultural institutions," "societal institutions," "institutions of the American society," or "widely-accepted-and-understood-institutions," etc. The meaning should be clear from the context.

Understanding Educational Organizations

To understand organizational dynamics and the importance of societal institutions, we must go back to the mid-1940s, when organizational theory emerged as a discipline in American universities. Max Weber's classic works on organizations were translated into English in 1946 and 1947.

Following his study of the Prussian military, Weber viewed organizations as rational bureaucracies,[2] as tools designed to attain predetermined goals with maximum efficiency through bureaucratic structures. An organization could be diagrammed as a pyramid, with the chief executive officer (CEO) at the apex and the staff members in their various roles below.

Is this view helpful in understanding colleges and universities? Certainly colleges and universities intending to meet real societal goals will typically have boards comprising responsible representatives of their mandating societies; the boards will need to name chief executive officers (presidents) to be responsible to work toward the goals between board meetings; the executives will need to name vice-presidents and other administrative officers; and the officers will need to provide for the appointment of faculty and staff members. Certainly the view of a college or a university as a rational bureaucracy is helpful if we want to understand how schools function.

Empirical studies of industries and other organizations have showed, however, that informal relationships among participants in an organization can be more important than formal structures in determining productivity. In one famous set of experiments, workers seemed to produce more when they felt they were noticed and given attention.[3] They were human beings whose interpersonal relationships were important; they were more than cogs in a pyramidal production machine. These studies led to what we can call a "human relations" view of organizations. In this view, organizations are not just neutral tools for meeting someone else's goals; they function also as systems interested in their own survival and well being. Sometimes an organization's readiness to adapt to its surroundings for survival is regarded with cynicism; sometimes it is seen more positively as the organization's attempt to meet needs in its surroundings.

A college or a university is certainly a community with a life of its own in which interpersonal relationships in departments, committees, faculty meetings, dormitories, and other settings are important. An educational organization does have an interest in its own survival and well being, as well as in its service to students and the wider society. Most people would say that faculty members and students should have important roles in decision-making. Participants in lively organizations are more than cogs in wheels. A "human relations" view of organizations explains some phenomena that the "rational bureaucracy" view does not adequately explain.

In the late 1970s, weaknesses in the explanatory power of the above views of organizations led to the emergence of a third view, the so-called "neo-institutional" view,[4] which is an important perspective among organizational theorists at present. The problem with the first two views is that they saw organizations as isolated systems. Empirical studies made it increasingly evident that organizations also had to be seen in their interactions with their environments, as "institutions of their societies." Organizations exist within institutional fields in their larger societies. According to rational bureaucracy or human relations understandings, organizations will normally move in rational ways that maximize their own interests or those of their stakeholders. But organizations sometimes follow leading organizations in their fields when it is not in their self-interest. Sometimes they do what is expected in their organizational fields when it is not a matter of following anyone's orders from the top. A neo-institutional view of organizations helps us to understand such phenomena.

When churches or other groups of Americans establish an organization they call a "college," they are buying into a well established institution of the American society. Almost all of the answers to questions anyone might have about the college will be taken for granted, not only by faculty members but also by prospective students, parents, donors, the local community, educational associations, government officials, and Americans at large. What a departmental faculty member might be expected to do, what kinds of officers might appear in the administrative cabinet, what the president and board might look like and how they should function, what the school year might be—even the kinds of gowns and hoods faculty members would wear at commencement—will be questions whose answers are generally taken for granted. The American college is a well-established and widely-understood American institution.[5]

Centuries ago on the American frontier, a "college" may have had only a president, and he might have stoked the pot-bellied stove. But then he needed and recruited a registrar. Then a dean. Then deans of men and deans of women. In more recent decades, colleges have acquired directors and vice-presidents of student development, vice-presidents of advancement, and still more recently, vice-presidents and directors of enrollment management. But why would colleges in California and New England and Texas all be creating these offices at roughly the same times? Because the whole concept of college is institutionalized in the American society, and there is a reasonable consensus among professionals and in the society across the land at a given time on what a good college might be expected to be and do.

Note that colleges do not make parallel changes at the same time because there is a rational bureaucracy headquartered in Washington or Chicago that tells colleges how they are supposed to organize themselves. American liberal arts colleges can be part of an institutionalized field in which there are powerful peer and societal forces toward conformity without being in a pyramidal structure in which someone at the top is telling them all what to do.

Neo-institutional theorists say that colleges and universities are subject to strong legitimacy forces (i.e., pressures to be accepted as excellent higher education institutions) and pressures toward mimetic isomorphism (i.e., toward being "morphed" into the shape of leading schools in their organizational fields). Theorists point out that the "neo-institutional" view is particularly useful in describing the functioning of organizations that have staffs of highly skilled professionals and strong organizational cultures. Colleges and universities do have skilled professional staffs. Many have strong cultures. Schools with staffs of professionals gathered together around distinctive

missions they share with distinctive church communities in their environments are particularly likely to have strong cultures. The neo-institutional
perspective is especially helpful in understanding the dynamics of such colleges and universities.

A Distinctive College in an Institutional Environment

Consider now a group of church people, or another group with distinctive
beliefs and practices, that gets together to establish a different kind of postsecondary educational organization. They want a school that is different
from the typical American college. They are not sure they should call it a
college, because the use of the term might evoke a whole set of understandings, myths, and symbols in the American context. They want to differentiate
themselves from other schools in their organizational field. They don't want
to call it a "university" or a "seminary," because that would be buying into
other different institutions of the American society and would elicit confus-
ing connotations of other kinds. They want a different kind of undergraduate liberal arts school.

If they want to avoid the prevailing institutionalization of the American
college, they could possibly call their new educational organization a
"school" (e.g., Juilliard School), an "institute" (e.g., Massachusetts Institute
of Technology, Kansas City Art Institute, Institute for Advanced Study),
a "conservatory" (e.g., Boston Conservatory, American Film Institute
Conservatory), an "academy" (e.g., Art Academy of Cincinnati, Air Force
Academy), or a "center" (e.g., Boston Architectural Center). But each of those
terms will likely have unhelpful connotations of other kinds.

The group of people who want to have this different post-secondary liberal arts school are faced with a choice. On the one hand, they can use an
unusual term to describe their new school and then try to fill the new term
with the meaning they want it to have by developing the kind of school they
envision and trying to explain what they are doing to their constituents and
the public. Or they can use a term like "college" which is already in use for a
kind of school currently institutionalized in the American society and then
mount a substantial and continuing effort to explain and demonstrate that
their school is really different from most American schools that call themselves by the same term. This can be a difficult choice for a school that wants
to be genuinely different.

We must understand that societal institutions like "the American college" can carry real freight and that a specific organization has to put forth a

serious and sustained effort if it wants to be different. A cultural institution is like an ideal pattern or a model. When a given organization wants to fit the pattern or model and uses the name most people in the society associate with the pattern, the organization finds that the institutionalization of the pattern in the society is helpful—the organization can easily explain who it is and what it is about. But when an organization wants to be distinctive and "cut new grooves," doing so in the midst of well-established institutional patterns can be a challenge.

An organizational theoretical understanding of the role of institutions in a society is foundational for an understanding of the phenomenon of secularization. Years ago, sociologist David Riesman referred to American higher education as a "snake-like procession" with Harvard at the head and other colleges and universities rather uniformly following a Harvard model of excellence.[6] More generally, *The History of Education Quarterly* has observed that much recent work in the field "casts research universities, which constitute only three percent of U.S. institutions of higher education, 'as the template against which other versions of higher education institutions are measured, and usually found wanting.'"[7] To the degree that this is an accurate description of higher education as it is currently institutionalized in the American society, churches and other groups with distinctive beliefs and practices that want to have schools that are different from the prevailing institutional pattern over the long term will need to be very clear with their internal and external constituencies about what they want to do and how they want to do it. Institutional dynamics can far outweigh the good intentions of such churches and other groups.

Churches, Colleges, and Organizational Theory

All three views of organizations are important for colleges and universities that want to be distinctive. We will begin with the most recent, the neo-institutional view, and then look at the human relations and the rational bureaucracy views, in that order.

1. From a neo-institutional view of organizations we begin to see the nature and importance of the powerful professional and peer-institutional forces toward conformity in the American environment. A board or administration of a school that wants to be different, but that does not take cognizance of environmental forces, can find itself swept along in a stream it does not

understand. An institutional perspective shows how a school can be led to engage in practices that are not in its self-interest, that are actually counter to its long-term interests and stated mission. Schools that do not adopt some policies and practices that differ at critical points from those characteristic of today's institutionalizations of college and university will typically find their best intentions frustrated.

2. A human relations perspective helps administrators, boards, and mandating societies understand the importance of creating and fostering lively faculty-student communities on their campuses to implement their missions. Boards and administrators can do much, if they will, to determine the nature of the composition of their faculty and student communities, but these communities then need to form chain reactions that favor learning and research. A governance or administrative bureaucracy that inhibits the formation of strong peer relationships and rewards for involvement and initiative will also inhibit energy, creativity, and "productivity." From the human relations perspective, a school community has a natural tendency to be interested in its own survival and well-being as an organization. But this tendency can be helpful when and to the degree that it motivates and energizes the school to make continuing adaptations to meet the changing needs of its mandating societies.

3. Finally, a rational bureaucracy view is important for understanding the unique roles of boards and their presidents and chief administrators. Boards and top administrators make it possible for a church or other group of thousands or millions of people with a distinctive mission to create and maintain lively long-term relationships with the organizations that the sponsoring societies need to implement their special missions. Boards and presidents channel only a very small part of the communication between an educational organization and its environment. By far the largest channel for communication with people outside a school is through students and faculty members with their peers, families, friends, and outside organizations. But boards and administrators through the departmental level have responsibility for policies and administrative procedures that, over time, can significantly influence

the composition of the faculty and student body. They monitor the interactions of the organization with its environment and can initiate needed course corrections. If the mandating society and the school want to have a school that is different from most schools over the long term, the boards and their executive administrators have key roles in keeping the school focused on its long-term mission and in monitoring the school's fulfillment of its mission.

Part IV will examine in a more detailed way key elements in the dynamics of church-school relationships.

Chapter 4 Endnotes

1   For example, a dictionary that appropriately differentiates between the sociological and popular usages of the word "institution" gives the sociological definition of
"institution" as "a well-established and structured pattern of behavior or of relationships that is accepted as a fundamental part of a culture, as marriage: *the institution
of the family*" (*The Random House Dictionary of the English Language, the Unabridged
Edition* [Avenel, N.J.: Random House Value Publishing, 1993]). See also W. Richard
Scott, *Organizations: Rational, Natural, and Open Systems*, 5th ed. (Upper Saddle
River, NJ: Prentice Hall, 2003).

2   Scott (ibid.) makes the interesting and helpful remark that "rationality" in this view
refers to the process through which the goals are implemented, not to the top executives' choice of goals or the behavior expected of those at the bottom of the pyramid.
Those at the bottom, for example, are expected to follow orders, not to engage in
independent reasoning.

3   Ibid., 54-55.

4   In its current form, this view is sometimes contrasted with some older institutional
views.

5   Burtchaell critiques the "dogma of 'institutional autonomy.'" In two full pages, he
cites over fifty specific linkages (in some cases involving formal accountability) of a
typical college or university with outside associations and agencies. He concludes:
"No university is an asteroid. It is an organic member of a complex, very endocrine
community" (James Tunstead Burtchaell, "Out of the Heartburn of the Church," *The
Journal of College and University Law* 25, no. 4 [1999]: 656–95).

6   David Riesman, "The Academic Procession," in Riesman, *Constraint and Variety in
American Education* (Lincoln: University of Nebraska Press, 1956), 25–65.

7   "A Glance at the Fall Issue of 'History of Education Quarterly': Broadening the History
of Higher Education," *Daily Report, The Chronicle of Higher Education,* September
16, 1999. Stephen Wu finds that "graduates from the [ten or twenty] top-rated PhD
programs continue to hold an overwhelming share of faculty positions at leading
colleges and universities." (See "Where Do Faculty Receive Their PhDs?" *Academe* 91
[July-August 2005]: 53–54.) Schools seek to follow the leaders in their organizational
fields.

5

GENERALIZATIONS FROM EXPERIENCE

A s we look to the future, we do well to learn from past experience.

Analytical Studies

In view of the dominance of the long-term trend toward church-school dissociation in North American higher education, it is remarkable that, until recent years, there were few studies analyzing the detailed dynamics of this phenomenon. Hundreds of institutional histories have described the evolution of given colleges and universities; dozens of denominational histories have recounted what has happened; and histories of American higher education have recorded the reality of dissociation. But until recent years there have been almost no serious analytical works on the dissociation process.[1]

It seems sometimes to have been assumed that the increasing distance between churches and their schools has been the product of a general secularization of certain cultural and intellectual elites in the North American society and the changing role of the church in the West. Certainly these are significant factors. But understanding these factors does not address the questions: Why does something happen that neither school nor church leaders initially intended? If dissociation is not what a church and school want, can they chart a different course? If so, how?

The secularization of certain subpopulations in the West is indeed a part of the landscape in which churches live and work today, but non-supportive or hostile environments have not always in the past meant that churches needed to withdraw from engagement.

From an organization-theoretical perspective, one of the reasons there have been so few analyses of the available data is that no one has been given the role of doing this in existing institutions. As Manning Pattillo and Donald Mackenzie reported in their Danforth Commission report already in the 1960s, most church bodies have not had strong denominational agencies and offices expected to be asking long-term questions about their involvements in higher education.[2] In their preliminary report in 1965, they called this "a major weakness of church-affiliated higher education."[3] Pattillo and Mackenzie reported that churches have typically asked their institutional presidents to represent their church interests in higher education. These presidents have typically served for relatively short terms and have needed to cope with short-term challenges. The institutional leaders have typically not been in a position to say, for example, that their institutions should make sacrifices in a three- to-five-year time frame in order to better fulfill their missions in a twenty- to thirty-year frame of reference. If they wanted to be "successful" leaders, they were expected by church and school people alike to meet shorter-term goals—and then these goals have often led in the long term toward dissociation.

In any case, the available historical studies and observations and the author's personal consultation visits to sixty or seventy North American colleges and universities over the years can serve as a database for preliminary generalizations in this chapter on the nature and dynamics of church-school dissociation as it has typically occurred in the past.

Lengthy Process

Dissociation is a process that typically occurs over relatively long periods of time. American college or university presidents are currently serving an average of 5.7 years.[4] The outcomes of steps taken by a given president or given denominational leaders are often not evident until years later. During his or her tenure, a president who is a denominational leader and an outgoing administrator who relates well personally to the institution's publics will sometimes gain the reputation of maintaining and even enhancing church-school relationships. While important factors may be contributing toward long-term dissociation, a charismatic president deeply committed to the church can, with the best of intentions, "warm up" personal relationships with church constituents and make the effects of the fundamental trend factors less visible. In a remarkable "cut flower" phenomenon, the ethos of a campus can reflect the nourishment of earlier roots for some time after the roots have been cut. It may become evident only years later that the president set in motion certain forces that resulted over the long term in the dissociation of the school from its church roots. By the time the long-term changes are obvious to everyone, it is often too late to reverse the fundamental factors, making further change inevitable.[5]

We can consider the case of a flagship Roman Catholic research university that has a distinctive campus ethos today. Most students are Catholic. There is a crucifix in every classroom. A recent president served with distinction for many years as a denominational and educational leader, with a deep commitment to the church relationship of his university. But in putting his university on the map with other leading research universities, he brought increasing numbers of faculty members to the campus largely on the basis of their conventional academic qualifications. The percentage of self-identified Catholic faculty members has fallen in recent decades— from sixty-four to fifty-six percent. In this time period, in spite of canon law, church statements, bishop's papers, and university policy on faculty composition, Catholics comprised only forty-five percent of the university's new regular faculty hires. Some of the new non-Catholic faculty members are deeply committed to the Catholic character of the institution. A 1995 study, however, showed (1) that many Catholic faculty members were not particularly committed to the Catholic mission of the university and (2) that the non-Catholic faculty members were, overall, less committed to the Catholic character of the school.[6] If the percentage of non-Catholic faculty hires at this university continues to increase as rapidly as it did in recent decades, the ethos will change over time.

Indeed, some changes have already become evident. Less than five years after the arrival of a new president, the university's faculty senate introduced a no-confidence resolution over the role of the faculty in university governance. The big faculty issue several years ago was the president's appointment of a member of the university's sponsoring religious order to the faculty, over the rejection of the candidate by the department involved. If the school's mission is to include the Pope's criterion that more than half of the faculty should be Catholic, past experience would indicate that the university cannot long maintain that mission without adequate support in the faculty for the mission.

At this university, changes initiated decades ago are having effects that are hardly visible in the campus ethos and public mind today. It may be several decades and several presidents from now before changes that may already be irreversible are fully visible.

Increasing Lack of Specificity

Dissociation typically involves a gradually increasing vagueness and lack of specificity about the school's mission. Observers detail the "progressive devolution of church-identifiers" of a denominational college, for example, "from Denomination X to generically Christian, then to generically religious, then to historically religious," and then to "value-oriented." The "rhetorical slide" in descriptions of the churchly involvement run from simply "Denomination X" through "ownership," "sponsorship," "patronage," "support," "affiliation," "relationship," to "historical relationship."[7]

Given the "cut-flower" phenomenon, the general ethos on campus may remain well after the specific church commitments that gave it birth are gone.[8]

Reversing the Course

Very few colleges and universities have reversed course after substantial dissociation—especially after faculty composition and student body mix have reached a certain level.[9] It is not hard to understand some of the dynamics involved. In today's higher educational environment, for example, important elements in faculty recruitment are often relegated to academic departments. Apart from very unusual situations in which a North American college or university has declared a department "academically bankrupt" (there are a very few recent instances), existing faculty members play key roles in choosing new faculty members. In colleges and universities, it is very difficult to terminate tenured faculty members who are not contributing adequately to the institution's distinctive mission or to get existing departments of faculty members not especially concerned about the institution's mission to appoint new faculty members who are.

The Church's Role

For example, a 1990 document of the Association of Presbyterian Colleges and Universities noted that although "education and the strong support of educational institutions" were "among the historic and theological hallmarks of . . . Presbyterianism," this "emphasis is lacking in current statement of mission and mission priority" of leading church bodies. Noting that "involvement in higher education is close to the essence of Presbyterianism," the document continued, "Next to the collective investment of human and financial resources in parish churches, . . . the collective investment of people . . . and money in . . . higher education represents, by far, the largest single domestic enterprise of our denomination. . . . This makes the lack of attention and concern about higher education [in official circles] all the more surprising. . . . The decline in membership which concerns us all is found . . . in the loss of our own young members." In looking to the future, the statement concluded that "some of the developments we have observed may be irreversible. The Presbyterian Church could be close to a point where its involvement in higher education might be lost forever."[10]

In 1993, in a budget crisis and time of re-structuring in the Presbyterian Church U.S.A., the denomination terminated its Committee on Higher Education, the church body which had been responsible for relationships with its sixty-eight colleges and universities, and reduced the role of its theological education office, the church group relating to its eleven seminaries. By 2009 there were only sixty-two members in the Association of Presbyterian Colleges and Universities. The staff of the Presbyterian Office of Collegiate Ministries was discontinued in further downsizing in 2009.

Chapter 5 Endnotes

1   The purpose of the present work is to ask what we can learn from the past, identify crucial variables, and then focus more specifically on ways of working that may help schools that want to be distinctive and their churches to realize their intentions in the future.

2   Manning M. Pattillo, Jr., and Donald M. Mackenzie, *Church-Sponsored Higher Education in the United States: Report of the Danforth Commission* Washington, DC: American Council on Education, (1966), 276–77.

3   Manning M. Pattillo, Jr., and Donald M. Mackenzie, *Eight Hundred Colleges Face The Future: A Preliminary Report of the Danforth Commission on Church Colleges and Universities* (Saint Louis: The Danforth Foundation, 1965), 49.

4   Private communication (May 13, 2005), James E. Samels, The Education Alliance, 205 Newbury Street, Framingham, Massachusetts 01701. In the December 10, 2004, issue of *The Chronicle Review, The Chronicle of Higher Education,* James Martin and James E. Samels write: ". . . College presidents leave their positions more frequently today than ever before. In the previous generation, the typical term of office might have been a decade or more . . .Various sources project that in a given year, one-fourth to one-third of the accredited colleges and universities in the United States are either preparing for or engaged in presidential searches."

5   In summary comments, both Burtchaell and Marsden make this point: "Short-term improvements often lead to long-term losses." (*Christian Scholar's Review* 29, no.1 [1999]: 177–81.)

6   Private communication from Michael Beaty and Larry Lyon of Baylor University, directors of a Lilly Endowment-supported study in 1995. The data from the respondents would in all likelihood have included a disproportionate percentage of faculty members committed to the Catholic character of the institution. Faculty members uninterested in religious considerations would have been more likely to discard the survey form and decline to respond. Even so, the data indicate that a majority (56.1%) agreed with the statement that their university should "hire faculty who have the highest levels of academic promise or prominence, regardless of religious beliefs or commitments."

7   James Tunstead Burtchaell, "The Alienation of Christian Higher Education in America: Diagnosis and Prognosis," in *Schooling Christians: "Holy Experiments" in American Education*, ed. Stanley Hauerwas and John H. Westerhoff (Grand Rapids: Wm. B. Eerdmans, 1992),129–63; George M. Marsden and Bradley Longfield, eds. *The Secularization of the Academy* (New York: Oxford University Press, 1992), 9–37; Duane Litfin, *Conceiving the Christian College* (Grand Rapids: Wm. B. Eerdmans, 2004), 238–39.

8   In the words of Hobbs and Meeth, "Perhaps a vestige of organizational attachment remains. . . constraints on appointments to the governing board . . . a modest financial contribution . . . courtesies extended to the denomination. . . . But . . . little [denominational involvement] at the functional level." (Walter C. Hobbs and L. Richard Meeth, *Diversity Among Christian Colleges* [Arlington, VA: *Studies in Higher Education*, 1980], 11.)

9   Reversing course has typically been difficult and painful. In their study of 179 colleges, Hobbs and Meeth refer to one that changed over an extended twelve-year

period and say, "Such stories are rare." (Hobbs and Meeth, *Diversity Among Christian Colleges*, 18). More recently, Kennedy and Simon cite a possible exception in James C. Kennedy and Caroline J. Simon, *Can Hope Endure? A Historical Case Study in Christian Higher Education* (Grand Rapids: Wm. B. Eerdmans, 2005). James K. Dittmar's title tells a story: "Against All Odds: An Investigation into the Transformation of Waynesburg College" (*Christian Higher Education* 8, no. 2 [2009], 85–114). At Baylor, which has sometimes been cited as a case in point, the board has accepted the resignations of two presidents in four years. In commenting on their survey findings, Lyon and Beaty of Baylor say, "Almost all religious colleges have moved toward secularization. . . .While . . . administrations may slow down the movement by hiring nonmarginal faculty and explicitly promoting the school's religious heritage, a true reversal is difficult." (Larry Lyon and Michael Beaty, "Integration, Secularization, and the Two-Spheres View at Religious Colleges," *Christian Scholar's Review* 29, no. 1 [1999]: 73.)

10 "A Statement of the Association of Presbyterian Colleges and Universities," March 25, 1990 (Presbyterian Colleges & Universities, 100 Witherspoon Street, Louisville, KY, 40202).

6

THE RECENT PAST AND THE PRESENT SITUATION

A vision for possibilities in the future needs to be rooted in an awareness of the trends of the past and the realities of the present.

Church Relationships and Reputational Excellence

One current reality is that there are relatively few contemporary cases of institutions with very close church relationships that are widely regarded as top models of educational leadership. This claim does not refer to measures of actual student learning but to reputations. At present, reputational academic strength is negatively correlated with religious distinctiveness.

U.S. News and World Report publishes the most popular of current rankings. It ranks 227 private institutions as "best liberal arts colleges" in its 2009 edition.[1] Of the top twenty-six, only two (eight percent) have a self-reported church relationship. Of the next twenty-six in the rankings, just over a third (thirty-five) have a self-reported church relationship. In order of declining ranking, the remaining groups,[2] had percentages of fifty-eight, seventy-three, and eighty-four, respectively. In other words, the higher the institution in the ratings for this kind of "reputational excellence," the less likely it was to have a church relationship.[3]

Ways of assessing educational effectiveness are being debated. Assessments have often been based on input variables (e.g., size of library, academic degrees held by faculty members, intellectual aptitudes of entering students) rather than on data on actual learning and growth of students during their college years. Reputations are not always based on realities. Some of the present rankings are based on conventional measurements of excellence that do not measure actual learning, and they frequently largely ignore student growth in non-cognitive areas that may be just as important for the futures of the students and their world.[4]

On a list of institutions with top academic reputations, many institutions have historical—rather than active and current—church ties. Some, of course, have severed their church relationships. At the same time, there are church colleges that most of us would not consider academically excellent. Even assuming that reputations are based on criteria that may not be entirely appropriate, and leaving aside the question of whether such reputations are justified or not, a negative correlation between reputational excellence and close church relationship is an environmental factor that can appear in the public consciousness and the media.

Student Personal, Social, and Spiritual Development

Some colleges and universities say that they are interested in the growth of the "whole student," in all dimensions of a maturing student's personal, social, and, sometimes, spiritual development. Assessing growth in these dimensions often presents challenges.

The problem of assessment exists in elite institutions as well as in institutions of more modest reputations. Columbia College and some other academically prestigious institutions in the East have professed to instill in students an interest in scholarship. A careful research report of the 1960s showed that forty-four percent of the entering first-year students at Columbia intended to enter scholarly careers—but that only nineteen percent of graduating seniors still wanted to enter scholarly careers. The net effect, contrary to the impression given in public statements at that time, was that Columbia College students were apparently not becoming more interested in entering scholarly careers![5]

Preparing future Ph.D.s may not be at the heart of the missions of most church colleges and universities, but one of very few data sets that can provide an objective way of measuring one kind of actual longer-term student outcome is the database for the baccalaureate origins of students who get earned doctorates. Studies of the undergraduate colleges from which Ph.D.s come show that, contrary to some popular impressions, private colleges and universities are overproducers. In a study of the rate of preparing doctorates awarded in the years 1991–2000, ninety-three of the top one hundred institutions were private institutions, and many of these were church-related. Indeed, ten of the top one hundred were Presbyterian, and this was more than the total number (seven) of public colleges and universities in the list.[6]

What is true in the cognitive area is often also true in the areas of personal and social development. Many colleges and universities that have said they would further the personal or social development of students have not produced hard data to support their claims. Many colleges that have said their students were growing spiritually have not had good data to support this claim.[7] In 1994, fifty institutions in the Council for Christian Colleges & Universities[8] launched a "Collaborative Assessment Project" with videotape interviews of sample populations as well as surveys of nineteen thousand students. The surveys included faculty members, and their longitudinal interviews and surveys included alumni two years after graduation. Their methods can provide researchers, administrators, and boards with data that have often not been available in the past.

In recent decades, the Lutheran Educational Conference of North America has sponsored alumni research on outcomes in student development and involvement in church and community life on the part of graduates of their institutions in comparison with the outcomes for graduates of public institutions.[9]

In a work on legal issues in higher education, Moots and Gaffney note that in a key Supreme Court case, one of the justices alluded to religious restrictions of a certain institution, "but dismissed them as . . . 'institutional rhetoric.'" Moots and Gaffney note that "some measure of 'institutional rhetoric' in college and university bulletins describing the general religious orientation of the institution appears to be acceptable, because the Court apparently does not believe that this sort of rhetoric describes the reality of what goes on in the classroom."[10]

As we have seen, public mistrust of institutions of the larger American society has increased in recent years. Mistrust of educational institutions has not increased as much as mistrust of political and economic institutions, but it has become a problem, particularly because colleges and universities are fragile institutions whose productivity is hard to quantify and because institutions of this kind are especially dependent upon public trust for their survival and health.[11]

An editorial in the *New York Times* summarizes the public's ambivalence about American colleges and universities and the increased interest in actual measures of student development:

Americans generally accept on faith that this country has the best higher education system in the world. . . . The business community has long disputed this view, citing the large numbers of college graduates who lack what should be basic skills. . . .[12] Colleges and universities should join in the hunt for acceptable ways to measure student progress. . . . Unless the higher education community wakes up to this problem . . . the movement aimed at regulating colleges and forcing them to demonstrate that students are actually learning will only keep growing.[13]

Clifford Adelman of the Institute for Higher Education Policy writes: "We've had a good run, but we are no longer at the cutting edge. U.S. higher education can no longer sail on the assumption of world dominance, oblivious to the creative energies, natural intelligence, and hard work of other nations."[14] America has been the world leader in higher education and in the rates of college attendance on the part of college-age young people, but other nations are becoming more competitive on the world scene.

The American public wants to know whether schools are doing what they say they are doing. The major regional accrediting associations want a "culture of evidence" and have asked institutions to assess and document student outcomes in all areas included in their public mission statements.

Public Statements about Church Relationships

Among church institutions, a discrepancy between rhetoric and reality sometimes seems to extend also to their public statements about changes in their church relationships. Substantial changes in structures and charters are sometimes accompanied by public statements that traditional and historic relationships with church bodies have not been changed.

In a March 1, 2005, announcement of a purchase of the Roman Catholic Franciscan University of the Prairies by the for-profit, on-line firm Bridgepoint Education, the chief executive officer of the purchaser said, "The university . . . would lose its religious identity . . . . They [the leaders of the Franciscans] were aware from the very beginning that that would be going away." The president of Franciscan, however, is reported as saying, "This is an event in the history of this place that is going to assure our heritage."[15] The Franciscan University of the Prairies is now Ashford University.

Developments in Various Church Groups

This chapter concludes with a brief overview of developments in several of the larger American church denominations and groups, including Roman Catholic, Presbyterian, Methodist, Lutheran, Adventist, Baptist, and Evangelical churches.

Discussion in the Roman Catholic Church, the largest American denomination with almost 60 million adult members, has centered around a draft of a document Pope John Paul II issued in the 1980s and, after much controversy, finalized in 1990 as an apostolic constitution, *Ex corde Ecclesiae*. Philip Gleason, a leading historian of Catholic higher education, has said that "a concern for the autonomy of the academic institution" has been the leitmotif in the thinking that led up to *Ex corde Ecclesiae*. He writes:

> It is essential to note that, in this context, "autonomy" means freedom from external ecclesiastical control, not all sorts of external controls, since no university is "autonomous" with respect to the requirements established by accrediting associations, governmental agencies, philanthropic institutions, and accepted academic procedures. The progressive sloughing off of external religious controls, while continuing to accommodate to the latter sort, can legitimately be spoken of as secularization.[16]

In her report to the Roman Catholic Bishops and Presidents Committee in November 1998, Monika Hellwig, at that time the executive director of the Association of Catholic Colleges and Universities, said: "There is an increasing awareness that the Catholic institutions need to take steps to assert and define themselves rather than be swallowed up in the secularizing trends endemic to the academy at large."

The religious orders, which historically actually provided the chief institutional link between Catholic higher education and the Catholic church, are in decline and no longer in a position to play the role they once played. Gleason agrees with others that "'proliferation' and 'duplication of effort'" have "militated against academic excellence in Catholic higher education."[17]

In brief, *Ex corde Ecclesiae* and canon law provide that the local bishop is responsible for (1) determining the "Catholicity" of universities (as with other local institutions in his diocese), (2) hiring a faculty that is predominantly Catholic, and (3) granting Catholic theologians mandates to teach Catholic theology in Catholic institutions. The American bishops approved the canonical requirements in 1999. But some Catholic institutions did not meet the requirements, and the requirements were not implemented as a test of Catholic identity.

Since 2005 there has been a new pope. A half year after his inauguration Pope Benedict XVI indicated in a speech at the University of Notre Dame that he might implement a policy of "evangelical pruning" of some Catholic colleges and universities that had become too secular, declaring them no longer Catholic. Future school-church relationships are not clear.[18]

Problems and tensions are not surprising. The Notre Dame faculty and administration, for example, would hardly see Bishop John D'Arcy of their diocese as having the staff or resources in his office in Fort Wayne to provide for appropriate evaluations of the University of Notre Dame and its theology professors.[19]

The Roman Catholic Church did not update its ways of relating to its colleges and universities decades ago when it began employing large numbers of faculty members who had not taken vows and when it placed the governance of many of its institutions in the hands of semi-autonomous or self-perpetuating lay boards of trustees. By 1999, the front page news releases reported that one of the moderate archbishops said: "The tension between the hierarchy and theologians now is the highest I have seen it in my 36 years as a superior in the Catholic church."[20]

Peter Steinfels writes: "It is part of a larger story that stretches far beyond the 200-plus Roman Catholic campuses to many other religiously affiliated colleges and universities in the United States."[21]

Ex corde Ecclesiae has contributed to a renewed interest in reflection on Catholic campus identity on many Catholic campuses. Philip Gleason has said that "church authorities are acting to keep Catholic universities from suffering the secularization that obliterated the religious identity of Protestant colleges a century ago."[22] Some colleges and universities, especially some Roman Catholic institutions, have included new vice presidents for mission and identity in their administrative cabinets.

The Presbyterian Church U.S.A., a Protestant denomination with roots in the Reformation and a historic emphasis on education, adopted statements in 1993 and made dramatic changes in its structures that made it clear that it was formally stepping back from its earlier involvement in higher education. As mentioned before, in a move that included retrenchment in the headquarters staff, top administrators were fired and the church's Committee on Higher Education was discontinued. There were further cuts in campus staffing in 2009.

In 1994 F. Thomas Trotter of the United Methodist Church wrote:

> The United Methodist Church, in a fit of distraction, passed a resolution in the 1968 General Conference that urged their colleges to

consider separation from all church connections so that they could survive as independent secular institutions. The Supreme Court decision in Roemer v. Maryland (1976) made such panic premature and misplaced, but it reflected the low estate of higher education in the denomination. The church could not articulate reasons. . .for its historical mission in learning. The churches generally held indifferent ideas about education and were prepared to move to other seemingly more urgent missions.[23]

In 1992, the presiding bishop of the Evangelical Lutheran Church in America, the largest Lutheran denomination in America, proposed to limit financial support of their colleges and universities from the churchwide budget. The institutional presidents and other supporters of ELCA higher education rallied, and the proposal was defeated, but the support has been reduced each time there has been a budget crisis.

Turning to more conservative denominations in America, we find two phenomena:

1. Although they are at different stages in the process, many have adopted institutional structures that are leading them toward increasing school-church distance. In this decade, the Seventh-day Adventists, who have close church-school relationships, have, in response to environmental pressures, come to refer to the "autonomy of institutional boards."[24] Their institutions used to have staff salaries that were coordinated with their church structures; now one or more of their institutions is setting salaries more independently. Robert Wuthnow, Princeton University professor and director of the University's Center for the Study of Religion has written: "Even among the students and faculty of the leading evangelical colleges, much ferment and accommodation with the secular culture has been in evidence."[25]
2. There are frequent headlines of church-school conflict. Some denominations have resorted to takeovers and attempted takeovers that have seriously damaged their educational efforts and will affect them adversely for years to come.

Such is the case with the Southern Baptists, by far the largest American Protestant denomination. Conservatives gained control of the national convention in 1979. Some colleges and universities with long histories have cut their ties with the church. Some faculty members with other options have left their church seminaries. Several of their universities have started new divinity schools to compete with the official Southern Baptist seminaries controlled by the convention.

A Southern Baptist who has been a university president, seminary president, and president of the Southern Baptist publishing house, has chronicled the events in these words:

> The almost total disruption of the largest non-Catholic denomination in America [the Southern Baptist Convention] has occurred in the last decade and a half. From a well-organized and cooperative body deeply involved in missions and education, it has moved toward fragmentation. Its institutions and agencies have suffered near catastrophic disruption. . . .[26]

The University of Richmond cut its governing and financial ties to the Virginia Baptist association that founded it 169 years earlier. A member of the committee set up by the association's governing body said, "We had come to the conclusion that the university has one mission and we have another. . . ."[27] Baylor University, the largest Baptist university in the nation, altered its relationship with the Southern Baptist Convention after 1979 and with the Baptist General Convention of Texas in 1990. Other Southern Baptist schools that have severed ties with their conventions include Wake Forest, Averett, Furman, Stetson, Richmond, and Georgetown College. Shorter College tried to cut its ties with the Georgia Baptist Convention, but this attempt was rejected by the Georgia Supreme Court in 2005. The Georgia Baptist Convention severed the ties with Mercer University in 2006. Although Belmont University tried to loosen its ties with the Tennessee Baptist Convention, the convention rejected this move in May 2006. However, it settled a lawsuit and severed the ties in 2007. A release in *Today's News, The Chronicle of Higher Education* for April 8, 2005 begins: "The Baptist General Association of Virginia and Averett University agreed to sever their ties last month, ending a 145-year relationship."

Hannah Lodwick writes: "The trend [string of defections] is well-established and accelerating: the largest and richest Baptist colleges are going it alone, and others who can will follow."[28]

Colleges of smaller conservative denominations and independent Christian colleges are also in the headlines from time to time.

A declining interest in denominational and "institutional church" structures and an increasing individualism in the American society have affected church partners in church-school relationships. In a *Christianity Today* survey article celebrating the fiftieth anniversary of the founding of the National Association of Evangelicals, evangelicals Nathan Hatch and Michael Hamilton wrote:

> The evangelical resurgence of the last half-century has unintentionally chipped away at the power and influence of the institutional church. . . . The result is that fewer evangelicals than a generation ago stand in a religious tradition that can provide ballast and long-term orientation. . . . Devaluing the church enfeebles Christians in two respects: it cuts us off from the past, and it relieves us of accountability. . . . Evangelicals. . . have difficulty seeing themselves as responsible and accountable to the church. . . .The very structures of evangelical life are attuned to the intense individualism of American culture. . . . Evangelicals have not won the right to be heard by twentieth-century intellectuals.[29]

In a modest reversal of the trend, some new conservative Catholic and Protestant schools are emerging, such as Christendom College (Roman Catholic), Ave Maria School of Law (Roman Catholic), Thomas Aquinas (Roman Catholic), and Regent University (Protestant, interdenominational).

Interest in Religion and Spirituality

Chapter 3 pointed out that religion and spirituality have found new life in much of the world and in the wider American culture and have been reflected on American public and private college campuses, especially since the early 1990s. On Roman Catholic campuses, interest and debate over church relationships were stimulated by intense discussions of bishops and Catholic educators about the Vatican's *Ex corde Ecclesiae*. On campuses of church-related institutions of many traditions, interest was stimulated by the foundation-supported researches and publications of Marsden, Burtchaell, Schwehn, Cuninggim, Sloan, O'Brien, and others in the first half of the decade of the 1990s. The Lilly Endowment led the way with a ten-year, $15.6 million initiative over the decade.[30] In the face of the "growing distance between many colleges and their sponsoring religious bodies," the Endowment's Initiative on Religion & Higher Education encouraged church-related colleges and universities "to strengthen institutional practices reflecting their religious heritage."

In a survey, Lilly evaluators found that seventy-three percent of the respondents at mainline Protestant schools, fifty-three percent of those at Catholic schools, and thirty-four percent of those at conservative Protestant schools agreed with the statement: "Faculty at my college/university are divided over the religious identity of the institution."

The Lilly Initiative supported a remarkable array of projects to strengthen the place of religion on public and independent campuses. Over 1200 administrators and faculty members from 177 colleges and universities took part in programs "designed to heighten a sense of faith and vocation." Lilly sponsored fifty regional and national meetings on religion in the academy. As a result, "Faculty members formed discussion groups on more than seventy college and university campuses." The Lilly Initiative funded major and influential faculty/staff formation programs: Collegium, the Lilly Fellows Program, the Rhodes Consultation, the Institute for Student Affairs at Catholic colleges, and the Association for Religion and Intellectual Life mentoring communities.

The University of Notre Dame initiated a Lilly-funded "Faculty Recruitment Network: A Web-Based Resource for Church-Related Higher Education" to help prospective faculty members and institutions find one another. To meet some Internal Revenue Service concerns and for other administrative reasons, the project was undertaken as a new "Career Center" by the Council for Christian Colleges & Universities in Washington, D.C. It has since been discontinued. The concept was apparently ahead of its time.

The 2000 evaluation report on Lilly's Initiative notes that historians were especially active in publishing new books on religion and higher education in the 1990s. They recommend social scientific research that can provide better current data. The evaluators further note that the impact of the Lilly Initiative was more on the "personal enrichment" of faculty members and less on "institutional change." The evaluators observe that "individuals as individuals can rarely affect substantive institutional change" and recommend "incentives and support for colleges and universities interested in making positive changes relative to their religious identity and mission." The evaluators also note "a paucity of religiously oriented programs for trustees and senior-level administrators who as leaders, set forth the vision for their colleges, determine policy, lead by example, and set the tone for much of the day-to-day operations of their institutions."

The present work is intended to move beyond existing historical studies and to focus on what trustees, administrators, and faculty members can do to effect needed institutional change.

Prospects

The interest in the larger American society in religion and spirituality has been heartening. Probably more books on religion and higher education have been authored in the past fifteen years than were published in the previous half-century. Some distinctive religious colleges have recently emerged or grown rapidly.[31] At the same time, the involvement of the major denominations in American higher education has declined, partly because they have followed traditional models of relationship that have made movement toward dissociation almost inevitable, and partly because of a recent megatrend toward "localism" in North American culture and church life. Church members have been hesitant to contribute financially to larger churchwide efforts beyond the local congregation or parish. And some churches and schools have taken actions that have led to conflict and served as models of what to avoid in future relationships.

In important ways, the experiences of churches working in education today parallel those of states in their relationships with their colleges and universities in earlier decades of the past century. Educational entrepreneurs wanted the freedom to use taxpayers' money to set up new colleges and technical schools and universities wherever they wanted to. In response, some legislatures took draconian steps that were sometimes ill informed and politically motivated and that did not further the development of good schools in their respective states. With a need for new structures and ways of working in the public sector, new models have been developed in recent decades.

As we have seen, the past trend has been one of increasing distance between churches and schools over time. If churches and schools would continue with the approaches and structures they have followed in the past, we would have to anticipate that this would continue in the future. But the destiny of groups interested in higher education in the future is not locked into the course of the past and present. Churches and other groups with distinctive beliefs and practices can learn from the past and develop different structures and ways of working for the future.

Chapter 6 Endnotes

1 *America's Best Colleges*, 2009 edition. The *U.S. News & World Report* uses the classifi-cations of the Carnegie Foundation for the Advancement of Teaching.

2 The remaining groups were of sixty-nine, sixty-three, and forty-three colleges, respectively.

3 In some cases, the church relationships might be categorized by some researchers as "nominal" or "historical." See Victor Stoltzfus, *Church-Affiliated Higher Education: Exploratory Case Studies* (Goshen, IN: Pinchpenny Press, 1992) for similar data using different categories for church-relatedness.

4 A problem in the *U.S. News* ratings was identified in an independent report commis-sioned by the *U.S. News* in 1997. Consultants from the National Opinion Research Center, a nonprofit corporation affiliated with the University of Chicago, wrote: "The principal weakness of the current approach is that the weights used to combine the various measures into an overall rating lack any defensible empirical or theoretical basis." (Leo Reisberg, *Independent Report in 1997 Assailed Substance of 'U.S. News' College Rankings* [August 28, 2000, accessed]; available from http://chronicle.com/daily/2000/08/2000082801n.htm .) More recently, David Leonhardt has said, "Measuring how well students learn is incredibly difficult." ("Rank Colleges, But Rank Them Right," *The New York Times*, August 16, 2006.) In a fall 2006 release, the Association of Governing Boards has said, "Consensus does not exist within higher education either on how best to measure educational quality and student progress or on how to communicate the subtleties of that information effectively to the public" (Washington, DC).

5 Stanley Raffel, "Some Effects of Columbia College on its Students," (unpublished report, New York: Columbia University, 1965).

6 Data corrected for sizes of graduating classes can be found in a report, "Proportional Ph.D. Productivity," by David Davis-Van Atta, director of institutional research and analysis, Carleton College, Northfield, MN (January 2004). See also Alfred E. Hall's earlier study, "Starting at the Beginning—the Baccalaureate Origins of Doctorate Recipients, 1920–1980," *Change: The Magazine of Higher Learning* 16, no. 3 (April 1984), 40.

7 Peter Schmidt, *Promoting Students' Moral Development Is Devilishly Tricky, Studies Suggest* (April 14, 2009, accessed); available at http://chronicle.com/daily/2009/03/13370n.htm. The Mennonite Education Agency (Goshen, Indiana) has had some limited data on student outcomes for students from various Mennonite congregations and conferences who attend Mennonite colleges in comparison with those who stay at home or attend public institutions. It may not be surprising to find that students who attend Mennonite colleges are more likely to be active members and leaders of in Mennonite and Christian churches in later life—they may well have gone to Mennonite colleges because they and their families were more interested in church life in the first place. One of the especially interesting findings, however, is that Mennonite students from some congregations and conferences, at least, are more likely to be active in church life in their later years if they attend state colleges and universities than if they stay in their home communities and do not attend post-secondary schools of any kind. It seems that, even with the possibility of involvement in local congregational life, staying at home is less likely to motivate a Mennonite young person to longer-term church involvement than the kind of serious reflection

on contemporary culture they can get in public and other non-religious colleges and universities.

8 329 8th Street, NE, Washington, DC 20002–6158. The project, which was initially funded by the U.S. Government's Fund for the Improvement of Postsecondary Education, has been merged with another project to form the present "Comprehensive Assessment Project."

9 A recent summary of some findings can be found at http://www.lutherancolleges. org.

10 Philip R. Moots and Edward McGlynn Gaffney Jr., *Church and Campus: Legal Issues in Religiously Affiliated Higher Education* (Notre Dame: University of Notre Dame Press, 1979), 76, 78.

11 Already more than fifteen years ago, the annual meeting of the American Association for Higher Education on April 5–8, 1992, was on the theme, "Regaining the Public Trust." No one in the meeting questioned the implication of the theme—that there had been a loss of public trust and that regaining it was important. Recently, Vice Provost Lucido of the University of Southern California and President Schapiro of Williams College have written, "Restoring public trust in education is as important as in other industries." (Jerome A. Lucido and Morton Owen Schapiro, "Joe, Mauricio, and the Public Trust," *Inside Higher Ed,* February 13, 2009, http://www.insidehigh-ered.com/views/2009/02/13/lucido.)

12 In the September 10–16, 2005, issue of the *Economist,* Adrian Wooldridge, the magazine's Washington bureau chief, does say that "America has the best system of higher education in the world." Wooldridge notes a recent ranking by a Chinese university that placed seventeen American colleges among the world's top twenty in such areas as Nobel Prize winners, publications in professional journals, etc.

13 Editorial, *The New York Times*, February 26, 2006.

14 "The Bologna Process for U.S. Eyes: Re-Learning Higher Education in the Age of Convergence" (Washington, DC: Institute for Higher Education Policy, April 8, 2009).

15 This is reported in Thomas Bartlett, "Catholic Company to Buy Roman Catholic University in Iowa and Turn It into a For-Profit Institution" in *Today's News, The Chronicle of Higher Education,* March 3, 2005. The release also indicated that the purchaser, a California company, would be changing the name of the university.

16 Philip Gleason, "The American Background of *Ex corde Ecclesiae*: A Historical Perspective," in *Catholic Universities in Church and Society: A Dialogue on* Ex corde Ecclesiae, ed. John P. Langan (Washington, DC: Georgetown University Press, 1993), 8. We noted in an earlier chapter Burtchaell's reference to the "dogma of 'institutional autonomy'" and his listing of ways in which a typical college or university is linked in a matrix of requirements and obligations with over fifty outside organizations and agencies. (Burtchaell, "Out of the Heartburn of the Church," 656–695.)

17 Gleason, "The American Background of *Ex corde Ecclesiae*," 5.

18 Stephen L. Trainor, "A Delicate Balance: The Catholic College in America," *Change: The Magazine of Higher Learning* 38, no. 2, March/April 2006, 14–21.

19 On February 2, 1999, Francis Cardinal George of Chicago summarized the situation in an address to the presidents and other administrators at the annual meeting of the Association of Catholic Colleges and Universities by saying that the expansion of hiring of faculty members from outside "the earlier pool" had "created a problem."

He noted that the papal mandates were asking the bishops to do something they did not want to do and indicated that he personally favored church-school relationships not now in existence. In 2005, Burton Bollag wrote, "The requirement [that theologians obtain a certificate from the local bishop] has been largely ignored. Few theologians have sought a *mandatum*. And despite attempts by a few American bishops to have Catholic institutions require it of job candidates, virtually no colleges have gone along" ("Mourning a Pope Who Stressed Orthodoxy," *The Chronicle of Higher Education,* April 15 2005).

The lack of clarity and agreement on structural relationships emerged recently in the local press in a front-page article, "D'Arcy Calls [Notre Dame President] Jenkins' Justification for Invite Flawed" (*Goshen News*, April 23, 2009). It concerned a Notre Dame pattern of inviting new U.S. presidents to give commencement addresses and receive honorary degrees. President Jenkins said their invitation to President Obama was "in compliance with a statement . . . passed by the U.S. bishops in 2004." The press report continues: "D'Arcy said the meaning of the statement is clear and that if Jenkins had questions he should have asked D'Arcy, not other university presidents. He wrote that the local bishop, 'who is the teacher and lawgiver in his diocese,' should provide the 'authentic interpretation' of such [bishops'] statements."

20 Archbishop Rembert G. Weakland of Milwaukee in Beth McMurtrie, "Bishops Approve Controversial Rules for Catholic Education," *The Chronicle of Higher Education,* November 26, 1999.

21 "Catholic Bishops and Educators near Another Round Over Effort to Resist Secularization," *The New York Times,* October 16, 1999.

22 In Gene Stowe, "Catholic Education Topic of Talk," *South Bend Tribune,* September 30, 2005.

23 F. Thomas Trotter, "Foreward," in Merrimon Cuninggim, *Uneasy Partners: The College and the Church* (Nashville: Abingdon Press, 1994), 12.

24 "Higher Education Policies" in *North American Division Working Policy 1996–97,* 217. In the light of the degree of collaboration and coordination among the thirteen American and ninety-four world-wide Adventist institutions, the author would raise a question as to the accuracy of the term "autonomy" in characterizing Adventist relationships. Perhaps the change is only an instance of "rhetorical slide."

25 Robert Wuthnow, *The Struggle for America's Soul: Evangelicals, Liberals, and Secularism* (Grand Rapids: Wm. B. Eerdmans, 1989), 158.

26 Grady C. Cothen, *What Happened to the Southern Baptist Convention? A Memoir of the Controversy* (Macon, GA: Smyth & Helwys Publishing, 1993), ix. See a recent front-page article, Alan Finder, "Baptist Colleges Scale Back Ties to their Church," *The New York Times*, July 22, 2006.

27 Frank A. Cain, cited in Beth McMurtie, "U. of Richmond Expects to Cut Ties to Baptists," *The Chronicle of Higher Education,* November 5, 1999.

28 Hannah Lodwick, "Largest Baptist Universities Face Watershed Leadership Changes," *Associated Baptist Press*, December 15, 2005. Also reported in the *Christian Century* 123, no. 1, January 10, 2006, 16.

29 *Christianity Today* 36, October 5, 1992, 29–30. Nathan Hatch was provost of the University of Notre Dame when he was chosen as president of Wake Forest University in 2005.

30 The citations in this section are from a report by Kathleen Mahoney, John Schmalzbauer, and James Youniss, "Revitalizing Religion in the Academy: Summary of the Evaluation of Lilly Endowment's Initiative on Religion & Higher Education" (Indianapolis: Lilly Endowment, 2000).

31 Naomi Schaefer Riley, *God on the Quad: How Religious Colleges and the Missionary Generation Are Changing America* (New York: St. Martin's Press, 2005).

PART II

⬿

WHO MIGHT WANT SCHOOLS THAT ARE DIFFERENT?

7

Curriculum:
A Different "What"

Many schools would like to emulate the traditional model of academic excellence, i.e., they would like to be more like Harvard. Some of what follows in Parts II, III, and IV will be relevant for schools aiming at traditional excellence. For example, schools that want to be excellent will need to have ways of recruiting excellent faculties.

Some schools serve special kinds of students. There are African American colleges, women's colleges, and a few men's colleges. There are institutes of technology. Some of my observations and recommendations will be relevant for them.

Historically, churches, more than any other special groups, have sponsored colleges and universities. Religious understandings attempt to integrate learning in various fields and attempt to deal with questions of ultimate reality. My continuing focus is on churches that are interested in having schools and on church schools that are rooted in distinctive epistemologies and have an interest in non-cognitive as well as cognitive student outcomes. My recommendations will be most immediately relevant for schools that want to be distinctively churchly in the longer-term future.

Distinctive Education and the Public Interest

Is having a variety of schools that are distinctive in various ways in the public interest? As we have seen, some commentators have seen the reduction in the ecological diversity in American higher education as an occasion for concern.[1] Some have seen the diversity of American institutions as one of the reasons for America's world leadership in higher education. After a ten-year study of European universities, sociologist Burton Clark, formerly of Yale and more recently of UCLA, writes of

> ... the important role private higher education can play in system differentiation. National systems around the globe with few, if any, private institutions are now seeking to develop them: Latin America has been a hothouse of such experimentation; Japan has a huge private sector; and even state-led Europe is now tiptoeing into permitting the growth of private institutions. . . . The American system . . . has long been blessed. . . .
>
> ... The ideal system of higher education in the 21st century will be reliably redundant, possessing a robust capacity to compensate for its own failures. . . . Higher education systems will need an even greater variety of institutional instruments than they now possess to self-correct and to respond more quickly and more widely to societal demands in the 21st century.[2]

Recent authors have had very different views on the past work of the Christian church in higher education. Some have seen it as a great success story—the pioneering work of churches has led to public and independent institutions that are the best in the world—and they would say that the church can now focus its efforts on other urgent needs. Other authors have looked differently at the past and have had a more critical perspective on the history of a drift toward greater church-school distance and secularization. In the following chapters we will look in greater detail at why these authors and other recent leaders have taken such different and sometimes opposing points of view.

Conversation on What Is Important

Education is a conversation between the older and younger generations on what is important. Sometimes the conversation is carried on in writing, involving books and libraries. Most of the excitement in the conversation surfaces, however, when the learners and teachers actually meet together in the curriculum and in the informal associations that are a part of school life.

The "what" of the educational conversation depends on who the teachers and learners are and what they and their friends and supporters think is important.

Although this point might seem obvious, it seems that it cannot be taken for granted. Some people seem to think the curriculum is a given that comes from the past. Educators have often been conventional in their program planning. Instead of seriously asking what is really important, educators have tended to ask what someone else is doing and to imitate that. Sometimes students ask why this or that particular matter is so terribly important and how it got into the curriculum and never got displaced.

From the perspective of organizational theory, we have observed that the American high school, the American college, and schools at several other levels are highly institutionalized entities in the American society. Everyone knows what something that calls itself a college is supposed to be and do. Educators are not the only ones who are conventional: parents, students, taxpayers, and citizens in general all have in mind some well-established conventions about what educators are expected to do and how schools are to work. School people are expected to follow their scripts. In the process, the question of what is really important may never get seriously raised.

When I was a ninth-grade student in a rural high school in Ohio, everyone in the ninth grade had to take ninth-grade algebra. It was "general education" for all students. In algebra we had to learn to solve quadratic equations (e.g., $2x^2 + 5x - 12 = 0$). Apparently it was considered important for all high school students to learn to solve quadratic equations as a part of their preparation for assuming adult roles in the State of Ohio.

A few years ago, in connection with other campus assignments, I conducted an informal survey of college presidents and deans. All were upstanding citizens of various states who had not only gotten through high school, but were college graduates and had doctorates. They were leaders chosen by our society to educate our youth.

I began with a former faculty member at Princeton and Harvard, an upstanding Rotarian, and a president and academic leader on his campus. I gave him a simple quadratic equation. He couldn't solve it. Then I asked nine other academic leaders on different campuses and in different states. Only one of the ten could solve the ninth-grade equation!

We can reflect on what this is saying. What if the high school children of a high school or college faculty member ask their parents for help with a quadratic equation? What impression will they get about how important quadratic equations and school really are for their elders?

These questions may not be entirely fair. Work in algebra can help students understand the importance of symbolic languages in our culture.

Perhaps at least some Americans in our world of technology should know about quadratic equations if we are to compete with the Chinese in years to come, and including quadratic equations in the ninth grade is a way of encouraging some of our students to continue in the world of mathematics. Maybe quadratic equations are like chess or Latin, good for a kind of mental discipline—but we don't require chess and Latin of all students. In any case, faculty members and administrators in other fields and other leaders in our society need to think seriously about their reasons for including what they include in required curricula. Requiring learning that many adults do not find important is not the best way of achieving educational ends.

How did quadratic equations get into the curriculum required of all Ohio high school students years ago? Those of us in academia (and increasingly others outside) know that that the curriculum is often a product of an extended faculty log-rolling process: "I'll vote for your physical science requirement, if you'll vote for my American government course." What results is a fragmented curriculum that does not have the full support of even the faculty that voted for it. The professors of political science and English ought to know something about what is going on in the physical science course and believe it is important for themselves if they want to require it of all students.

Sometimes when someone proposes something important that should be in the curriculum, everyone says the curriculum is crowded. Is it too full of topics that even faculty colleagues do not consider very important? As educational leaders and supporters of education, we have to be ready to engage in the hard work of asking what we and our fellow citizens think is really important and building curricula with integrity out of the results of our corporate discernment.

Many of us are concerned about a kind of liberal arts education that prepares students for more than entry-level jobs. We are by now aware that our students will change jobs many times in their working lives, and that they need a broad arts preparation in some fundamental fields and in learning how to learn. They need more than preparation for specific jobs. Even in our older generation, many have needed to be prepared for different job roles in business, the professions, and administration. We anticipate that our students will change roles even more frequently. Beyond that, most of us believe that what is important in life involves more than work.

I will never forget a visit with an old school friend and classmate at a reunion a few years ago. He had spent his life working in a tire factory and had just retired. I asked my friend about his old job. He said he had carried bags of a chemical used in the manufacturing process from one place to another. After some years, he had been promoted. Before retiring, he had become a foreman overseeing the transport of the bags of chemicals. I asked him what the chemicals were. Were they making better tires? Would changes in the chemicals increase tire life? I drew a blank. He said he had never asked what the chemicals were.

Most of us would hope that, whatever their work, our college graduates would ask a few questions about what they were doing. When we were younger, many of us had summer jobs in construction or manufacturing. We will have students who may carry bags as we did, but we hope that they will wonder what is in the bags, whether they can find ways of streamlining the operations to everyone's benefit, and, indeed, if they are in manufacturing or construction, whether there are contents of the bags or processes that would make their products last longer or be more useful and in those ways make the world a better place.

Many of us in education do our work in the hope that through it and our students we can be making the world a better place for humankind.

Making the World a Better Place

What is important in working at making the world a better place? Good people differ. Before 1870, American schools taught the great truths and values of the Western tradition. Students read the classics and pondered the great questions of the Greek and Judeo-Christian forebears of western culture. Then came a revolution in education. The discovery of new truth became a central purpose. To learn about nature you did not read the classics—you did experiments. The natural sciences became a major part of the curriculum. To learn about humankind and society, you collected data and tested hypotheses. Studies in the classical works in ethics and social philosophy gave way to the modern social sciences.

Practical truth also came to the fore. Instead of reading about the eternal truths, people wanted to know how to grow better wheat. States established publicly supported land-grant institutions for the study of agricultural and mechanical arts. Americans needed knowledge to tame the frontier and things to make life more than a struggle for survival. The society needed educated people in medicine, teaching, and the other professions.

One could say that, in the early period of American schooling, people looked to the past for meaning. The revolution in scholarship and education in middle and later years of the nineteenth century was a turn to the present—trying to get in touch with what is real and important by observing and describing what we find in the world around us through the modes of inquiry of the specialized disciplines, especially those of the natural and social sciences.

Now we are in the twenty-first century. It is not clear that what we need most now is more things. Indeed, we are polluted by some of the things we have made and their byproducts. By now, some professions are crowded. We ask about the needs of our world in a new way. What should schools be doing now? What is important now?

Before answering these questions directly, we need to recall an observation made earlier. When students read the great classics in early American schools, and later when scholars discovered new knowledge using the supposedly objective methods of inquiry of the various academic disciplines, there was a generalized American religion of the educated white Anglo-Saxon Protestant citizenry. It provided a universe of discourse and certain understandings on moral questions and values that were shared by liberally educated members and leaders in the society. In the major periods of classical and then experimental-pragmatic education, there was a kind of consensus among leadership groups in American society about the great truths and moral values of the Greek and Judeo-Christian traditions.

In our time, that consensus has come unglued. We are not agreed on what is "true." We disagree on fundamental values. In the post-Christendom era, we are more aware that we are living in a pluralistic society and world.

The discipline-oriented, pragmatic-utilitarian approach to education symbolized by the older multiversity is still dominant in American education, but it is being challenged. A people's education is ultimately based on that people's vision of the good society and of what it means to participate in it. A school cannot be viewed apart from the vision and purposes of the people it represents.

"Religionists" in a Pluralistic Society

In a pluralistic society the ways start to part. Jewish people believe that God was acting in history in a special way in Abraham and his descendents and that the people of Israel have a special calling as God's agents in the world today. Christians also see God acting in Abraham and his descendents, but in a unique way in Jesus Christ and those who confess his name. Free Church descendents of the sixteenth century Anabaptists have differed from

Establishment Christians in their vision of what God intends human life in society to be. However, as we have seen, mainline Protestants, Evangelicals, and American Catholics all increasingly recognize that they are not in control of the levers of power in our post-Christendom world and that our society must be seen as genuinely pluralistic.

Jews, Anabaptists, African American Christians, Muslims, and many others are not surprised to find that the larger American society is really a collection of many different societies and that they live among many peoples gathered about all kinds of special loyalties, interests, and understandings of reality. It is not at all surprising that groups with distinctive beliefs and practices want educational conversations with the next generation of young people who are interested in exploring their visions to see how the visions grow out of their histories and contribute to their future lives and missions as peoples.

We live in a world with problems and needs—poverty, crime, broken family relationships, ethnic rivalries, tensions between tribes and nations, alienation from meaning and purpose, to begin a list. There is more to do than can be done. And yet, with all of these problems, there are people who cannot find jobs. Somehow, whether through miscalculation or misplaced values or for other reasons, our society isn't matching the available people with the tasks that need to be done. We have not found a way of packaging as jobs some things that need to be done in our society and in the world.

Some Christians and church educators have a particular point of view in this situation. Jesus lived in a society of serious need. He saw some needs in the world of his time. He saw a need for change, for a new way of doing things. The people of his time did not have job slots for some of the things he thought should be done. They had a slot for a carpenter. He could make furniture. But when Jesus started meeting people's more urgent needs, his society didn't have a place for him. His contemporaries didn't know what to do with him. To say there wasn't a good market for his skills and understanding is understatement. They killed him.

Martin Luther King Jr.'s calling in the American society of our time was not and is not universally appreciated either.

There are times when education in Jesus' love, sacrificial service, and living as though God's intended order were already partly here—what Jesus called "the kingdom"—may seem to have a limited market. At least some Christian educators should see their callings as providing a kind of education that, at least in part, prepares students for jobs that don't yet exist. Some of us may be able to develop and shape jobs that meet real needs in the name of Christ. We need to be creative.

One church-related college had a program in environmental studies years before environmental studies were in vogue. Were there jobs? It wasn't always clear. What was sure to the college was that it was preparing students in an area of real human need. The students were preparing for jobs that were urgently needed and should be created, if they did not already exist.

Some church colleges have had peace and conflict resolution studies well before people realized that they were needed in American higher education more generally. Chapter 15 discusses other distinctive missions.

A curriculum needs to arise out of what people think is really important. If they have distinctive beliefs and practices, they may need to have institutions with distinctive curricula.

Ultimately, a curriculum needs to arise out of a people's vision of the good society. Especially today, a curriculum should be based on a vision of the world as it should be, not just the world as it is. If religious and other groups have distinctive visions of the good society, they may well need to have institutions in which their visions can be shared and tested with the younger generations for whom they may be helpful in years to come.

Do Church People Have a Distinctive Vision?

Do most religious groups these days profess to any particular wisdom on the world as it might or could be? Or regarding what the responsibilities of their groups and members in such a world might be?

Christians have for centuries been moved by Jesus' response to someone in his time who asked those questions. Jesus told him and his fellow Jews a story about a disrespected foreigner who came across a Jew in need, treated him as a neighbor, and helped him.[3] Church people who are engaged in education that calls itself in any way Christian in our time can hardly ignore Jesus' response.

Perhaps we can hear Jesus' response best when we consider a story enacted in our own times—for example, a story from the 1993 Reginald Denny beating trial in Los Angeles. Denny was a white truck driver pulled from his truck and battered till he was almost dead in a crime that was captured on TV and seen around the world. At the time, four different African Americans, who lived within blocks but did not previously know each other, saw the crime on TV as it happened. In spite of the obvious danger in going into the angry mob, each independently rushed to the scene to try to be helpful.

Later, in a trial, the four African Americans who came to Denny's aid were asked why they did what they did. Bobby Green, an African American truck driver, saw the brick when it hit Denny's face. He said simply, "It felt like I got hit myself." He crowded his way into the truck cab and, leaning out of the side window because the windshield was shattered, drove Denny and the truck to the hospital. Terri Barnett, an unemployed data-control clerk, said, "Anyone who had seen the way he looked . . . . He was so badly beaten. . . . The reaction was just, go." Finally, Lei Yuille, a nutritionist who had just come in from work and was watching TV, testified: "My brother was in the room. He looked at me and said, 'We are Christians. We've got to go help him out,' and I said, 'Right.' Then he went and got his keys."[4]

There are different kinds of learning. A student can learn something about Nicaragua by researching facts in a library. A student can learn something else about Nicaragua by meeting people there. A student can go still farther by beginning to empathize with peers in Nicaragua—by saying, "How would I feel if I had been born and reared there?" But a still different kind of learning is that of a student who, in the face of a new awareness of life in Nicaragua, begins to say, "I am going to change my life plans and spend some of those days and years God has given me to make a difference in Nicaragua (or Botswana or Los Angeles or wherever)." That is a different kind of growth and change.

The catalogs of many Christian colleges use the name of Christ and say that they promote Christian values. If these claims are authentic, the colleges should presumably include in the spiritual development they expect of students development of the kinds of behavior exhibited by the Good Samaritan of Jesus' story or by the "Good Samaritans" of the Reginald Denny story.

Accrediting associations are asking colleges and universities to assess the degree to which they are doing what they say, not only in promoting the cognitive development of their students but also in the other areas of development included in their missions. We could put an assessment question straightforwardly: Would the seniors in a church school with a distinctively Christian mission be more ready than its first-year students to do what the four Los Angeles African Americans did?

One time I was a consultant and leader of a two-day faculty workshop at a formerly church-sponsored university. They asked me to devote one of the two days to assessment. I studied the institution's documents and mission statements. In one of the assessment sessions, I asked, among other things, if they could show that their seniors were more "loving" than their incoming first-year students. A professor on the first row blurted out a question: "Dr. Meyer, are we supposed to be teaching 'loving'?" Well, I said, when I had read in their mission statements the commitments and the reference to seeing Jesus Christ as a model, I got the impression that they might be trying to go beyond helping students gain knowledge about others in the world, and even beyond helping students gain empathy for others. I wondered what they thought it would mean to help students be more Christ-like in the area of "loving." Did they really have that as one of their objectives? Could they give evidence to the accreditors and to the public of actual change in students?

A More Fundamental Look—A Different Epistemology?

Before we turn from the "what" questions to the "how" questions, we should take a further look at what it means for the church that uses the name "Christian" to be involved in education in our kind of post-Christendom, post-Enlightenment culture.

At the heart of the work of any higher educational institution is, after all, a conception of truth. A Christian institution is more than chapels or courses in religion or treating students as "whole persons." It has to be built on an understanding of what is true.

The Enlightenment thought around us has assumed, at least until the deconstructionism of the recent past, that reality consists of autonomous objects "out there." To arrive at the truth according to this understanding we need to handle the objects out there from a distance in order to minimize our subjective biases. We need to develop propositions that conform to the canons of evidence and reason about such objects, and we need to break the objects into pieces and sub-pieces for analysis in order to get to what they really are.

Probably more than any of our other contemporaries, Parker Palmer has written and spoken in leading American educational associations on the need to move beyond this "objectivist" view of truth.[5] Douglas Sloan of Columbia Teachers College has also published a book on the impact of an "objectivist" view of truth on mainline church education.[6]

Palmer, a Berkeley-trained sociologist, reminds us of the dramatic moment when Jesus was brought before Pilate to be tried. Pilate said to Jesus, "So you are a king?" Jesus answered, "You say that I am a king. For this I was born, and for this I have come into the world, to bear witness to the truth. Everyone who is of the truth hears my voice." Pilate said to him, "What is truth?"[7] Palmer comments:

Pilate's final question can be asked with a cynical sneer or a despair-
ing sigh, or both. But the cynicism and despair are not to be located
in the word "truth".... The problem is in the word "what.".... From
the outset ... Pilate tried to reduce Jesus to an object by forcing
him in the category of "king," thus making him both comprehensi-
ble and dispensable in the political framework of the time.... Pilate
is the model objectivist, focusing on the "whatness" of truth, while
before him stands a person in whom truth is embodied, a person
who is not an object "out there," but a subject who wants to enter
into Pilate's life.... By reducing truth to nonpersonal terms, Pilate
puts truth beyond reach, and finally assents to that violence which
wants to murder truth.

Palmer is not talking about a subjectivism of personal feeling or expressive
individualism. When Pilate was in front of Jesus, Pilate was not just being
called "to do his own thing." To paraphrase Palmer, personal truth is neither
"out there" nor "in here" but is always found in dialogue, in relationship, in
community.... The words "truth" and "troth" come from the same root: both
are rooted in deep relationships and community.

Other words from Palmer resonate deeply with foundational Christian
understandings:

When academics speak of "the pursuit of truth," ... there is a con-
ceit hidden in that image: that we can close the gap by tracking an
elusive truth down. This gap exists not because truth is evasive but
because we are.... Subjective truth is truth to which we subject ourselves.... This is also the sense of our word "understand," meaning
"to stand under" some truth.

And finally, perhaps most significantly:

... The objectivist approach to education is so tenacious because it
is a defense against transformation.[8]

These words remind us of the counsel of Isaac Penington, the seventeenth-
century son of the mayor of London who became a Quaker and spent five
years of his life in prison because he felt called to worship God in a manner
other than that prescribed by the Established Church: "O keep out of that
wisdom which does not know the truth."[9]

We have noted that in the early history of American higher education
the curriculum was built around the great truths of the classics and, later,

around the discovered truth of the sciences. Some Christians who are interested in a kind of education that authentically represents their vision will want a kind of education centered on personal, people-of-God truth that looks forward to the transformation needed as we face the future, rather than only on the great truths of the past or scientific discoveries about the world of the present. The work of at least some church people in education will have a special focus on "people-truth"—what it means in all areas of life to live in relationship to God and as a part of a community of God's people. They will want to go beyond describing the world as it is. They will want to image a world that, in God's providence, can and should be.

Chapter 7 Endnotes

1   Raymond F. Zammuto, "Are the Liberal Arts an Endangered Species?," *Journal of Higher Education* 55, no. 2 (1984): 184–211. In an interesting empirical study of private elementary and secondary schools, Sikkink shows that parents who choose church or home schooling for their children are not withdrawing from public life and creating isolated religious enclaves, but engaged in greater civic participation. Church-related private schooling at these levels "leads to greater civic involvement" and contributes to the formation of "social capital." (David Sikkink, "Conservative Protestants, Schooling, and Democracy," in *Evangelicals and Democracy in America, Volume 1: Religion and Society*, ed. Steven Brint and Jean Reith Schroedel [New York: Russell Sage Foundation, forthcoming].) Having a variety of schooling opportunities can contribute to the public interest.

2   Burton R. Clark, "Collegial Entrepreneurialism in Proactive Universities," *Change: The Magazine of Higher Learning* 32, no. 1 (2000): 10–19, 13.

3   Luke 10:25–37.

4   *Newsweek*, September 13, 1993, http://www.newsweek.com/id/115481. See John F. Dovidio, et al., *The Social Psychology of Prosocial Behavior* (Mahwah, NJ: Lawrence Erlbaum Associates, 2006).

5   *The Christian Century*, October 21, 1981, 1051. Parker J. Palmer, Barbara G. Wheeler, and James W. Fowler, *Caring for the Commonweal: Education for Religious and Public Life* (Macon, GA: Mercer University Press, 1990).

6   Douglas Sloan, *Faith and Knowledge: Mainline Protestantism and American Higher Education*, 1st ed. (Louisville: Westminster John Knox Press, 1994).

7   John 18:37–38.

8   The citations are from Parker J. Palmer, "Truth Is Personal: A Deeply Christian Education," *The Christian Century*, October 21, 1981, 1051–55.

9   Richard J. Foster and James Bryan Smith, eds. *Devotional Classics: Selected Readings for Individuals and Groups* (San Francisco, CA: HarperCollins Publishers, 1993), 236–41.

8

Instruction:
A Different "How"

Schools, churches, and other groups that want a different kind of education may want education that is different not only in what is taught but also in how it is taught.

Modeling as Well as Verbalizing

Church educators who understand truth as, first of all, personal will, for example, expect that faculty members will model what they think is important with their lives as well as their words.

I was once asked to spend a day as a consultant with a church college faculty that had voted on a new requirement. Each student was now to have three hours of academic credit in a service activity in the local community. The new requirement was to be a general education requirement for all students in all fields. The college had hired a director for the program. Now the college wanted a consultant interested in service learning to meet with them to work on the criteria for the kinds of activities that might be approved or developed to meet the new requirement.

I was with their principal faculty committee at nine o'clock in the morning. On impulse, I began the session by saying that we were, as faculty members, all college graduates. We all knew that students learn by what they see as well as by what they hear. I proposed that we might just go around the table and have each of us mention one of the kinds of service activities we each were engaged in in our communities, and then we could perhaps talk about the kinds of activities we would like to encourage and recognize among our students. It quickly became clear that I had had a bad idea. Before we even had a chance to start, a professor halfway around the table broke in, saying, in effect: "Dr. Meyer, I am a psychologist. I am already overloaded with my teaching. We hired a director to handle the service requirement!"

What should be talked about and taught and learned in an academic community that has integrity? We have said that the content of the curriculum is not just an inherited body of knowledge from the past, or experimental findings about the world as it is. The curricular structure and content of at least the general education program of expectations of all students ought to flow with integrity out of what faculty members think is really important, i.e., what they model with their lives, as well as their words.

In the oldest document in the New Testament—perhaps the oldest Christian document anywhere—the Apostle Paul says his friends at Thessalonica became "imitators of me [Paul] and of the Lord" and then "became an example to all the believers" in their region. Certainly people who call themselves Christians or followers of Christ have to go beyond verbalizing and express in their very lives what they think is important.

The connotations of the words "profession" and "professional" have changed significantly since the origins of those terms. There was a time when "professionals" were those who had made the "profession"—i.e., taken the vows to enter a religious order—and who were ready to give their lives to God and to humankind. The professionalization of the faculty of the past half-century has brought benefits, but that professionalism and disciplinary fragmentation have also brought problems. Today we find that even some ethics professors insist that their promotions and tenure be based solely on their classroom lectures and professional activities, without any regard for what they do in their personal lives.

If a school and its friends believe that the truth is first of all personal, and if education is fundamentally a conversation between the generations about what is important, the faculty members in that setting can appropriately commit themselves to modeling what they think is important with their lives as well as their words.

Teaching and Learning in Community

The truth that we are seeking in education is truth for us in community, not just for individuals among us as isolated individuals. The shape of the learning situation is therefore important.

The importance of human-scale communities in even large institutions has been recognized in recent years. Harvard has had "houses" and Yale its colleges for years. More recently Princeton underclass students have been clustered in colleges.[1] Baylor, a church-related university with over 14,500 students, began its Brooks College of 370 students in 2007. Many colleges and universities have small-group sessions in at least some classes. Princeton has had small preceptorials or their equivalent in all undergraduate classes since Woodrow Wilson's presidency in the early 1900s.

On one consultation visit to a small church college, I attended a large general-education art lecture followed by a meeting of one of the small groups into which all of the underclass students were divided. The lecture had been on five principles of art. The assignment for each small group was to photograph five scenes, each one illustrating one of the principles, and to bring them to class the next week. It became evident that the students in the group I attended were experienced at working as a group. One chaired. They had to decide how many cameras they had in the group and whether they were each going to take five photos and choose the best or whether they were going to work in subgroups, with each subgroup working on one photo. They were going to be graded as a group. The professor sitting in was also monitoring the contributions of individuals to the group. I was struck by the degree to which what they were doing corresponded to activities I have found important in my own community and professional life.

The shape of the learning community is particularly crucial for educators in traditions with distinctive ecclesiologies that have distinctive visions of the kinds of community life they see as God's intention for humankind.

Moving beyond Describing to Imagining

If education is viewed not just as describing what has been, but as participating in the creation of what could be, a school's instructional program needs to reflect this reality.

As a worst-case example, some American and international students have known the authors' names and titles of English masterpieces but have never read any of the works. In some schools, a course in "Short Story" is a reading course; in others, students are expected also to write short stories of their own. An "Introduction to Art" course can be a course in art appreciation, or it can include studio work in which students try their hands at creative work themselves.

In the physical sciences, a colleague and I started an undergraduate laboratory for original physics research in the late 1960s. Undergraduate research in the sciences was much less common forty years ago than it is today. In starting the special laboratory years ago, we thought students who were learning about scientific modes of inquiry and who were making career choices needed to know more than the physics of the past. They needed an idea of what is involved in work at the edge of our present knowledge. A student should not need to be in a master's program before finding that physics research is not quite like listening to lectures and solving textbook problems.

If church people are interested in envisioning the order of God's intention for humankind, they will have a special interest in a kind of education that elicits from students creative responses that go beyond describing the past and the present and project what could be in the future.

A Calling for Church Educators

Some of the measures highlighted in this chapter were called for in reform documents produced by American educational leaders already in the 1980s.[2] The teacher-student and student-student relationships, and the learning-centered instruction that leading researchers are advocating look structurally very much like those found in many small church colleges in the United States today.[3] Some of the distinctive emphases of these future-oriented church-related colleges may not be what everyone would want—they are not necessarily trying to be all things to all people—but current studies certainly indicate that such instructional structures and strategies have the potential of offering significant and life-changing possibilities for students.

Chapter 8 Endnotes

1   Actually organizing undergraduates into colleges was one of the three principal innovations Woodrow Wilson proposed just after the turn of the century when he was president of Princeton. His proposal was not accepted at that time. In 2006 President Shirley Tilghman of Princeton said that the most significant change at Princeton since she became president five years earlier was the creation of a four-year residential college system to be implemented in 2007—a century after Woodrow Wilson first proposed such colleges. (Eric Quinones, "A Vision for Princeton," *Princeton Weekly Bulletin* 96, no. 3 [September 25, 2006]).

2   Among the most significant from the 1980s are: Association of American Colleges and Universities, *Integrity in the College Curriculum: A Report to the Academic Community* (1985), and the final report on AAC&U's project on Redefining the Meaning and Purpose of Baccalaureate Degrees; and National Institute of Education, *Involvement in Learning: Realizing the Potential of American Higher Education* (Washington, DC: National Institute of Education, U.S. Department of Education, 1984), final report of the NIE's Study Group on the Conditions of Excellence in American Higher Education.

3   Alexander W. Astin, *What Matters in College? Four Critical Years Revisited*, The Jossey-Bass Higher and Adult Education Series (San Francisco: Jossey-Bass, 1993); Ernest T. Pascarella and Patrick T. Terenzini, *How College Affects Students: Findings and Insights from Twenty Years of Research*, ed. Kenneth A. Feldman, The Jossey-Bass Higher and Adult Education Series (San Francisco: Jossey-Bass, 1991); and Pascarella and Terenzini, *How College Affects Students: A Third Decade of Research*, The Jossey-Bass Higher and Adult Education Series (San Francisco: Jossey-Bass, 2005).

9

WHY MIGHT SOME CHURCHES WANT SCHOOLS THAT ARE DIFFERENT?

In the past 150 years, and particularly the past fifty years, the church sector in higher education has shrunk to the point where, for example, not even one out of every eight students in the United States is attending an institution with any kind of church relationship. The almost-universal trend of recent years has been one of dissociation—of increasing distance between schools and the churches that gave them birth and early sustenance.

Observers have had different perspectives on the trend partly because they have differed with one another on the mission or missions they thought the church should have in education. The differences have arisen even more fundamentally from differences in their views on the church's role in society.

We need to look more specifically, then, at the different missions the church might accomplish today in higher education.

Missions

In their mission statements, some schools focus on the "development of the life of the mind." Other schools encourage personal and social development, the "development of the whole person." Some schools award degrees based on the completion of coursework. Others have much broader missions and expectations of graduates.[1] Some schools say in their mission statements that they differ from others in the ways they teach, their methods of instruction, and the structures of their learning communities.

Churches and their higher education institutions are frequently vague in their mission statements. They sometimes speak about their church founders and origins without reference to their church relationships today. A college that speaks of "providing an education rooted in a unifying Christian worldview" may have worthy goals but may not be very clear on which worldview it is talking about in these pluralistic times. A college or university that does not want to identify itself as confessionally Christian may speak of its dedication to the pursuit and sharing of truth, again without noting that good people differ in their understandings of truth.

Some differences in school missions are rooted in differences in the ways churches see their roles in the larger society. Churches from Establishment traditions will tend to identify with Michael Novak: "They lend their energies to altering [the] world in its basic institutions, even if ever so slightly, in the direction of caritas."[2] Churches of Free Church traditions (e.g., "Believers' Church," or "Anabaptist") will tend to think that some of the institutions of the larger society need more basic challenge and that, in their church life, Christians should try to model better and, possibly, more radical alternatives. Establishment churches are more likely to support existing public and quasi-public models of colleges and university life. Free Churches are more likely to support alternative models.

Merrimon Cuninggim, former executive of the Danforth Foundation and president of Salem College, expressed the Establishment vision for church-related higher education very clearly. He wrote, "A church-related college must have an understanding of, and must practice, the essential academic values."[3] He listed these as "truth, freedom, justice, and kinship." He made it clear that he was not proposing anything as "grandiose as love, not even respect."[4] He wrote: "Then let me come clean: the academic values at the heart of the church-related endeavor are the same values that are at the heart of all other types of colleges, independent, tax-supported, even profit-making if there are such."[5]

A profound difference clearly exists between Cuninggim's perspective and the ecclesiological vision of other leading contemporary thinkers, such as Stanley Hauerwas and William Willimon, at that time at Duke; James McClendon, who was reared in the Baptist tradition and spent much of his long academic career as a systematic theologian at the Episcopal seminary in the Graduate Theological Union in Berkeley, California; George Marsden of the Christian Reformed Church and faculty member at the University of Notre Dame; "Dorothy Day" Catholics and many other Roman Catholic educators; as well as John Howard Yoder of the Mennonites and many members of the Society of Friends and Church of the Brethren in the Anabaptist tradition.

Hauerwas and Willimon see Christians as "resident aliens."[6] Marsden proposes "alternatives to secular colleges and universities."[7] Episcopalian Loren Mead speaks of the break-up of the "culture of establishment," the "Christendom Paradigm," in which the church was viewed as identical with its environment. Now, Mead says, "We are surrounded by the relics of the Christendom Paradigm, a paradigm that has largely ceased to work."[8]

These different understandings of the missions of the church in society lead to different understandings of what church-related schools should be doing. In seven chapters, Cuninggim devotes a full chapter to an attack on Hauerwas, Marsden, and others.[9] Others who have viewed trends of the past half-century less positively have spoken of "secularization" with equal intensity. It is the "Dying of the Light."[10] The differences between these interlocutors arise fundamentally from their different ecclesiologies.

In going beyond abstractions and vagueness in identifying some of the different missions churches have had for their colleges and universities, we can begin by speaking in terms of the students or others being served. Of course, a given institution can assume or try to assume a mission that incorporates several "sub-missions" simultaneously.

Some different possible church-related college or university missions:

1. *Preparing students who are interested from the outset in exploring the church and its mission for their future participation in the life and mission of the church.* Many older universities were once established to prepare members and leaders for church and their mission in the world.

2. *Serving as a direct resource and "think tank" for the church as the church works with the challenges and opportunities with which it is confronted as it faces the future.* A church can have "institutes of advanced study" that do not have any students at all, since the "think tank" mission is different from the mission of educating students. In most educational institutions, however, even think-tank research scholars do some teaching and, in many, they involve students also in their work.

3. *Educating students from the society at large with a view to inviting them to join in the church's mission in the world.* Some students attend church colleges at first primarily because of proximity, convenience, or academic interest, rather than because of their interest in or commitment to the church's distinctive vision. A college or university may engage in this mission thinking that a free and fair exposition of various worldviews and their serious consideration will lead some initially uninterested students to choose to join the church in its mission.

4. *Modeling educational innovations and reforms in the interest of pointing the way to improvements in public and independent higher education.* Most students are in public and other independent institutions. The church can pioneer in the testing of educational innovations and help schools that are not church-related to be what they can be. Public school educators have often welcomed the initiatives of private school educators. The leaders of public colleges and universities have often in the past been able to advocate for their schools programs that have been tested and modeled by private schools.

5. *Meeting basic, but unmet, educational needs of students in the larger society.* Students may have real educational needs, even though many of them may have no particular interest in the church's mission in the world. A church may start schools or programs intending to transfer them to public responsibility when the public is ready to assume responsibility for the schools as institutions that are established and running well. Or a church may use its people and dollars in operating and supporting indefinitely some schools as a contribution to education in the society.

Most institutional mission statements speak about their aim to further the intellectual, social, and personal growth of their students (with implications for the schools' programs) and about the education of their students for thoughtful and productive lives (an outcome) without speaking very specifically about the kinds of students they aim to educate (an input) or, apart from educating students, the ways they want to serve their supporting constituencies in the achievement of their missions. A school cannot say everything in a brief mission statement. It is, however, important that a school be clear on the individuals or groups it is trying to serve. In a popular article, Robert Samuelson summarizes a recent serious research paper in these words: "What students bring to college matters more than what colleges bring to students."[11]

Which students a teaching institution wants to teach is a particularly important question for a church college or university in the Free Church tradition. Churches in this stream of history believe that churches should be places of giving and receiving counsel and that people should consciously decide they want to join and engage seriously in this kind of group process before they are considered members. Colleges in this tradition do not see themselves as "cookie cutters" turning out a specified product regardless of the input. At their best, colleges in this tradition have clear missions and give special attention to the kinds of students they encourage to enroll and agree to educate.

Church colleges and universities have engaged in each of the five missions listed above at various times and places. Since churches do not have infinite resources, they need to consider mission priorities appropriate to their particular situations in North America today. Let us look at the different missions in greater detail.

Preparing Interested Students

"Preparing students who are interested from the outset in exploring the church and its mission for their future participation in the life and mission of the church" is the first of the mission options listed above, and one of the first in early America. Preparing church students for ministry was the mission of Harvard and of other Colonial colleges in their early years. Churches have founded many other colleges, universities, and theological schools with this mission since the Colonial era.

Communicating Christian beliefs and practices to especially interested students, including but not limited to young church members and future leaders, is a priority mission for many churches with beliefs and practices different in some ways from those of the surrounding American culture today. The intergenerational conversation that is education involves a continuing testing of the implications and relevance of those beliefs and practices for the future. Interacting with younger members and future leaders, and with others enrolling because of their interest in the Christian beliefs and practices of the sponsoring churches, is a central mission for these church schools.

The "Think Tank" Mission

The second mission listed in the previous section is "serving as a direct resource and 'think tank' for the church as the church works with the challenges and opportunities with which it is confronted as it faces the future."

In their major Danforth Foundation study in 1965, Pattillo and Mackenzie deplored the weakness of many church colleges and universities in working at this mission. Some institutions have, however, contributed very significantly to the welfare and direction of their respective churches. In such institutions this mission is usually carried on by a community of faculty members gathered primarily around a teaching mission.

Groups of church scholars can prepare historical, theological, sociological, and other scientific studies that can help a church as it faces the challenges of changing times. They can prepare materials for the education of church members generally. Scholars can serve in church leadership positions.

Individual church members with professional roles in institutions across the land can make contributions to the lives of their churches. Groups of church scholars at church-related colleges and universities have the advantage of the mutual stimulation and support, and sometimes of special library and other reference resources, as they make their contributions to church life.

Colleges and universities have traditionally said that they have three functions: teaching, research, and public service. Church schools need not and, in many situations, should not assume that their responsibilities are limited to teaching students.

A Mission to Students-at-large

The third mission invites students-at-large to enroll in the standard disciplines and generally accepted degree programs in the hope that, although the students were initially uninterested in the schools' religious offerings, the students would become interested in religious questions. Some students who initially attended church colleges only to get the benefits of locally accessible education have indeed become active members in the Christian movement in the process.

However, some questions need serious attention as a church considers giving priority to this as its mission or part of its mission:

1. Much of the learning that goes on in a college is peer learning. Colleges where most of the peers are not interested in the

church mission of the institution can undermine the learning environments for students seeking and paying special tuition for learning in Christian community. For instance, in another context, we would say that a college with almost no students interested in physics might not be the best place for a student who wanted to become a physicist. A church and its schools need to ask to what degree a substantial mission in educating local students interferes with or enhances the mission of preparing really interested students for leadership in the church's mission.

Some denominations are discovering that the absolute numbers of the students from their sponsoring churches have actually declined as the total enrollments at their institutions have increased.

2. Some major denominations are becoming concerned that the flow of future leaders going through their colleges and universities to their theological seminaries has decreased. A phenomenon of this kind is potentially much more of a problem for a church with a more distinctive—and even countercultural—vision than it is for the large American mainline denominations. It is a problem for a church with distinctive beliefs and practices if most of its congregational and churchwide leaders come from "generic" universities and seminaries and have not wrestled seriously with its distinctive church vision.

Good teaching begins where the learners begin. Teachers whose classes have substantial numbers of students not interested in the church mission of the college—especially the college of a church with distinctive and countercultural convictions—are often under great pressure to water down unpopular convictions in their teaching.

3. Using proximity or convenience as a means of attracting uninterested local students to the Christian cause raises special problems, especially for Free Church people. It raises the same kinds of questions that have arisen when churches took advantage of overseas nationals' eagerness for the benefits of education to try to convert them in the mission compounds of an earlier era, or when some churches have taken advantage of rescue mission attendees' hunger to preach to them.

One of the major historical arguments that leaders of the Establishment churches of the Reformation used against the Anabaptist pioneers of the Free Church vision was that state-enforced religious education assured that children of unbelievers as well as those of believers would be exposed to the gospel. But by now it has become clear that the use of social or political incentives and pressures to encourage or force people to hear or agree with the Christian message can be counterproductive. In my view, the day when the church should act like an Establishment church is past—indeed, some say, it should never have existed. As a point on which Christians have disagreed in the past and on which they disagree today, it is an occasion for conversation as we face the future.

4. A church needs to engage in serious discernment on the ways it wants its members and agencies to use their mission outreach dollars among the many available options in today's environment.

    The American college model is an expensive model. But the pressures on most college administrators and admissions staffs to increase enrollments at just about any cost are enormous.[12] Members and denominations can find that they are spending millions of dollars educating students at large.

    In most denominations, increasing the numbers of students at large in their schools and the resultant reallocating of church resources have arisen from a school-based interest in increasing enrollments. The increases were not usually a matter of deliberate denominational strategy developed by their denominational general boards in cooperation with their mission and service agencies. If the purpose is outreach, these latter boards need to speak to the use of the church resources of their members and agencies.

Educating students at large was an important service of the church when there were no other schools. But there are other schools in America at this time. In many denominations, the colleges and universities have recruited more local students, not because they gave priority to this mission, but because they wanted to grow and there were fewer students from their sponsoring churches.

Modeling Educational Innovation

"Modeling educational innovations and reforms in the interest of pointing the way to improvements in public and independent higher education" is the fourth listed mission option for church schools.

I have referred earlier to the role of the post-World War II Mennonite mental health centers in meeting unmet needs for psychiatric care in their respective geographical regions. They did not, however, just bring to new communities the outdated methods of psychiatric treatment that their con-scientious objectors had observed in the state hospitals where they had been sent to serve during the War. They pioneered in new approaches to psychotherapy. (This mission has become less urgent and distinctive today. Practices that were innovative fifty years ago have now become widely accepted in good psychotherapeutic practice.)

Modeling educational innovations requires resources, but where these are available, it is a mission church colleges and universities have accepted in the past and can fulfill in the future.

Meeting Unmet Student Needs

As a fifth possible mission, I have listed "starting new institutions or pro-grams intended to meet the unmet educational needs of students in the larger society who may have no particular commitment to or interest in the church's mission in the world."

The denominations that merged to form the United Church of Christ and other denominations started schools on the American frontier. Many churches have started mission schools to meet unmet student needs in other parts of the world.

Different Missions and Different Views on Dissociation

How does a church's view of the dissociation of its schools from close school-church relationships depend on the mission or missions it has projected for its schools? How does the church's view depend on its understanding of its own churchly mission in the larger society?

A church will be especially interested in having schools of its own if it believes that its Christian message and the understandings constitutive of its Christian peoplehood will not be adequately communicated to its young people and future leaders otherwise through the work of public schools in the larger society.[13]

In Europe and early America, the church pioneered in establishing institutions of higher education, as it did in establishing hospitals and other societal institutions. The church had to establish schools if there were to be any schools. In some places in the world, church or private schools are still the only schools in existence. Churches can well see a Christian calling and mission in founding and supporting schools that help children learn to read and write or help older students in liberal arts, pre-professional, and professional studies to become medical doctors, agricultural specialists, and persons in other roles urgently needed in their societies, even where any overtly Christian emphases in their curricula are not permitted or appropriate.

There are, however, fewer and fewer places around the world where the only available education is church education. More governments and peoples generally are seeing education as important for their futures. With the coming of stronger public institutions in the past 150 years, and particularly in times of tight budgets, churches in North America have been asking questions about priorities. In these situations, it is understandable that many church and school leaders will come to the belief that churches should not allocate large amounts of their limited resources to operate general hospitals when the public is ready to assume that responsibility—or to operate colleges or universities that simply duplicate what the larger society is ready to provide through public funding.

In any case, the question about how the church might see its colleges and universities as important for the church's present and foreseeable future is a church question, not just a question for the schools to answer. Certainly the colleges and their leaders need to be clear on their institutional missions. But there are problems from the outset if a church that intends to sponsor or have special relationships with educational institutions is not clear on its own churchly role and the reasons for this role. Someone has to speak for the long-term interests and educational part of the mission of the church.

A Look to the Future

Historically, dissociation has often been the unintended outcome of actions taken to meet short-term objectives. The next chapter will examine ways in which churches and schools that really wish to do so can move more intentionally toward dissociation.

But if a church or other group has a strong sense of identity and mission, it will give high priority and substantial resources to sponsoring and supporting schools to communicate its sense of identity and destiny to oncoming generations.

In their 1968 classic work on American higher education, Christopher Jencks and David Riesman of Harvard wrote:

> The survival of recognizably Protestant colleges . . . seems to depend on the survival within the larger society of Protestant enclaves whose members believe passionately in a way of life radically different from that of the majority, and who are both willing and able to pay for a brand of higher education that embodies their vision.[14]

What Jencks and Riesman said about Protestants and their colleges could have been said about other groups that have been different from majorities in their cultures.

Throughout the history of the church, and from times well before the Protestant Reformation, there have been important minority groups that have had a strong sense of identity and mission—the earliest Christians in the Roman Empire, the Christians coming into the world of the Norse and Anglo-Saxon culture in England, dissidents in the Medieval Roman Catholic church, the Radical Reformation groups of the sixteenth century, the English Separatists and Quakers a century later, and other dissenters down to our own times.

There are churches and other groups in America today with beliefs and practices and a vision for the good society that differ from the American majority.[15] They see their vision as relevant for the larger American society, but they also know that theirs are minority voices, at least at present. It is understandable that they would want to have and support educational institutions in which they would be in conversation with the oncoming generations about their vision.

Chapter 9 Endnotes

1 Professional schools differ in their understandings of their requirements for degrees. In awarding a Master of Divinity degree, some theological schools are saying that a graduate is qualified to pastor a congregation; others are saying the student completed course requirements. Nursing schools differ on whether they should award degrees to prospects who have passed the courses, but whom they do not see as qualified for actual nursing practice. Liberal arts schools differ even more in their missions and requirements. In March 2000, an appeals court reversed a lower court decision and said Johns Hopkins University was within its rights in denying a diploma to a student who had completed his coursework, but who had killed another student and was serving a thirty-five-year prison sentence. The Conduct Code of the university says that students "who harm or have the potential of harming others . . . will be disciplined and may forfeit their right to be members of the university community." The opinion said that "the policy outlined in the [student] handbook clearly states that a student will not receive a degree based solely on the completion of coursework" (Ben Gose, "Court Upholds Right of Johns Hopkins U. to Deny Diploma to Convicted Killer," *Today's News, The Chronicle of Higher Education,* March 7, 2000, http://chronicle.com/daily/2000/2000030703n.htm).

2 "Controversial Engagements," *First Things*, no. 92 (April 1999): 23.

3 Merrimon Cuninggim, *Uneasy Partners: The College and the Church* (Nashville: Abingdon Press, 1994), 102.

4 Ibid., 108-111.

5 Ibid., 113.

6 Stanley Hauerwas and William H. Willimon, *Resident Aliens* (Nashville: Abingdon, 1990); Stanley Hauerwas, *After Christendom?* (Nashville: Abingdon, 1991).

7 George M. Marsden, "The Soul of the American University: A Historical Overview," in *The Secularization of the Academy*, ed. George M. Marsden and Bradley J. Longfield (New York: Oxford University Press, 1992), 41.

8 Loren B. Mead, *The Once and Future Church* (New York: The Alban Institute, 1991), 18.

9 An indication of the passion with which Cuninggim writes is his repeated reference to the Council for Christian Colleges & Universities in Washington, D.C., as "ultraconservative." It is interesting, however, that he includes some of the Council colleges in an appendix as representing some of the kinds of schools he sees as models. It is also interesting that, in his criticism, Cuninggim says Marsden "reads as if he thought of himself as spokesman more for the church than for the college" (72) as though that were enough in itself to discredit Marsden's work.

10 Burtchaell, *The Dying of the Light: The Disengagement of Colleges and Universities from Their Christian Churches* (Grand Rapids: Wm. B. Eerdmans, 1998).

11 Robert J. Samuelson, "The Worthless Ivy League?," *Newsweek*, November 1, 1999, 45. The paper Samuelson is summarizing is a December 1998 Princeton University working paper by Stacy Berg Dale of the Andrew W. Mellon Foundation and Alan B. Krueger, a Princeton University economist. Their paper was later published as "Estimating the Payoff to Attending a More Selective College: An Application of Selection on Observables and Unobservables," *The Quarterly Journal of Economics* 117, no. 4 (Cambridge, MA: MIT Press, 2002), 1491–1527. In the October 2004

Atlantic Monthly, (vol. 294, no. 3), Gregg Easterbrook of the Brookings Institution writes that the paper by Dale and Krueger "dropped a bomb on the notion of elite-college attendance as essential to success later in life" (128-133).

12 There is a widespread belief that enrollment growth leads to financial strength. Chapter 14 reports on a study showing that this is often not the case.

13 I have referred especially to the relationships of colleges and universities with Christian churches, the case of particular prominence in the American history, but I would note again that the considerations given here apply also to the interests of Jewish groups, African Americans, Muslims, and other minority subpopulations in the American society.

14 Jencks and Riesman, *The Academic Revolution* (Garden City, NY: Doubleday, 1968), 330.

15 John Wright emphasizes the challenge church institutions face when they exist within the space provided by a liberal nation-state their educational programs are supposed to serve. See Wright's chapter in Michael L. Budde and John Wright, eds. *Conflicting Allegiances: The Church-Based University in a Liberal Democratic Society* (Grand Rapids: Brazos Press, 2004).

10

INTENTIONAL "SECULARIZATION"

Before turning to elements in healthy long-term church relationships, we need to consider the situations of churches that do not want to sponsor schools that are different—or, indeed, in some cases, that do not want to sponsor any schools at all. There are circumstances under which a changing church in a changing environment will and should choose dissociation for some or all of its educational institutions. We need to consider the "how" of good dissociation as well as the "how" of avoiding unintended dissociation.

Intentionality Rather than Drift

Consider what can happen when a church institution drifts into dissociation. In the late 1950s, the president of a church-related university in Canada had a vision. He wanted his denomination to have his liberal arts college become a sub-college among other church sub-colleges at the heart of a new provincial university that would have engineering and other specialized faculties. He was ready to help form the new university. The church could focus its resources on its priorities in liberal arts education. The professional and technical programs would be developed with public funding. But the president was stymied by short-sighted denominational leaders. His church leaders wanted to have their church-related college as an independent denominational school, not a denominational sub-college at the proposed new "secular university"![1] The president and his denominational board parted ways. The president helped form and lead the proposed new provincial university, which emerged with liberal arts sub-colleges from other denominations.

After some years and several presidents, the original denominational university "went secular" after all and became a second provincial university in the city. After stumbling and mistakes, the church people in the province awakened to find nothing remaining of their denomination's venture in undergraduate and arts education in the province. And instead of having one provincial university in the city in this time of tight budgets and retrenchment, the province now faces the inefficiency of having two provincial universities within a mile of each other in the same city.[2]

A Case of Successful Dissociation

Now consider a story of intentional and successful dissociation: A college started in the early years of the past century had four years of high school and a two-year college. Its church academy was the only high school in its rural community. With the support and encouragement of his denomination, a new president helped the local community form a legal school district and select a public high school board. The church contracted with the local district to get the new public high school started, with the college president as the legal superintendent in the transition. The church saw the need to focus its churchly educational efforts on having a good two-year college, rather than on spreading its resources over six or even eight high school and college years.

In the first of the three transition years, the community public high school was held on the church's junior college campus. The new president worked with the teachers. No one lost a job in the transfer. In the transition years, the church served the community as the community geared up to meet its educational needs. To further focus the church's use of its resources, the new president radically reduced the number of junior college courses. Some vocational and professional programs were added later as enrollments grew.

In recent years, the two-year college has had strong church and other constituency support. Its contributions per student have been at or near the top of those for private and public two-year colleges in the United States

Observations

What can we say about intentional church-school dissociation?

1. *Where a church has carried legal responsibility for a college or university and the relationship is to be changed, the new relationship must be clear and outlined in appropriate documents and releases.* If the church is not in a position to make decisions and to take effective action in areas where it once carried responsibility, the church must not allow itself to become vulnerable to ascending liability suits.[3]

2. *In dissociation arrangements, the church must be clear about the ways in which the institution can and cannot use the church's name in student recruitment and fundraising efforts.*

   The following is a hypothetical composite account of what has occurred in more than one denomination: The denomination was facing tight budgets and did not want to channel church funds to one of its universities. Indeed, the denominational executives thought that the school, with its advancement officers and development staffs, was in a better position to raise funds than the denomination itself. The church gradually reduced and then discontinued forwarding church funds to its school. But it did not develop understandings concerning the school's use of the denominational name in fund-raising contacts with church members and donors. In fact, the church leaders were pleased that the university continued to allow a denominationally funded chaplain to have an office on campus and to have a department of religion—they were pleased that the university was giving at least this recognition to its historical relationship to the church. (Actually, the new arrangements did not provide for much more of an official place for the church on campus than churches have had at some major state universities.)

   In news releases, the university said, "Nothing in our historic relationship to the church has changed." The president used the church's name in mass mailings to church members and in contacts with major donors. Contributions from church members continued. At the same time, the university increased its appeals to non-church constituents. The university president was respected by faculty, donors, and church alike as a highly successful leader and fundraiser.

In the meantime, the financial situation of the church became even more critical. It had to cut its staff drastically in a major retrenchment move. It eliminated its board of higher education and had to discontinue other programs in the cut-backs.

A study later showed that the giving of members of the church had increased substantially. Their giving to causes outside their local congregations was also increasing, even when corrected for inflation. But the members of the church were giving more of their outside giving as individuals to the university and to other institutions they thought were a part of the denominational network than to any other causes outside their local congregations. They were giving less to the denominational offices and other denominational efforts.

Because of its failure to project its goals more carefully and then to plan with greater integrity, the church found itself in greater trouble after the dissociation than before. It had not reduced the flow of dollars from denominational members to the university. It had only abdicated its responsibility to give clear guidance to its members concerning their stewardship of their dollars. Because of its failure to anticipate the dynamics in the dissociation, the church found itself in a situation in which, while the members of the denomination thought they were increasing their giving to "the church," the denomination was facing an increasingly serious financial crisis.

Alert church leaders and trustees will want to be sure either (1) that the church can fulfill its churchly responsibility in its relationship with its school or (2) that the school-church relationship has changed and that the school is now clearly independent.

3. *Dissociation takes time. A church and its institution can well develop a clear, multi-year plan for who is to do what at various stages of the process and project a definite terminal date beyond which both church and school will regard the school as independent.*

More attention needs to be given to the "how" of desired and intentional dissociation. There are current studies on retrenchment. There are fewer studies on mergers. Churches are challenged today to find ways of proceeding expeditiously and with grace and intentionality in dissociating the church from educational institutions that have served well as church institutions and that now can serve better as public or independent institutions in today's changed church and school environments.

Chapter 10 Endnotes

1   The next chapter will refer at greater length to "sub-colleges" of this kind, colleges on larger university campuses. Sometimes called "cluster colleges," these sub-colleges exist in different forms at Oxford, Cambridge, Harvard, Yale, Princeton, University of California at Santa Cruz, and other Western universities. The English universities have religious, as well as non-church-related, colleges.

2   In July 2004, due to financial problems, one of two remaining liberal arts colleges of the same Canadian denomination in another province became a secular campus of a public university.

3   See also Chapter 18.

PART III

CURRENT ISSUES

11

Diversity, Pluralism, and Community

Arthur Levine, former president of Teachers College, Columbia University, writes:

> Today diversity is the largest cause of student unrest on campus. . . . Discourse is dominated by two small, but vociferous groups—one yelling that diversity has eclipsed all other aspects of college life and the other shouting that colleges remain impervious to diversity. . . .[1]

Levine noted that 1979 undergraduates described themselves in terms of commonalities they shared with their generation. Asked the same question in his 1997 study, students emphasized the characteristics that made them unique.

Understanding how diversity issues relate particularly to colleges and universities with special missions is one of the goals of this chapter.

A Societal Challenge

One of the battles currently being fought on the larger U.S. political scene is over affirmative action.[2] A major challenge for the U.S. society and its institutions is making the transition from a culture dominated by white Protestant males to one that is more equitable. As settings in which representatives of the older generations meet with the upcoming generation for reflecting on the past and for visioning possible futures, schools find themselves in important and contested roles in this transition.

Churches of various kinds bring a combination of assets and liabilities to the scene. Some churches bring histories of intolerance and suppressing dissidents. It has been said that Sunday morning is the most segregated hour in the United States. On the other hand, in recent decades some civil rights-minded Christian churches, especially African American churches, have led in the struggle for civil rights for minority groups.

Diversity in Education

We cannot consider the present and the future without reckoning with the history of discrimination against women and racial-ethnic minority groups. Colleges and universities have participated in the discriminatory systems of the larger United States society.

College and university administrators need to be concerned about the representation of various groups in their faculties and student bodies for at least three reasons:

1. Liberal arts education involves leading students out of earlier experiences that may have been more limited into today's world of national and global diversity. Having students encounter people of differing backgrounds and perspectives can further their learning and preparation for life in today's world.[3]
2. With changes in the demographic composition of churches and other societal populations, higher education institutions that want to be in the market in the future have to make changes to meet the changing needs of the populations they serve. Colleges and universities exist to serve the needs of their mandating societies, and their societies are increasingly diverse.
3. The representation of various groups in our higher education institutions is a matter of fairness and justice. College and university graduates have increasing occupational and other advantages in our society. At their best, Christians and citizens generally have a concern for justice for everyone.

Church educators ought to be interested in diversity for all three of these reasons. They certainly ought to be interested in having all of their students grow in cross-cultural experiences. In the long-term interest of their institutions, if for no other reasons, they ought to be meeting real student needs, not planning to educate students that do not exist. And they ought to be concerned about fairness and justice.

Many independent four-year institutions and their public counterparts are trying to provide access to students from diverse racial and ethnic backgrounds. Full-time equivalent minority enrollments analyzed in 2004 indicated that they were at twenty-nine percent of the total student bodies at private four-year institutions and twenty-eight percent at state institutions.[4] Major universities are enrolling minority students.

Gender and Racial-Ethnic Diversity in Recruitment

Many institutions say they want to recruit more faculty members and students from the underrepresented groups of women and people of color. Hiring faculty is especially important, but challenging.[5] An unconscious racial or gender bias may play a role, even where search committees are trying to look for promising candidates without regard for race. Some candidates may find the atmosphere of a campus unwelcoming.

Women academics have faced barriers. For example, "Do Babies Matter?," a foundation-supported research report based on surveys of 160,000 people who earned Ph.D.s, found that having babies interferes with the tenure aspirations of women, but "enhances the academic prospects of men."[6]

Salaries a search committee is working with may not be competitive. School budgets reflect institutional priorities, and some school budgets reflect a higher priority on bricks and mortar or on athletic teams than they do on faculty diversity. Schools with a commitment to salary scales uniform across disciplines may find themselves unable to attract gifted prospects in high-demand fields.

The fact that a school is distinctive in some ways may increase the numbers of good prospects. A researcher may prefer a school in which he or she can teach young people, as well as do research. A candidate may want to be in a school committed to diversity. A school's religious mission may attract some candidates who would not otherwise be interested.

In hiring desired faculty members, goals and institutional commitment are important. Schools with distinctive missions need to think proactively about searching seriously for faculty members and students, rather than selecting faculty members and students from traditional populations of those who apply. Moving toward identifying gifted faculty and student prospects years in advance and helping them prepare are longer-term efforts that can increase the pools of prospects.

Years ago one small church school developed a coordinated long-term program for identifying and recruiting promising women faculty members in areas not traditional for women scholars. The substantial program included identifying gifted prospects and providing institutional financial support for women ready to enter graduate studies, annually bringing women on leave from their graduate studies to the campus as one-year visiting faculty members, appointing a woman scholar to a senior position in academic administration, and bringing women to the campus as special lecturers. The program eventuated in the appointment of new gifted women to tenured positions.

Recruiting the best prospects to church college and university faculty teams requires a change in the way faculty recruitment has been institutionalized in U.S. academia. Assuming that women and minority Ph.D.s are always eager to get to our campuses is an illusion. It takes years to cultivate most big donors, and it can take years to cultivate the very top faculty prospects for campuses with special missions. In some instances, colleges and universities will have to "grow their own." It will take dollars to work with prospects over the years of their preparation and to overstaff to some degree to employ them when they are available. (It takes dollars to work with prospective donors, too.) Some donors may be interested in endowing new efforts to provide for future faculties. The need to cultivate and develop prospects is particularly critical in fields with small numbers of doctoral-level prospects. (See Chapter 13.)

The challenge cannot be taken lightly. The March 1, 2005, *New York Times* reports that "in 2003, Ivy League campuses hired 433 new professors into tenure-track jobs, but only fourteen were African American and eight were Hispanic." The release also says that one of the problems has been the shortage of Ph.D.s from underrepresented minorities in the arts and sciences and engineering.[7]

Substantial change will require long-term efforts. Unfulfilled promises of quick fixes to underrepresented groups can lead to cynicism. In 1988 Duke University approved a policy in which each of its fifty-six departments was to have added an additional African American faculty member by the fall of 1993. Five years later, the September 19, 1993, *New York Times* had a top front-page article entitled, "Duke Learns of Pitfalls in Promise of Hiring More Black Professors." Instead of having at least fifty-six additional African American faculty members, its fifty-six departments had shown a net gain of only eight. A later paragraph says, "Black students . . . say they feel betrayed."

We can applaud Duke's setting of a goal. We can learn from their experience that the goals need to include the allocation of necessary resources and aggressive efforts to provide for needed candidates from underrepresented groups.

International Diversity

Recent events have highlighted the way events in one part of the world can have global consequences. Followers of the major world religions worship a God whose reign, they believe, transcends the tribe or nation. Religious people of one nation have interests and loyalties that involve people of other nations and cultures. Preparing U.S. students for life in today's world ideally involves some first-hand awareness of the ninety-four percent of the world's population that lives outside the United States.

The most recent data from the Institute for International Education indicate that growth in the number of American students who have traveled overseas to study in the past decade has been unparalleled. Many educators are eager to see more students studying abroad, but at present the percentage of all college students who actually go abroad remains very low. Churches and their colleges and universities can lead in educating for global awareness and involvement.

The preliminary headline findings of Harvard's recent general education study, its first such study in almost thirty years, were (1) that its students were not participating in study abroad as much as students of some other leading universities and (2) that its general education program needed to be changed to provide a greater place for international education.[8] U.S. Secretaries of Education under Presidents Clinton, Bush, and Obama have urged colleges and universities to give greater emphasis to study abroad.

After 9/11, colleges and universities across the country protested visa restrictions that reduced the numbers of international students coming to U.S. campuses.[9] This reduction occurs at a time when some schools in Europe and the Far East have begun offering programs in English to attract some of the international students who had been coming to the United States.

International faculty members were also victims of "ideological exclusion"—barred as foreign intellectuals based on their views or associations. In the fall of 2004, the U.S. government revoked the visa of Tariq Ramadan, a world-renowned Swiss Islamics scholar who had had a clear visa and appointment at the University of Notre Dame, and who had already arranged for housing, furnishings, and schools for his children. Actions like these occurred at a time when it was common knowledge that Americans have had far too little understanding of the Muslim world and that far too few Americans can use Arabic.[10]

Building international study into the curricula of U.S. students has had less attention than providing for international students and faculty members from overseas. Preparation for life in today's world is more than a matter of preparation for life in the diversity of the U.S. society.

Religious Colleges in a Diverse World

Moving toward a more appropriate gender and racial/ethnic diversity of faculties and student bodies in typical U.S. colleges and universities is important. But the fact that some kinds of diversity enhance education is not to say that every imaginable kind of diversity in every institution is good. There is a place for women's colleges—for colleges that do not admit men and that are not gender diverse. There is a place for African American colleges. And there is a place for colleges with special religious missions.

In promoting diversity, schools face a special challenge that derives from the nature of education itself. Schools bring students into learning communities that are not intended to be representative of the larger society in every dimension. For instance, schools bring history students together in history classes and business students in business classes. These settings are intentionally created places where students and faculty members of common interests are brought together and some kinds of diversity are intentionally reduced. Students have different interests, and students not interested in French are not enrolled in advanced French classes with French majors.

Theodore Newcomb was the father of social psychological researches on the changes colleges produce in students. Forty years ago, he and a younger colleague, Kenneth Feldman, published *The Impact of College on Students*,[11] a classic in educational literature. They surveyed all research studies of the previous forty years on the impact of college on students and summarized the findings in two volumes. More recently, Ernest Pascarella and Patrick Terenzini have published sequels summarizing the work of empirical studies of more recent years.[12]

One could summarize the life work of Newcomb with the word "accentuation." Out of the diversity of the larger society, a college or university brings together people with certain common characteristics, and those initial characteristics then get accentuated through their mutual interactions. College students begin to act more like college graduates. Architecture students start acting more like professional architects. In a medical school, students begin to act more like doctors. In a department within a whole college, the institution brings together the history majors or the physics students, and the students start acting more and more like historians and physicists.

Students' initial characteristics are "accentuated" in their life in the intentional communities we call "departments," "medical schools," etc. The students pay their thousands of dollars; they live for a while with peers and professors in these very specialized kinds of intentional community; and they end up looking and acting like graduates and specialists in their respective fields.

The goal is to bring together students representing some different initial characteristics (e.g., to provide for racial and ethnic diversity) and those representing some similar initial interests (e.g., to provide for the "accentuation" that occurs among college majors in an academic field or among people committed to a common mission).

Pascarella and Terenzini cite the conclusions of *Four Critical Years*, an earlier classic by Alexander Astin of UCLA,[13] who has authored a more recent work, *What Matters in College*.[14] Astin confirms the "accentuation" concept. In speaking of cognitive, affective, psychological, and behavioral changes, Astin says, *"The student's peer group is the single most potent source of influence on growth and development during the undergraduate years."*[15] He also finds that faculty characteristics and faculty-student relationships are important.

Pascarella and Terenzini note that, already in 1977, "Astin identified seven trends in American educational policy that ran counter to what his extensive analyses suggested would be sound educational policy . . . ."[16] Three of the trends Astin deplores are as follows[17]:

1. Trend toward larger institutions. Astin critiques "the assumption that bigness is somehow better" and shows how it is denied by research results. Astin also cites a widespread belief in "economics of scale" and says that "These . . . are mainly illusory. Large institutions actually spend somewhat more per student for educational purposes than small institutions. . . ."
2. Disappearance of single-sex colleges.
3. Deemphasis of the residential experience.

In his reference to colleges with special student populations, Astin refers especially to single-sex colleges, but he also reports some findings on African

American colleges and religious colleges. His findings are relevant for religious colleges with distinctive missions, because many of them are small residential institutions, not large research multiversities.

Astin discovered that small, private, residential colleges that have communities of faculty members and students typically have a greater educational impact than other kinds of higher education institutions. He states "the underlying principle" behind this impact: *Students in similar circumstances and with common needs and interests have been afforded an opportunity to interact and learn together.*[18] He says, "This kind of peer community has developed more or less naturally in many small, private, residential colleges that serve primarily eighteen- to twenty-two-year-olds."

More recent results of the National Survey on Student Engagement ("NSSE") have also given high scores to small residential colleges.

Colleges are special communities populated by members with certain common interests in learning. Astin says that those institutions and institutional subgroups with the greatest educational impact are precisely those in which the sense of community among the members of the community provide for optimal educational accentuation and resultant impact.[19]

College supporters and campus people can differ on the kind of campus community they see as implementing their mission. If a church-related college and its church want their campus to be a happy family of racially homogeneous students and faculty members, racial characteristics will be accentuated. Church-related colleges and universities can successfully work for gender, racial/ethnic, and international diversity while recruiting faculty members and students supportive of their missions to the extent that they and their churches are open to transformation and being inclusive.

If a church or a college has problems with diversity, the problems will pose a special challenge. If the problem is located primarily in the college, the church may need to clarify agreement on the mission. If the problem is located primarily in racism or sexism in the church, the church and college may both see the college as a resource for effecting needed change.

In speaking to presidents of Christian colleges, Arnold Mitchem, president of the Council for Opportunity in Education, said, "The data show that ethnic minority students do better at your kinds of institutions [i.e., Christian colleges] than at public institutions."[20]

In a church-related institution, *religious* diversity that tried to replicate the composition of the larger society would reflect mission diffusion. But some kinds of racial-ethnic and gender diversity are important for good church-related education. Colleges and universities that want to be distinctive will have to discern which kinds of diversity are helpful and which are not helpful as they seek to implement their missions.

Epistemological Pluralism

The interest in gender, racial-ethnic, and international diversity on U.S. campuses arises partly out of the fact that the American society and the global environment are increasingly pluralistic. "Pluralism" is a term with several different meanings. We need to differentiate "ordinary" pluralism from "theoretical," or "philosophical," pluralism.[21]

"Ordinary pluralism" (or "mere pluralism") describes a situation in which people with cultural differences exist and need to be taken into account. Affirming pluralism in this sense is saying that one can and should recognize a great diversity of views and lifestyles, on the one hand, and maintain conditions for order and communication necessary for corporate life, on the other. Larson and Marty call these kinds of pluralism "ordinary" or "conventional" pluralism.

"Theoretical pluralism" (or "philosophical" or "ultimate" pluralism) refers to the denial of the possibility of the existence of any all-encompassing truth. It is not the tolerance of a diversity of systems under a larger umbrella, but the denial of the existence of the umbrella. One of its advocates, Raimundo Panikkar, says that this kind of "pluralism entails ... the dethronement of reason and the abandonment of the monotheistic paradigm."[22]

Most academics would affirm ordinary pluralism but would object to theoretical pluralism's "dethronement of reason." Church people and most Americans generally would not be ready to abandon the "monotheistic paradigm." Churches and church educators who recognize the pluralism of our postmodern culture and who want diversity and innovation in educational programs will heartily affirm and welcome "ordinary" pluralism and, at the same time, affirm the existence of truth and the importance of searching for it.

Diversity among Institutions

Just as different academic communities in different settings may agree on the use of English or French or Japanese as their languages of discourse, so academic communities in different settings gather around rather different understandings of knowledge and truth.

Communities within a pluralistic society differ from one another in important ways. Faculty members and interested students united by certain common Christian understandings or other comprehensive perspectives on reality can differ from faculty members in institutions with other understandings. Churches and other groups with distinctive beliefs, practices, and epistemological understandings can benefit from having communities of faculty members and students gathered around special missions. (See Chapters 13 and 14.)

Trying to have the student bodies and faculties of all schools represent a statistical sample of the larger United States or world population in all respects is not furthering good education. A "standardized diversity" is an oxymoron! There is an important place for diversity among schools, as well as among students and faculty members within a school.[23]

Practical Arrangements for Diversity and Community

The most obvious and important way of providing for both diversity and community in a college is by having the kinds of diversity desired represented in a faculty and student community of members committed to a common educational mission. The diversity in the faculty and commitment to the mission are particularly important.

The curriculum of a church college can "teach" diversity in many ways. In every college and university, as young people study classic and contemporary works in literature, the arts, and the sciences, they reflect on the pluralism of our society and world.

Schools can provide for a combination of diversity and community experiences for students by having their students spend part of their school years in off-campus groups in cross-cultural settings. Some colleges include cross-cultural terms as parts of their core general education programs. Students are expected to have experiences of these kinds as a part of their studies about the world of human beings and societies, in the same way that all students are expected to have some laboratory work in their studies of the natural world.

Secondary schools can also have off-campus terms. One high school I visited was one of the first high schools in its state to offer a one-week January interterm in which students could get experiences in diversity not available on the home campus. The authorities in the state offices discouraged the attempt and were not sure they would approve and accredit the unconventional program. Then, within only two or three years, the state authorities made an about-face. They became so convinced of the value of the innovation that they were actively recommending it to other high schools in the state.

Another way colleges and churches can provide for the combination of religious commonality and diversity they may seek for their students is to follow a pattern for higher education much older than Harvard. Oxford and Cambridge in England and some other universities in England and Canada have had individual colleges located as "cluster colleges" on their university campuses, as was actually the original intention for Harvard. The Harvard in Cambridge in New England was to follow the lead of its Cambridge prototype in old England; Harvard College was to be the first of a series of colleges. But other colleges were never started on the Massachusetts campus and Harvard College just got larger as a single unit. Then other U.S. colleges and universities followed the Harvard single undergraduate college pattern.

Having colleges of various church and private groups on a university campus can provide for a combination of intentional diversity and commonality particularly appropriate for the post-Christendom paradigm of the church as a minority community in a larger pluralistic society. Students and faculty members live in intentional community in their colleges; at the same time, they have daily contact with the variety of members of the university at which their colleges are located.

Already in their 1966 Danforth Commission publication, Pattillo and Mackenzie wrote:

> The pattern developed at the University of Waterloo [in Ontario, Canada] between a public university and church-related colleges has advantages which might very well be explored by institutions in the United States. Not only does the arrangement afford substantial financial savings, particularly for the colleges, but also enriches the environment of the University and tends to sharpen the distinctive character of each cooperating college. . . . It fits the realities of a religiously pluralistic society.[24]

In the past four decades, few U.S. churches and colleges have pursued this suggestion of Pattillo and Mackenzie, although George Marsden continues to note this as an attractive option for today:

> Perhaps what post-Enlightenment universities, which presumably recognize that there is no universal scientific or moral vision that will unite the race, need to do, in addition to making a pragmatic search for some functional common ground, is to conceive of themselves as federations for competing intellectual communities of

faith or commitment. This might be more difficult for U.S. universities than for British or some Canadian universities, which have always seen themselves as federations of colleges among which there was sometimes diversity. U.S. schools, by contrast, were shaped first by sectarian Christian and then by Enlightenment and liberal Protestant ideals that assumed that everyone ought to think alike. Nonetheless, if American schools were willing to recognize diversity and perhaps even to incorporate colleges with diverse commitments, whether religious, feminist, gay, politically conservative, humanist, liberationist, or whatever, pluralism might have a better chance.[25]

Even if individual residential colleges are not on one larger campus, colleges may gain some of the advantages of experiences in diversity (and wider ranges of curricular offerings) through "strategic alliances" with other institutions. Technology has made possible some cooperative relationships that would have been impossible in the past.

For optimal learning, college students need a combination of experiences in diversity and community. A physics department can bring together a diverse group of women and men, Hispanics and Caucasians, and Americans and Indonesians with a common interest in physics. In today's world, a church and a church institution will often seek racial-ethnic and gender diversity, and it can do this while focusing its mission and avoiding "mission diversity." Churches and schools can provide for the accentuation of some desired student characteristics by bringing together students and faculty members with these common characteristics who represent also the racial-ethnic, gender, and international diversity the schools seek to enhance.

Chapter 11 Endnotes

1 Arthur Levine, "The Campus Divided, and Divided Again," *The New York Times*, June 11, 2000.

2 Providing for immigrant and other underrepresented peoples is controversial also in other parts of the world.

3 The work of William G. Bowen and Derek Bok, formerly presidents of Princeton and Harvard, respectively, and a study by the Civil Rights Project at Harvard say that a diverse education environment "confers benefits on all students, members of majority and minority groups alike" (Gary Orfield, "Affirmative Action Works—But Judges and Policy Makers Need to Hear That Verdict," *The Chronicle of Higher Education*, December 10, 1999). An interview with one of the authors summarizing findings in a recent work by four psychologists, *The Diversity Challenge: Social Identity and Intergroup Relations on the College Campus* (New York: Russell Sage Foundation, 2008) can be found in Peter Schmidt, "The Mixed Benefits of Diversity," *The Chronicle of Higher Education*, February 27, 2009. Daryl G. Smith and Associates, *Diversity Works: The Emerging Picture of How Students Benefit* (Washington, DC: Association of American Colleges and Universities, 1997) provides a survey of research to the late 1990s. Pascarella and Terenzini, in *How College Affects Students: A Third Decade of Research,* The Jossey-Bass Higher and Adult Education Series (San Francisco: Jossey-Bass, 2005), say: "Our review of the research since 1990 indicates that what we have called 'diversity experiences' are positively related to both cognitive and affective learning outcomes" (638).

4 Analysis in 2004 of 2002 data from the U.S. Department of Education and the National Center for Education Statistics by the National Association of Independent Colleges and Universities, 1025 Connecticut Avenue, N.W., Suite 700, Washington, DC 20036.

5 Debra Humphreys, *General Education and American Commitments: A National Report on Diversity Courses and Requirements* (Washington, DC: Association of American Colleges and Universities, 1997). This work includes an extensive annotated bibliography. Excellent and very practical suggestions will be found in Caroline Sotello Viernes Turner, *Diversifying the Faculty: A Guidebook for Search Committees* (Washington, DC: Association of American Colleges and Universities, 2002). A recent bibliography by William Kraft on diversity issues as they relate to Christian colleges and universities can be found in the Fall 2004 issue of *CCCU Advance*, Council for Christian Colleges & Universities, Washington, D.C.

6 The study, by Marc Goulden and Mary Ann Mason of Berkeley, is reported in Robin Wilson, *The Chronicle of Higher Education,* July 15, 2005.

7 After some controversy over his commitment to diversity, then President Lawrence Summers of Harvard announced that his university would "spend at least $50 million over the next decade to recruit, support and promote women and underrepresented members of minority groups on its faculty" (Alan Finder, "Harvard Will Spend $50 Million To Make Faculty More Diverse," *New York Times*, May 17, 2005). This could have been a helpful initiative, but it was too little too late, and President Summers resigned in 2006. Data on minority enrollments can be found in "Minorities in Higher Education: Twenty-Second Annual Status Report," American Council on Education, Washington, D.C. (2006).

8 "Some universities which had not promoted study abroad have begun to encourage it" (Karen W. Arenson, "A Decline in Foreign Students Is Reversed," *New York Times,* November 13, 2006). In Harvard's 2004 review of its undergraduate program, the first specific recommendation of its committee's report was: "Every Harvard College student should be expected to complete an international experience. . . ." (*A Report on the Harvard College Curricular Review: Summary of Principal Recommendations,* April 2004.) The new general education curriculum approved by the Harvard faculty on May 15, 2007, however, does not include a study abroad expectation. In 2006 Yale became the first major university to require its MBA students to study abroad.

9 Several years ago, the Institute of International Education reported: "The drop in enrollments in 2003–04 is the first absolute decline in foreign enrollments since 1971–72" (*Open Doors 2004: International Students in the U.S.* [New York: IIE, 2004]). IIE data released in November 2008 indicate that foreign enrollments in the United States have just bounced back to the previous all-time high of 2002–2003. See Cornelia Dean, "Scientists Fear Visa Trouble Will Drive Foreign Students Away," *The New York Times,* March 3, 2009.

10 John Schwartz, "U.S. Is Urged to Lift Ban on Foreign Scholars," *The New York Times*, March 18, 2009. Bollag reports on foreign academics barred by the U.S.in Burton Bollag, "Scholars Kept Out," *The Chronicle of Higher Education*, June 15, 2007.

11 Kenneth A. Feldman and Theodore M. Newcomb, *The Impact of College on Students* (San Francisco: Jossey-Bass, 1969).

12 Pascarella and Terenzini, *How College Affects Students: Findings and Insights from Twenty Years of Research*, ed. Kenneth A. Feldman, The Jossey-Bass Higher and Adult Education Series (San Francisco: Jossey-Bass, 1991); Pascarella and Terenzini, *How College Affects Students: A Third Decade of Research*, The Jossey-Bass Higher and Adult Education Series (San Francisco: Jossey-Bass, 2005).

13 Alexander W. Astin, *Four Critical Years: Effects of College on Beliefs, Attitudes, and Knowledge* (San Francisco: Jossey-Bass, 1977). In 1990, J. M. Budd found that Astin's book was the single most frequently cited work in the higher education literature. ("Higher Education Literature: Characteristics of Citation Patterns," *Journal of Higher Education* 61, no. 1 [1990], 2).

14 Astin, *What Matters in College? Four Critical Years Revisited* (San Francisco: Jossey-Bass, 1993).

15 Astin, *Four Critical Years*, 398. (Italics in original.)

16 Pascarella and Terenzini, *How College Affects Students*, 647.

17 The citations from pages 244-47 of Astin's work.

18 Astin, *What Matters in College,* 415. (Italics in original.)

19 In reviewing and summarizing the research, Daryl G. Smith et al. write: "The evidence grows showing that involvement in specialized student groups, such as ethnic residential theme houses, support centers, and academic departments benefits students of color and others. Indeed, these activities appear to contribute to increased satisfaction and retention, despite prodigious commentary of their negative effect on the development of community on campus. . . . Special mission institutions—historically African American colleges and universities. . . . American Indian controlled colleges, women's colleges, and Latino/a serving institutions are important in higher education for the student groups they serve." (*Diversity Works: The Emerging Picture*

of How Students Benefit [Washington, DC: Association of American Colleges and Universities, 1997], vi, vii.)

20 Address at the Council for Christian Colleges & Universities, Washington, DC, February 1, 2000.

21 In distinguishing these meanings of pluralism, I am using designations proposed in Gerald James Larson, "Contra Pluralism," *Soundings* 73, no. 2–3 (1990): 303–26.

22 Cited in Larson, "Contra-Pluralism," 309.

23 David Solomon, a Protestant philosopher at the University of Notre Dame, is one of many who emphasize the fact that a concern with pluralism is consistent with a commitment to preserving the religious character of schools: "In the name of pluralism, then, Notre Dame and Baylor surely have an *obligation* to continue to pursue hiring policies that will preserve their distinctive characters" ("What Baylor & Notre Dame Can Learn From Each Other," *New Oxford Review*, December 1995, 17–18). Litfin makes the same point: "The right of the individual scholar to work and teach from whatever perspective he or she saw fit was to be held inviolate: the right of voluntary communities of like-minded scholars to do the same was somehow delegitimized. . . . Academic freedom was considered crucial to the vitality of the intellectual conversation, but at the institutional level homogeneity was to be encouraged" (*Conceiving the Christian College*, 257).

24 Pattillo and Mackenzie, *Church-Sponsored Higher Education in the United States: Report of the Danforth Commission* (Washington, DC: American Council on Education, 1966), 182.

25 Marsden, "The Soul of the American University: A Historical Overview," 40–41.

12

ACADEMIC FREEDOM

"College," "university," and "professoriate" are well-established North American institutions. Schools that want to be different from colleges and universities as widely understood need to be very clear about their missions and how they seek to be different. United States regional accrediting associations are ready to work with schools with distinctive missions and to evaluate them in terms of their own missions, but schools need to know what those missions are. A school can hire and promote faculty members who further its mission, but the mission needs to be clearly stated to prospects for employment and promotion, or the prospects will understandably assume that the school is using criteria like those of most other schools across the land.

As college and university are presently institutionalized, for example, faculty members at some schools are evaluated primarily in terms of their "productivity," i.e., their research and publications. If a college values teaching undergraduates as a part of its mission, it will have to make that clear and find appropriate ways of assessing teaching effectiveness in employing and promoting faculty members.

Is a faculty member's moral character an appropriate consideration? Most schools would consider fabricating experimental data by a faculty member as unacceptable dishonesty. It might not be necessary for a given school to be very explicit about that kind of widely held moral consideration. On the other hand, while avoiding sexual harassment of students has received attention in recent decades, understandings about faculty members dating students and having consensual relationships have varied from school to school. A school that felt that modeling integrity in keeping family commitments was a moral, personal, or religious consideration that was a part of its institutional mission would do well to be fairly clear about such expectations of faculty members. Which considerations and expectations are seen as "professional" depends on the way a profession is institutionalized in a particular society at a given time. In some professions, widely accepted rules and understandings on sexual harassment and racial discrimination have changed in recent decades.

Chapter 12 advocates the academic freedom for groups to have colleges and universities with distinctive missions in their search for truth, as well as the academic freedom of individual faculty members and students to join and work within such institutions of higher learning.

The American Association of University Professors

Stanley Fish cites what he calls "a famous passage in the declaration of principles of the American Association of University Professors, first published in 1915 and left in place (if only by silence) in subsequent declarations": "The A.A.U.P. denies to religiously based institutions the name of 'university' because 'they do not, at least as regards one particular subject, accept the principles of freedom of inquiry.'"[1]

In 1940 the American Association of University Professors (AAUP) issued its "Statement of Principles on Academic Freedom and Tenure," a document issued following a series of conferences begun in 1934. The 1940 document contains the well-known "limitations" clause: "Teachers are entitled to freedom in the classroom in discussing their subject. . . . Limitations of academic freedom because of religious or other aims of the institution should be clearly stated in writing at the time of the appointment."[2] Then in 1970, the AAUP issued an "Interpretive Comments" document with numbered references to specific portions of its 1940 Statement. The interpretive comment referring to the "limitations" clause cited above reads as follows: "Most church-related institutions no longer need or desire the departure from the principle of academic freedom implied in the 1940 Statement, and we do not now endorse such a departure."

In other words, rightly or wrongly, AAUP was saying that hiring faculty members committed to the distinctive religious or other mission of a school was a "limitation of academic freedom" and that, by 1970, most church-related institutions no longer wanted to hire faculty team members with commitments of those kinds. In any case, the AAUP did not favor hiring faculty members that way.

In its January–February 1997 issue, *Academe*, the AAUP journal, published a report of an AAUP subcommittee called, "The 'Limitations' Clause in the 1940 Statement of Principles: Some Operating Guidelines." It includes the following significant footnote:

> From its beginning days, the American Association of University Professors has found it necessary to distinguish between institutions of higher learning that are committed to academic freedom and those essentially proprietary institutions where free inquiry is subordinated to a religious (or to some other) mission. (49)

In its further comments, however, the subcommittee report notes that an institution can be "somewhere between an institution committed to academic freedom and one that pervasively restricts it" by being "an institution that provides academic freedom in most respects save for a carefully crafted core . . . of creedal or doctrinal conformity" (50). The subcommittee then takes a kind of mediating position and allows for invocation of the limitations clause in such instances, provided that the institutions in question have been sufficiently clear and explicit about their distinctive missions.

The AAUP was earlier trying to say that any institution with a distinctive religious mission should not be allowed to call itself a college or university and that any institution calling itself a college or university should not then be allowed to hire faculty members committed to a distinctive religious (or other) mission. But then the AAUP found that that earlier position was out of touch with reality and backed off from it.

The AAUP has generally seen religious considerations as obstacles and "limitations" in the search for truth. But some Christians think that there might be a special kind of freedom and helpful orientation in the search for truth about the Creation in a living relationship with the Creator revealed supremely in Jesus Christ—that perspective being one among many in today's pluralistic thought-world. Certainly that memory and the weaknesses of the church and Christendom throughout the centuries are partly responsible for the ambivalence of many today regarding the contribution of the church to the academy. But the AAUP and others today also need to take into account the fact that deeply committed Christians and Christian churches were involved in the origins and development of both the modern university and modern science.

On October 24–26, 1997, the AAUP sponsored a precedent-setting conference on "Academic Freedom at Religiously Affiliated Institutions." The event was initiated and arranged by a new, young staff member and legal counsel who had also been a Presbyterian elder. Religiously affiliated institutions were well represented. Also, as might have been expected and certainly as appropriate, some panelists and speakers represented traditional AAUP perspectives. At several points, AAUP spokespersons said that what is taught should, "of course," ultimately be left to the judgment of the professoriate. (This should probably not be surprising in an association that functions partly as a professors' trade union.) The comments of these AAUP representatives seemed to assume that the professional judgments needed would be those of the respective disciplinary associations in the several fields—e.g., the American Physical Society, the American Political Science Association, the American Sociological Association and their international counterparts. The AAUP representatives seemed to assume a kind of Enlightenment and pre-postmodern epistemology—that there are hard facts on which professionals would agree, and that religious considerations would be in the area of feelings and values which would not really bear on the kind of truth the professionals would be working with in their academic roles.

In the past, the AAUP has focused on the academic freedom of individual academic professionals to represent diverse points of view. It has not focused on the academic freedom of institutional communities of faculty members to be different from other academic communities in the larger society. It has tended to favor the freedom of diverse individuals over the freedom of diverse academic communities. The AAUP has failed to recognize the way these two kinds of freedom are related. An individual is not fully free if he or she does not have the freedom to join an academic community that is distinctive religiously or otherwise unusual.

We should, however, affirm the AAUP's initiative in finally calling the conference in 1997. The AAUP expressed its openness to hearing different points of view. The majority of the conference presenters the AAUP invited to speak at the conference were church-related college and university spokespersons. The AAUP was open to discussion and sponsored the conference. Some of us who attended got the impression that the AAUP is becoming aware that its earlier approach has not been working and needs to be changed.

This impression was confirmed in a second conference held by the AAUP jointly with the American Academy of Religion and the Society of Biblical Literature on March 31 to April 2, 2000, at Baylor University, a Baptist-related institution in Texas. Again, the program included speakers of various perspectives, including Nicholas Wolterstorff of Yale and William J. Abraham of Southern Methodist and Harvard. Many speakers noted—and the AAUP representatives seemed to recognize—that some limitations on a faculty member's academic freedom (e.g., what a professor might say in class) may be greater at public universities than at church-related ones, and that the AAUP should at least be even-handed if it wants to continue to use "limitations" as a term and frame of reference. At one point there emerged the beginning of a general agreement that faculty contracts should be clear on expectations—that faculty handbooks were not enough. But no one was aware of models of faculty contracts that were actually long enough to contain all of the proposed detail. Neither public nor independent universities can very well have faculty contracts of tens of pages or more that list all of the expectations that need to be in faculty handbooks!

In any case, let us hope that the recent AAUP conferences are the beginning of a fruitful and long-overdue conversation and that North American higher education will continue to include schools with different missions.

Academic Freedom for Individuals and Groups

If faculty members of a French university were recruited with the understanding that French would be the language of instruction and discourse, would that mean that the faculty members were not academically free? Would it be a "limitation of academic freedom"? It would clearly exclude a faculty prospect who did not want to speak French. But most academics would say that a university in which faculty members and students spoke a thousand different tribal languages could hardly be called a university at all. There could be no instruction or conversation, and the participants would not be free to have any kind of academic community under those circumstances. Having a common language of instruction and conversation in a school enhances the free exchange of ideas and the development of the kind of campus academic community that facilitates the search for knowledge and understanding.[3]

One can support the academic freedom of the individual, on the one hand, but one must also support the freedom of groups to form academic communities and of individuals to join such communities.[4]

Chapter 12 Endnotes

1   Stanley Fish, "Academic Freedom: When Sauce for the Goose Isn't Sauce for the Gander," *The Chronicle of Higher Education,* November 26, 1999. Fish continues: "Academic freedom, rather than being open to all points of view, is open to all points of view only so long as they offer themselves with the reserve and diffidence appropriate to Enlightenment decorums. . . . Academic freedom is not a defense against orthodoxy; it *is* an orthodoxy and a faith." He continues: "Academic freedom invites forceful agendas in only on its terms, and refuses to grant legitimacy to the terms within which such agendas define themselves. We are right back to the 1915 A.A.U.P. declaration, with a slight modification: Religion can be a part of university life so long as it renounces its claim to have a privileged purchase on the truth, which of course is the claim that defines a religion as a religion, as opposed to a mere opinion."

2   One might reflect on the meanings of "freedom" and "limitations" here. Would a geographer teaching that the earth is flat be "free" to do this without jeopardizing his or her possibilities of promotion? What about a sociologist promoting the superiority of Caucasian "Aryans" in the classroom? Or a class burning flags in a state institution?

3   This is not a hypothetical question in many universities around the world where English has become the lingua franca. See, for example, Burton Bollag, "The New Latin: English Dominates in Academe: As Students and the Internet Cross Borders, Academics Find They Must Speak the Same Tongue," *The Chronicle of Higher Education,* September 8, 2000.

4   See Anthony J. Diekema, *Academic Freedom and Christian Scholarship* (Grand Rapids: Wm. B. Eerdmans, 2000) and William Cavanaugh, "Sailing Under True Colors: Academic Freedom and the Ecclesially Based University," in *Conflicting Allegiances: The Church-Based University in a Liberal Democratic Society*, ed. Michael L. Budde and John Wright (Grand Rapids: Brazos Press, 2004), 31–52.

PART IV

HEALTHY LONG-TERM CHURCH-SCHOOL RELATIONSHIPS

13

Faculty Teams for Distinctive Missions

Except for the concluding chapter, each chapter of Part IV begins with information from published sources and campus visits on a key element in present academic systems that has tended to lead over the long term to increased church-school distance. Then the chapters each turn from science to visioning, from observation and analysis of what is to considering what could be. Each chapter projects practical ways in which churches and schools with distinctive commitments might realize their shared intentions more fully in the future.

While the front pages of their catalogs have continued to affirm church missions, many church colleges have adopted models and ways of working that have made change over time almost inevitable. Lacking clarity on how to get from here to there, American church colleges have frequently found themselves carried along in processes that led to unintended outcomes. The path away from church relationships and toward the prevailing model of excellence is paved with good intentions. Churches and church institutions that want to maintain longer-term church-school relationships will need to move beyond good intentions. They will need to understand better than they have in the past the dynamics of dissociation and the alternative strategies needed for maintaining lively and healthy continuing college-school relationships.

Educational practitioners have not taken seriously enough what organizational theorists have found in their studies of institutions and what theologians have described as "principalities and powers."[1] Institutions can render a needed service by providing stability in times of social change. Under the influence of prevailing external and internal forces, however, an organization in an institutional field can tend to develop a life and momentum quite apart from the intentions of its founders and sponsors. Educational institutions thus become "principalities and powers" that express themselves in agencies and organizations, like governmental and market-system institutions, parts of the good order that God intended for humankind, but also entities tempted by self-interest and a desire for autonomy.

Church-affiliated colleges and universities have had many different kinds of church relationships. Various authors have tried to gain perspective on the differences by identifying the degree to which the various institutions have been church-related.[2] But schools have differed not only in the degree to which they have been church-related, but also in the various ways in which they have been church-related. Schools cannot easily be mapped on a single degree-of-church-relatedness continuum—it would take a two- or multi-dimensional mapping to represent the variations adequately.

Part IV does not try to describe the various past categorizations and then to develop them further, but to deal directly with the basic elements in lively, long-term church-school relationship systems. What is ultimately important in education is what happens among teachers and students, and among students and students in classroom, office, convocation, and residence hall. But we begin at a more fundamental level than the curriculum. We focus on the basic need for assembling faculty teams that will provide leadership in setting appropriate curricular and extracurricular requirements and expectations and in relating to students. We deal with the administrators that provide leadership in the staffing of their institutions. We deal with the boards that carry the primary responsibility for the choice of chief executive officers and for a clear focus on the long-term relationships of their schools. In brief, we focus on foundational elements in church-school educational systems that can provide for education that is distinctive over the longer term.

The key elements are parts of a system. An institution cannot recruit faculty members interested in its mission if it is not clear on its mission. A church cannot have the kinds of schools it might want to have if it does not have boards through which its thousands or millions of members can express themselves authentically. A church and a school will have to have dollars to provide for a kind of education that is different from what others in the larger society are ready or able to support. A church may want to have schools that can effectively transmit the best of its traditions to the younger generations, but the church can get out of touch with the younger generations and the findings of researchers if it does not ask its teachers and scholars to be testing its traditions and helping it face the challenges of life and mission in a changing world. None of the elements will relate to each other optimally without effective administrative leadership. These elements undergird the day-to-day experiences of students and faculty members.

We need to be practical and specific. Many writers, for example, have talked in generalities about the importance of a "critical mass" of faculty members or students, or of a church relationship of a church-related school. But how can a school actually reach goals in these areas? Administrators too often face enormous pressures for short-term results. We need to consider practical ways they can be supported as they work toward longer-term objectives.

The order in which we will be looking at the various elements in this section is somewhat arbitrary. Change can be initiated at different points. A change can be initiated by a creative and farsighted president. Or a faculty researcher can raise questions that lead others to promote change. Board members who come with outside perspectives can ask whether "the emperor is really wearing any clothes." Sometimes environmental forces lead institutions to ask questions about their long-term missions. Actors in college and university organizational systems who want to initiate change can begin where they are.

Faculty—Key to Mission Fulfillment

Many observers agree that the hiring of faculty members is a key to the fulfillment of a school's mission. But few have asked about the kinds of systemic changes in faculty recruitment that will be helpful—or necessary—if distinctive long-term missions are to be implemented.

Schools with a distinctive mission will have to have at least some faculty members committed to the mission. Earl McGrath, a U.S. Commissioner of Education in the Truman and Eisenhower administrations and higher education leader and consultant to many colleges in his lifetime, said, "[An important] step to be taken by Christian colleges to restore their identity and status is to select proper teachers."[3]

Faculty members teach the students and meet with them in their laboratories and offices. Faculty members develop curricula and co-curricular programs. In most schools, faculty members in departments play key roles in hiring new faculty members. Faculty members have a voice in presidential searches and searches for other administrators. Where faculty members and academic departments choose their leaders and successors, the values and interests of one faculty generation are transmitted to and often enhanced in succeeding generations. Board members and top administrators can play a role in outlining procedures and some criteria for faculty recruitment, but there is little they can do if they have employed too many faculty members who are not interested in a school's long-term goals and mission.

Is it enough to ask only that faculty members refrain from actively opposing the mission? If the institution calls itself Christian, for example, does that mean asking only that faculty members refrain from actively opposing the idea of a Christian institution? Would a physics department find it adequate to ask that physics instructors refrain from actively opposing the idea of physics as a discipline? Would it not want to have enough physics instructors who know something about physics and are actual practicing physicists? Should not these physicists show a little enthusiasm for the study of nature?[4]

In a public session at the conference sponsored by the American Association of University Professors in October 1997,[5] the director of a series of consultations on "The Future of the Church-Related College" funded by the Lilly Endowment, said:

> I'm the only [member of my denomination] in our [denominational] college's religion faculty of 12. I can't think of anyone in the middle-age group at our college that is behind our institutional mission. I'm not sure we can go back . . . . Unless an institution has an adequate body of faculty members who in some way affirm and live out the mission, it might as well close its doors. It will not be meaningfully church-related for long. Faculty hiring is the crucial issue."

A dean of a Catholic law school, who has taught at Notre Dame and Creighton and served on the accreditation committee of the American Bar Association's legal education division, said:

> Over the years, a lot of Catholic law schools began to hire people who didn't care about the Catholic mission of the school, and these people

are now tenured, full professors. In this situation, it's difficult to reaffirm your mission because faculty governance is so important.[6]

How many faculty members need to model active involvement in the school's mission? The Pope says that more than fifty percent of the faculty members of a university that calls itself Catholic need to be Catholic.[7] Some churches and schools speak of a "critical mass," often without specifying quantitatively what that mass might be.[8]

Clearly the criteria for faculty recruitment and overall faculty composition depend on the particular mission in which the church and school are engaged. If a church's mission involves having schools trying to be like Princeton, the church may want its schools to have chaplaincy services like those at Princeton, but it will not use religious criteria in its recruitment of departmental faculty members. On the other hand, an institution with a distinctively churchly as well as an academic mission, for example, will need to have at least some faculty members who sense a calling to communicate in a positive and warm and outgoing way their vision for participating in God's cause in the world.

In the past century, the professionalization of the faculty by discipline (the "Academic Revolution" of Jencks and Riesman[9]) and the long-term effect of prevailing faculty recruitment practices have probably contributed more to the distancing of church colleges and universities from their churches than any other single factor.[10] The long-term relationship of schools to a church or other societal group with a distinctive mission will depend more on getting key faculty members than on any other factor.

Traditional Faculty Recruitment

A major problem for schools with distinctive missions is that the way faculty recruitment is presently institutionalized in North American academia is inimical to the development of strong faculty teams committed to distinctive missions. Faculty recruitment criteria and practices at a given school are frequently influenced largely by criteria and practices of practitioners of a discipline at other schools, to the neglect of organization-specific considerations. The traditional recruitment criteria and practices in North American academia can be obstacles to the recruitment of strong faculties prepared to implement distinctive missions.

Traditional approaches involve waiting until a vacancy appears, advertising for candidates who have already obtained Ph.D.s or equivalent terminal degrees, and choosing among those who apply. The department wants a top Ph.D. now. In reviewing lists of candidates, there is some room for considering religious qualifications, but sometimes even that hardly occurs. A typical North American church college or university that does exercise religious preference in a search does it by working with the group of candidates that a given department considers academically most "excellent." It then tries to find someone whose beliefs and practices are not incompatible with the institution's religious mission. In some instances, this is someone who is hardly aware of the background of the religious movement of which the school is a part or who is not personally active in any religious community.

Peter Steinfels sees the problem: "If questions about a new faculty member's fit with a school's religious identity were to be part of [the] process, they could not be left to a last-minute conversation."[11]

A college or university with a distinctive churchly mission and an interest in academic quality is often looking for candidates who bring an unusual combination of qualifications: (1) potential for exciting classroom teaching and inspiring mentoring relationships with students, (2) cutting-edge involvement in one of the school's academic fields, and (3) rootage in the life of the church and a clear sense of calling and commitment to the churchly mission of the school. In some cases, schools are looking for candidates from underrepresented groups to develop greater racial-ethnic and gender diversity in their faculties.[12]

An advertisement in the *Chronicle of Higher Education* may bring hundreds of responses in today's market. In some searches, none of the candidates who apply really bring outstanding qualifications in all of the above areas. Perhaps another candidate who would have had all the qualifications graduated with his or her Ph.D. two years before and is now in a tenure-track position in an Ivy League university. Perhaps an outstanding prospect is in graduate school and needs an additional year or two of residence. In today's market, where there are few openings for new Ph.D.s in some fields, some of the most promising and enterprising prospects—prospects who could easily have completed Ph.D.s—have not undertaken doctoral studies at all.

The present institutionalization of faculty recruitment in American academia is certainly as frustrating for young faculty prospects as it is for church colleges and universities trying to assemble good faculty teams. Some qualified applicants submit application after application and travel from interview to interview, then still wind up with no job offers.[13] The present system for matching institutional needs with the gifts and abilities of faculty prospects needs to be changed.

The fundamental problem is that traditional approaches to faculty recruitment are based on a selection paradigm rather than a search paradigm. One of the great obstacles to change in today's recruitment procedures is the idea that "there are lots of good people out there." There are lots of people. But searching within a five-month vacancy window for the combination of theological maturity, teaching ability, and demonstrated experience in creative work in an academic discipline can pose serious challenges. A multi-dimensional search can start with hundreds of applicants and end up with none.

There are not many Nobel laureates. How many Baptist-interested African American women Ph.D. physicists who have a gift for exciting teaching will a Baptist college interested in racial and gender diversity be able to recruit if the outstanding candidates also have invitations from Harvard?[14] If Tony Dungy of the Indianapolis Colts would have said that "there are lots of Peyton Mannings and tight ends out there" and waited for them to apply, he would have been at the bottom of the league. Teams of academic and athletic professionals may get hundreds of applicants, but they do not get Nobel Prize winners or star quarterbacks by advertising in professional journals and assuming that top candidates will come running.[15]

In recruiting Nobel Prize winners and other academic stars around which they can build great departments, the leading North American research universities follow search and recruitment procedures very different from those that are otherwise traditional in North American academia.[16] They do not assume that there are lots of good Nobel Prize winners available and that they will apply in response to advertisements in the *Chronicle of Higher Education*! An institution that assumes that the best candidates will come running when a vacancy is announced can maintain a kind of status quo academically, but is headed over the long run toward mediocrity. And, when a church-related institution wants to fill a vacancy within a five-month hiring window and needs to compromise in its selection from a list of immediately-available candidates, it is frequently the criterion of excellence in potential for implementing the institution's distinctive religious mission that gets lost. In meeting a short-term need to fill a vacancy, an institution can find itself with a faculty member of less-than-optimal gifts who may serve for thirty or more years.

Saying that a president or academic vice president will carry the responsibility for bringing institution-specific, as opposed to disciplinary, considerations to bear in recruitment decisions is in most instances simply inadequate. In one college I visited, for example, the president refused to approve a candidate proposed by a department. Several months later, another department proposed an unqualified candidate in its field. Sensing that he had used up about as much of his presidential "capital" as he could without stirring up an insurrection, the president reluctantly approved the second candidate. The institution now has a less-than-qualified faculty member, and will probably have that faculty member for the next several decades.

In describing Waynesburg College's move toward a more distinctive religious identity, James Dittmar emphasizes the importance of faculty recruitment. He observes that one important element at Waynesburg was a change in 1996 in the structure of faculty search committees to include "one or two members from the department in which a position was open, at least one faculty member from another department, and at least one other senior administrative staff person in addition to the Academic Dean." He says that the change "supported the developing mission and character of Waynesburg's church-related and Christian identity."[17]

Theodore Marchese emphasizes the importance of active search, as opposed to the more routine processing of applications and suggestions submitted by others. He provides some time-tested and detailed suggestions that can help faculty search committees, as well as committees responsible for recommending administrators.[18]

Faculty Recruitment and Faculty Development

Some administrators have focused their efforts on the development of new faculty members after their initial employment. Faculty development can be helpful, but it cannot replace good recruitment. The problem has been that it has not been easy to make significant changes in the religious orientations and other life commitments of faculty members already in their twenties or thirties and busy meeting the other requirements for tenure at their institutions. Indeed, some faculty development efforts almost seem to be an invasion of the personal privacy of new faculty members, especially when expectations were not clear at the time of their hiring.

Case Study: Roman Catholic Institutions

More than any other Catholic educator, James L. Heft, S.M., former chancellor of the University of Dayton and former chair of the board of the 230-plus-member Association of Catholic Colleges and Universities, has focused on the importance of faculty hiring. He and a Dayton colleague have said, "In the 60's and 70's many Catholic colleges and universities believed that they were forbidden to ask candidates for faculty positions about their willingness to support the mission of the institution. From the mid 80's to the present, however, that understanding has disappeared. Now, many institutions are being more forthright."[19]

Heft and Pestello refer to a study published in the Winter 1996 issue of *Current Issues in Catholic Higher Education* that found that only two to seven percent of Catholic colleges and universities specified any preference for Catholic faculty. Thinking that this was inaccurate, they conducted an extensive set of interviews with administrators and faculty members in 1998. They found that all institutions surveyed sent mission documents to faculty prospects, and all had administrators assigned to interview and approve of candidates for hiring. Several schools requested written statements from candidates. However, Heft and Pestello observe that most administrators had difficulty defining how a prospect would "fit" with the mission of the institution. "Administrators had an easier time describing the 'ideal' faculty member than they did defining 'fit.'. . .The characteristic of the ideal faculty member which was mentioned most often . . . was a commitment to teaching and students," hardly a religious qualification. They further found that, apart from theology and philosophy hires, "most administrators feel that hiring should occur without primary regard to faith as a major criterion." "One of the ideas rarely mentioned explicitly in any of the interviews was the importance of hiring Catholic intellectuals and intellectuals immersed in the Catholic tradition."[20]

Heft and Pestello write that "administrators are keenly aware of the threats to the Catholic identity of their institutions." But is having an administrator interviewing candidates toward the end of the hiring process an effective way of choosing prospects enthusiastic about an institution's mission for the long run? How many proposals from strong departments could such an administrator veto before running into hopeless conflicts—are vetoes the most effective way of achieving the desired ends? What if, as Heft and Pestello found, the administrators in the church institution do not see faith as a major criterion in their decision-making?

Hiring adequate numbers of Catholic intellectuals is a criterion mentioned by the Pope. If it is not the best criterion, then perhaps better criteria need to be clearly stated. The point here is only that, whatever the criteria, conventional recruitment procedures have frequently not been adequate as ways of meeting stated goals.

A Challenge

People who have not reflected on the long-term outcomes of traditional procedures in faculty recruitment are not likely to want to innovate. Educational leaders proposing systemic change face a challenge.

Most institutions do not have anyone given specific responsibility and time for the identification and cultivation of contacts with gifted persons who might not be immediately needed and available, but could be excellent faculty prospects for the longer-term future. Recruitment is sometimes colloquially called "head-hunting," but what we are talking about here includes preparation for future service. Academic deans and provosts have increasingly felt overloaded with immediate faculty needs and other day–to-day tasks. With the increasing pressures they are coping with now and in the foreseeable future, they will typically not be in a position to allocate time and energy for implementing needed change in faculty recruitment and employment procedures. With the removal of age as a factor in mandatory retirement policies, school administrators are finding it even more difficult to do long-term faculty planning than in the past, since they are not sure when they will have vacancies.

An alternative or alternatives to traditional faculty recruitment procedures will need to meet challenges in two areas: (1) searching for and maintaining contacts with prospects, whether or not they are needed for immediate employment; and (2) employing outstanding prospects when they are available, even though they may not be needed to fill specific vacancies at precisely the time of their initial employment. Both of these are significant challenges. Both involve funding. Identifying and staying in touch with prospects for years before they may become available or are needed requires the allocation of staff time. "Over-hiring"—hiring prospects as backup team players for several years before a specific vacancy exists—may well require salary funding that would not be required otherwise.

If restricted funds for the implementation of over-hiring and other long-term hiring objectives are not available, changes of these kinds can hardly be initiated in a time of overall institutional consolidation and retrenchment. And yet an investment in initiatives of these kinds can have a long-term return even greater than the long-term investments institutions make in bricks and mortar. Funding strategic faculty recruitment could be very attractive to donors interested in the long-term effects of their contributions on the missions of their institutions. Listing the names of donors to a special fund could publicize the cause. Alumni memories of their college days usually center on professors who changed their lives more than on buildings on the campus. A denomination with an interest in higher education might want to contribute in a special way to the faculty recruitment needs of its institutions.

Major research universities have sometimes both "searched" and "overhired" as they have recruited internationally recognized scholars. They have worked creatively with prospects over years in recruiting them to create new departments and to initiate new programs in old ones. They have employed academic stars when they were available, whether or not they were needed to fill previously existing vacancies.

The hot news in many issues of the *Chronicle of Higher Education* is on universities' successes in landing faculty recruits. A lead article on a well-known educator and columnist in one *Chronicle* was subtitled: "Stanley Fish surprised academe by becoming a dean at the U. of Illinois at Chicago. Now he's going after other big names and landing them." The inside title: "Stanley Fish, as a College Dean, Makes a Big Splash and Spares No Expense."[21] The article listed fifteen of Fish's recruits and five offers he had made.

"Shoulder-tapping" gifted candidates used to be more common at many kinds of institutions. Some universities, including Harvard, hired productive scholars and administrators, including some who did not have terminal degrees. David Hoekema, then provost at Calvin College, describes a time when Calvin needed a faculty member in French.[22] The Calvin president at that time went out and asked a specially gifted recent graduate who was teaching high school to go to graduate school to get advanced degrees. The candidate did this and became a valued member of Calvin's French department. The histories of some other institutions have stories of this kind.

Liberal arts institutions, churches, and other groups with distinctive missions will need to make investments in recruiting faculty members with unusual combinations of gifts for the achievement of their long-term goals. They cannot turn the clock back. Older kinds of "shoulder-tapping" sometimes involved "old boys networking" that often excluded minority candidates. However, shoulder-tapping can now be a part of targeted recruiting for minority candidates.

Where Can an Institution Begin?

An administration, board, and church can begin by highlighting the importance of calling gifted prospects who are already interested in the mission of the church and school to teaching as a vocation and ministry.

In actual practice, such "calling" may involve obstacles. How can administrators or a board stimulate needed change without highlighting the weaknesses of some existing departments that may be the result of bad faculty recruiting in the past? How can one be specific without antagonizing continuing faculty members whose support is desired? How can one talk about faculty needs without discouraging students? One cannot easily highlight needs in specific departments even when it is common knowledge that a school has some departments that are weak in their enthusiasm about the school's church mission or in attracting and inspiring strong students. However, school leaders can often say: "It is not that our school is worse than other schools. If we do what others do, we will tend to be average. We do not want to be average. We want to be excellent! We cannot be different from others in this regard unless we are willing to adopt some practices that are different from theirs." School leaders can ask faculty members and administrators: "Do we want to stay where we are in our academic performance, image, and present church relationship? If so, we need only to continue the kind of faculty recruitment everyone else is doing. If we want to move toward leadership in the pack, we'll have to be ready to be different."

Long-term faculty planning—including arranging for faculty members not needed in the next two years—can be called "planning for deferred service," and the parallel between deferred service and deferred giving can be highlighted. Years ago many school people didn't understand the importance of deferred giving. Now almost everyone does. I remember well when, years ago, some faculty members asked: "Why in the world should we pay staff people to raise endowment when what we need is operating money now? Other schools like ours aren't spending that much on raising endowment!" On today's scene one can make the parallel of deferred service with deferred giving and then put the question: "Which is more important in making a school great, money or people?"

A board has a special responsibility for the long-term mission achievement of its institution. It can play a key role.

Creating a "Strategic Faculty Recruitment" Role

After consultation with a board, an administration can appoint a top-level staff administrator as "associate vice president for strategic faculty recruitment."[23] The associate vice president would develop and maintain contacts with faculty prospects not necessarily needed in the next eighteen months, but needed for the longer-term future.

The board can ask for the appointment of an associate vice president for strategic faculty recruitment with a full-time equivalent load assignment of a minimum of one-half of the total full-time equivalent (FTE) assignment the institution gives to staffing deferred giving assignments. For example, a board might ask that a university with 1.6 FTE per thousand full-time students in deferred giving would have half that much, or 0.8 FTE per thousand, for strategic faculty recruitment or "deferred service." Strategic faculty recruitment, like deferred fundraising, requires special gifts and expertise. It does not have an immediate pay-off. Recruiting for deferred service also does not have an immediate pay-off, but it is important for the long-term accomplishment of the institution's mission. In fact, recruitment for deferred faculty service can have a more immediate pay-off than deferred giving.

The job description of the associate vice president for strategic faculty recruitment could begin with preparing a confidential list with the name of a good back-up prospect for every position in the faculty held by a person over fifty-five years of age.[24] Years ago, in his first years, a dean at one school I visited tried to have at least one back-up person in mind for every faculty position.

Full consideration should be given to prospects for mid-career moves, as well as to encouraging younger candidates to enter graduate studies. Universities are increasingly making headlines with news of good mid-career recruits.

Other specific elements in the job description of an administrator for strategic faculty recruitment could include:

- Surveying academic administrators of other church-related institutions and constituency leaders in order to develop a database of names of especially promising young and mid-career prospects for possible recruitment.
- Providing workshops for members of all new departmental search committees before they begin their work.
- Working with search committees and individuals in finding and agreeing on prospects for later active service as successors to faculty members nearing retirement.
- Working with prospects for later service by providing them with opportunities and expectations for university teaching internships, theological preparation, and other experiences to

prepare them academically, intellectually, and spiritually for teaching positions.

- Visiting lively prospects from time to time (e.g., once a year).
- Having e-mail or telephone contact with each prospect on a regular schedule (e.g., every six months).
- Hosting each prospect at a campus visit and arranging for an informal visit of the prospect with the academic department and academic vice president or dean from time to time.
- Creating awareness on campus of the need for and importance of working with prospects years before they may be needed for service.

With Lilly Endowment support, the University of Notre Dame and now the Council for Christian Colleges & Universities have done some work on a new national or international recruiting network for faculty members and administrators, but that project has been discontinued for the present. A campus-based staff administrator for strategic faculty recruiting at a church-related institution could use the resources of such a network.

Involving the Academic Vice President

Vice presidents for academic affairs and academic deans can consult with senior faculty members on their retirement wishes in order to facilitate arrangements for good transitions. Retirement at a given age can no longer be required by an institution, but retirement incentives have been ruled by the courts as legal. Incentives (e.g., greater medical benefits for those who retire by certain deadlines) can be used to facilitate advance planning. New "voluntary tenure-buyout" plans can make such arrangements attractive to both faculty members and administrators.

The goal would be, where possible, to have understandings about the retirement preferences of individual faculty members five or more years before their dates of actual retirement. Given the opportunity, some or many faculty members would be ready to do advance planning in order to see that the work to which they had given many years of their lives would be picked up by good successors in the best way. Discussions with senior faculty members would be within the scope of the responsibilities of academic vice presidents, not the new associate vice presidents for strategic faculty recruitment.

Advance Recruitment and Preparation

If informed of the prospect of an opening several years in advance, the administrator can work with a search committee to initiate a public search for a candidate or candidates. The search can include initiating contacts with gifted minority persons and women who may not have entered advanced studies because of the job market for Ph.D.s in their fields.

Announcements would make it clear that, in the interest of employing persons with special qualifications, and especially of eliciting the interest of persons from underrepresented groups, the search is an equal-opportunity search at this advanced time. The search would be for a person with whom some mutual commitments can be made, although there could be changes in the commitments as outlined below.

The interviews involved in the selection of the candidate or candidates of choice would appropriately include campus visits with presentations to classes or faculty groups. In the interviews with departmental faculty members and administrators, the candidates could be asked about the kinds of further preparation they would propose if selected as candidates of choice for a faculty position.

When a candidate or candidates who are interested in preparing to fill the opening have been identified,[25] the institution and the candidates would cooperate in providing for the best preparation the candidates could have in the years available.

- Typically, for many candidates, the largest part of the time would be spent in graduate study or post-graduate research.
- The candidate might be asked to spend a semester or a year in a teaching internship at the institution as a way of further discerning the prospect's teaching gifts at an early stage of his or her preparation and the mutual interest of candidate and institution in a long-term appointment. This used to be an option in the old Danforth Fellowship program for the preparation of college teachers. As mentioned previously, it was also a part of the program for recruiting more women faculty members at one institution we have studied.
- For a church institution, theological study and reflection, as well as discipline-based preparation, could be included.
- A candidate might spend a block of time working with students in overseas study-service terms or in another educational or

church service assignment. If it sounds reasonable in academic circles that a candidate could be expected to take four to six years to earn a Ph.D., it should not be seen as unreasonable for a church-related institution to want a candidate to have at least a semester of theological study and/or directed church-based experience commensurate with the candidate's gifts.

- The preparation could well include a candidate's reflection, anticipatory note-taking, and consultation on specific resources and ideas for the creative preparation of new courses he or she would be preparing to teach. The fact that a course might have an old name should not mean that new teachers should not creatively develop new "productions." Creative work of this kind takes time.

Whether or not the institution would want to provide some financial assistance to the candidate during the time of preparation would depend on the circumstances. A policy to guide decisions in this area could be drafted by the associate dean for strategic faculty recruitment. Ideally, an institution would provide some financing for the candidate's preparation with the understanding that either the institution or the candidate could decide to terminate the arrangement at any point. The goal might be to have enough of a financial contribution from the institution that the candidate would not see it as unfair if the institution terminated the arrangement and a contribution from the institution small enough that the institution would not see it as unfair if the candidate terminated the arrangement. The arrangement might involve a loan that would be forgiven for certain amounts per year of later service as a faculty member at the institution.

After completing the main part of the preparation, a candidate might be available for full-time employment at a time earlier or later than the time of the institution's greatest need. The associate dean for strategic faculty recruitment would need to have some limited budget resources for facilitating such transitions.

In referring to the hiring of minority scholars, Turner says: "Rather than waiting for a vacancy to occur, some institutions create funding pools from which departments can draw to hire qualified minority scholars when an opportunity presents itself. These funding pools [are] often called Target of Opportunity Appointments."[26]

Restricted funds (i.e., funds apart from regular unrestricted current budget amounts) would be needed to employ outstanding prospects when they are available. Such prospects could be given full-time duties that would contribute to curricular development and academic innovation (or to releasing some regular faculty members for work in such areas), but there would be some above-budget costs in getting them "on line" for regular tenure-track appointments.

If a candidate were available earlier than anticipated or before the full-time position was vacant, other possibilities might also be considered:

- A post-doctoral appointment for further research.
- Preparation of a dissertation or research papers for publication.
- A domestic or foreign educational or church service assignment, if that had not been included previously.
- Leadership of a group of students in an off-campus term, as mentioned above.

If the candidate were available later than anticipated, the institution might employ a short-term teacher or agree with a retiring faculty member to continue for an additional term or two.

Sometimes candidates would enter preparation and then decide that they did not wish to continue, or the institution would decide that the candidate was not a good prospect for a long-term appointment. Of course, sometimes faculty members hired with a view to tenure are not given tenure or decide to leave for other reasons. And sometimes prospects with whom development officers have worked for years for deferred gifts also do not in the end come through.

Reporting

The associate vice president or dean for strategic faculty recruitment would report regularly to and work cooperatively with the institution's vice president for academic affairs or academic dean.

In implementing its special responsibility for the long-term well-being of the institution, the institution's board could well require reporting on deferred service recruiting through the president to the board at least equal in time, docket space, etc., to that provided by the president on enrollment prospects and on deferred giving. The information on staffing, time allocation, and procedures would be included in regular session reporting. Because some of the information on deferred giving and deferred service is confidential, some of the reporting and discussion in these areas could be included in executive sessions of the board.

A Moment of Opportunity

The years immediately ahead seem to promise a special opportunity for institutions ready to initiate more creative and forward-looking faculty recruitment policies and practices. Despite new uncertainties about ages when faculty members will retire, professors of the baby-boomer generation are entering their sixties. Institutions wanting to build new faculties will soon be able to hire new teachers,[27] and they can work creatively with this opportunity.

The biggest challenge could well be in arranging for the appointment of a top innovator and "people-person" to the new associate vice president or dean for strategic faculty recruitment position. Appointing a weak faculty member without enough contagious enthusiasm to fill classes just because the faculty member had nothing else to do or asking a vice president or academic dean to do this in addition to his or her existing responsibilities could be little better than doing nothing.

The deferred giving staff role has been institutionalized in North American academia; the strategic recruiting ("deferred service") role has not. It is recognized by everyone that a staff person working in deferred giving needs to have specialized information on estate and retirement planning options, information not needed by a staff person working in annual giving or other advancement roles. Similarly, working in a deferred faculty service role can and will, at best, utilize information and expertise not usually a part of present North American roles in academic administration. The new staff roles in strategic faculty recruitment must be initiated by appropriately gifted and creative personnel.

Finding Good Matches in Recruitment, Retention, and Tenure

How can an institution, on one hand, and a prospect for faculty status, on the other, discern whether or not they are a good long-term match for one another?

Academic promise is hard to evaluate using purely quantitative criteria. In the case of experienced candidates, one can get information from the record and the portfolio of publications. Determining the promise of gifted but younger and less-experienced prospects is more of a challenge. Evaluating the potential contribution of a candidate to the religious or other distinctive missions of a school is also a challenge.

Some institutions from more creedal traditions ask new candidates to respond to questionnaires concerning their beliefs. This procedure has the advantage of a certain kind of clarity and objectivity. Candidates can be informed of written religious or other special expectations by mail. There is no question about what a candidate has said if the response is preserved in writing. It avoids trying to interpret what a candidate might have said in response to an inquiry phrased orally by an administrator in the privacy of the administrator's office.

However, church and school leaders of a more communitarian orientation do not find an approach that relies heavily on written questionnaires satisfactory. In the task of assembling a faculty team enthusiastic about a distinctive school mission and showing promise for creative work in the academic disciplines of the institution, interpersonal conversations are helpful. By analogy, the manager of a National Football League team does not try to evaluate quarterback prospects through the use of written questionnaires! The manager could perhaps determine how well the prospect understood the offenses and whether the candidate was willing to use the kinds of plays the team was projecting, but quarterbacking and leading a team is more than knowing plays and having good intentions.[28]

A board and its school need to have (1) procedures for initial recruitment to temporary or tenure-track positions, (2) procedures for granting year-to-year contracts, and (3) procedures for granting tenure or continuing employment. The procedures may differ from stage to stage, but the institution and a candidate for initial employment should have a clear—meaning written, in today's contexts—and common understanding of the procedures to be followed and criteria to be used in all later stages.

These days academic administrators and boards need to have policies on hiring faculty couples. Nationally, the proportion of faculty members hired as couples is rising. Institutions need ways of working that benefit from the advantages of hiring couples without raising questions of fairness and academic standards.

Ordinarily, there are several years during which a new faculty member can decide on his or her interest in joining the long-term faculty team and the institution can also discern the prospects for a good long-term contribution to the institution's mission. Also, a faculty member, perhaps including his or her family may need to actually live in the academic community with colleagues before deciding on the desirability of a longer-term commitment to the institution's mission and membership in the institution's faculty team. In such instances, the really critical long-term decisions are made at tenure time. (This situation resembles the general schedule followed in Ivy League universities where only a small percentage of instructors and assistant professors actually get tenure and can continue at the schools.) In these cases it is particularly important that a board and its administrators have policies that can assure everyone involved that new candidates understand the procedures and criteria to be used at tenure time. Moving professional staff people and their spouses and families after the instructors and their spouses have found employment and their children are situated in schools is stressful. There need to be procedures for determining with integrity the degree to which a staff member's gifts and abilities match the needs of institutions, but every effort should be made to avoid unnecessary surprises that add to stresses in these situations.

An institution cannot implement a distinctive mission unless it has enough faculty members ready to give time and energy to the mission. Obviously the procedures and criteria for hiring faculty at given institutions need to be based on the missions of the institutions. The typical problem at present is that the procedures currently in use at most institutions depend too heavily on traditional academic practices supplemented by relatively unstructured personal interviews with one or two administrators, sometimes in circumstances in which the need for filling vacancies is pressing.

The literature on alternatives to conventional procedures in both recruitment and retention of members of faculty teams suitable for institutions with distinctive missions is limited. We anticipate a higher-than-average return for an investment of energy and creative work by leaders and institutions of this kind in faculty recruitment.

Chapter 13 Endnotes

1   H. Berkhof, *Christ and the Powers*, trans. John Howard Yoder (Scottdale, PA: Herald
    Press, 1962) and Walter Wink, *Engaging the Powers: Discernment and Resistance in a
    World of Domination* (Minneapolis, MN: Fortress Press, 1992).

2   Pattillo and Mackenzie, *Church-Sponsored Higher Education in the United States:
    Report of the Danforth Commission* (Washington, DC: American Council on Education,
    1966); C. Robert Pace, *Education and Evangelism: A Profile of Protestant Colleges*, ed.
    Clark Kerr, The Carnegie Commission on Higher Education (New York: McGraw-Hill,
    1972); Merrimon Cuninggim, "Varieties of Church-Relatedness in Higher Education,"
    in *Church Related Higher Eductation*, ed. Robert Rue Parsonage (Valley Forge, PA:
    Judson Press, 1978), 15–132; Robert T. Sandin, "A Taxonomy of Religiously Affiliated
    Higher Education," in *Autonomy and Faith: Religious Preference in Employment
    Decisions in Religiously Affiliated Higher Education*, ed. Robert T. Sandin (Atlanta:
    Omega Publications, 1990), 19–44. Benne, *Quality with Soul* (Grand Rapids:
    Eerdmans, 2001), categorizes institutions in terms of their criteria for faculty
    appointments.

3   Earl J. McGrath, "Between Jerusalem and Athens: The Position of the Christian
    Institution," in *Diversity among Christian Colleges*, ed. Walter C. Hobbs and L. Richard
    Meeth (Arlington, VA: Studies in Higher Education, 1980), 70–93. In a review of
    two recent books, Ronald A. Wells says, "As all commentators on the church-related
    college agree, faculty hiring is vital to institutional identity," in "The Church-based
    University: Back to School," *The Christian Century* 122, no. 15 (July 26, 2005), 30. In
    his popular book, *Good to Great*, Jim Collins says, "You have to get the right people on
    the bus" (New York: HarperCollins, 2001). Peter Steinfels of the *New York Times* is
    one of many observers who sees the challenge. For example, he writes: "The future
    of Catholic identity in higher education is inescapably linked to hiring practices." (*A
    People Adrift: The Crisis of the Roman Catholic Church in America* [New York: Simon
    & Schuster, 2004], 152). However, along with many others, he does not propose
    the specific kinds of structural changes in faculty recruitment that might be ways
    of meeting the challenge. Scott Barge, a Harvard graduate student, has written on
    the relationship of faculty recruitment to church relationship at Goshen College in
    "Renegotiating the Goshen College-Mennonite Church Relationship: Harold S. Bender
    and Faculty Development at Goshen College, 1931–1944," *Mennonite Quarterly
    Review* 81, no. 4 (2007): 549–76.

4   I was reminded of prevailing attitudes in our American context recently in a con-
    versation with a friend who was not hired at a school with a church mission. He
    told me, "They were fairly upfront about saying that they wanted someone relating
    to their church's interests and someone going to church." He seemed surprised. He
    said, "I could always find and go to a church somewhere, if that's what they wanted."
    It did not seem to occur to him that showing a little spontaneous enthusiasm for the
    school's church mission and showing a little interest in a department's academic dis-
    cipline might both be reasonable qualifications for employment at the institution.

5   Conference on "Academic Freedom at Religiously Affiliated Institutions," Chicago,
    October 24–26, 1997. This is the conference referred to in Chapter 4.

6   Bernard Dobranski, cited in Katherine S. Mangan, "Ave Maria: a 'Seriously Catholic'
    Law School," *The Chronicle of Higher Education,* February 18, 2000.

7   "In order not to endanger the Catholic identity of the university or institute of higher studies, the number of non-Catholic teachers should not be allowed to constitute a majority within the institution" (Part II, Article 4, Section 4 of *Ex corde Ecclesiae*, the 1990 apostolic constitution of Pope John Paul II on Catholic universities). See John P. Langen, ed., *Catholic University in Church and Society: A Dialogue on* Ex corde Ecclesiae (Washington, DC: Georgetown University Press, 1993), 247. Some major American Roman Catholic universities have not followed this guideline in their hiring practices.

8   The concept of critical mass is also used by some educators to refer to students, and, again, usually without indicating how large that mass might be in specific situations. See Chapter 14.

9   Jencks and Riesman, *The Academic Revolution* (Garden City, NY: Doubleday, 1968).

10 One cannot easily observe the effects of single factors viewed in isolation. For example, a school cannot hire faculty members to implement a mission if the mission is not clear. I identify some of the factors and examine them in detail in the analysis that follows, but we need to remember that the various elements in the prevailing institutionalization of higher education are closely interwoven as parts of a system.

11 Steinfels, *A People Adrift,* 157.

12 In addressing problems in the recruitment of faculty members of color, Turner says: "Search committees often approach their charge in a passive, routine way: advertise the position in publications (e.g., *The Chronicle of Higher Education* . . .), evaluate resumes, invite three to five candidates for campus interviews, and then make an offer. . . . Search committees must take a more proactive approach and genuinely *search* for candidates of color." (Turner, *Diversifying the Faculty: A Guidebook for Search Committees*, 13.) When Lawrence Summers announced that Harvard would allocate $50 million to implement his institution's interest in hiring more women and underrepresented members of minority groups, he said that some of the funds would be used for what he called "pre-hiring."

13 Just one of many first-hand accounts is in Michael Loyd Gray, "To: All Search Committees; From: A Stymied Job Seeker," *The Chronicle of Higher Education*, July 2, 1999.

14 I am aware of some instances of the recruitment of highly gifted prospects of underrepresented populations in which the prospects chose even relatively small church colleges when they actually had invitations from Harvard or Princeton. The colleges' strong church relationships were positive, not negative, factors—indeed, they were the deciding factors. But these unusual instances of the successful recruitment of outstanding but unlikely prospects have typically been the product of years of search and courting, not of assuming good candidates would suddenly appear in response to advertisements in the *Chronicle of Higher Education.*

15 Gary Olson writes, "Perhaps the single most-important strategy in building a strong institution is aggressive recruiting of first-rate candidates (as opposed to passive 'searching'—i.e., posting an ad and waiting to see who applies)" ("The Proper Way to Court," *Chronicle Careers, The Chronicle of Higher Education*, January 22, 2009).

16 Studies in Princeton's 250th anniversary year pointed again to the role of Dean Henry Burchard Fine's work in faculty recruitment (supported by his presidents) in transforming the small colonial College of New Jersey of the 1800s into the major research university Princeton became in the 1900s. Theron Schlabach highlights

the importance for Goshen College in the past century of President Sanford Yoder's hiring of Noah Oyer, Harold Bender, and other remarkably gifted leaders for his renewed faculty in 1924. (Theron F. Schlabach, "Goshen College and Its Church Relations: History and Reflections," in *Models for Christian Higher Education: Strategies for Success in the Twenty-First Century*, ed. Richard T. Hughes and William B. Adrian [Grand Rapids: Wm. B. Eerdmans, 1997], 200–221). In recent years, *The Chronicle of Higher Education* and the daily press have increasingly reported on strategies for longer-term departmental development in major universities and the "hot pursuit" of leading scholars.

17 James K. Dittmar, "Against All Odds: An Investigation into the Transformation of Waynesburg College," *Christian Higher Education* 8, no. 2 (2009): 85–114.

18 Theodore J. Marchese and Jane Fiori Lawrence, *The Search Committee Handbook: A Guide to Recruiting Administrators*, 2nd rev. ed. (Sterling, VA: Stylus Publishing, LLC, 2005).

19 James L. Heft, S.M., and Fred P. Pestello, "Hiring Practices in Catholic Colleges and Universities," *Current Issues in Catholic Higher Education* 20, no. 1 (1999): 89–97. One can appropriately ask how these institutions mistakenly believed that they could not ask about support for an institutional mission and acted on this belief for perhaps two decades. It seems that the dominant force behind the mistaken belief arose, not from any legal requirements, but rather from the American institutional environment within which these Catholic institutions were aspiring for a new kind of recognition. Colleges and universities often follow the lead of institutions widely recognized as successful rather than risk following practices that are legal but less conventional.

20 Ibid.

21 February 4, 2000.

22 Hoekema recounted this story from Calvin's past at the October 1997 AAUP-sponsored conference on "Academic Freedom at Religiously Affiliated Institutions" in Chicago.

23 To emphasize the importance of this role for the long-term future and the parallelism of strategic faculty recruitment with deferred giving, this position might be called "Associate Vice President for Deferred Service" or "Associate Dean for Deferred Service." The title might be different in larger and smaller institutions.

24 Some institutions might wish to request that a younger age be set in this requirement. For example, an associate dean for strategic faculty recruitment might report with some pride that he or she had a list of back-up prospects for every position held by a person over thirty-five.

25 In some situations the institution might want to reach agreements with more than one candidate.

26 Caroline Sotello ViernesTurner, *Diversifying the Faculty: A Guidebook for Search Committees* (Washington, DC: Association of American Colleges and Universities, 2002), 9. Turner also refers to faculty fellows programs as a strategy for hiring graduate students for "recruitment of potential faculty of color, sometimes from outside of academe."

27 Denise K. Magner, "The Imminent Surge in Retirements: Colleges Face a Generational Shift as Professors Hired for the Baby Boom Enter Their 60's," *The Chronicle of Higher Education*, March 17, 2000. Magner notes examples of institutions with large

numbers of faculty members over fifty-five or sixty and refers to Robert L. Clark and P. Brett Hammond, eds., *To Retire or Not: Retirement Policy and Practice in Higher Education* (Philadelphia: University of Pennsylvania Press, 2000). Ann E. Austin and Donald H. Wolff say, "Universities and colleges are moving into a period when they will be hiring in significant numbers" ("New Path to the Professoriate," *New Educator* 10, no. 2 [East Lansing: Michigan State University College of Education], [spring 2005]).

28 A suitor trying to determine the degree to which he or she and a prospective spouse had the potential of being good marriage partners should hardly rely too heavily on the use of written questionnaires!

14

A Student Peer Environment
that Furthers the Mission

Whether or not a school with a mission of providing for the spiritual, social, and academic growth of its students can carry out this mission effectively depends in part on whether it has some students committed to its mission and on the student peer environment they provide.

Peer Culture and Education

In some situations, recruiting interested students has not been as important as recruiting committed faculty members in furthering long-term relationships of schools with churches. Under some circumstances, for example, Christian churches have sent workers overseas to mission schools in which very few of the students were Christian. Where such teachers are needed, teaching children of other traditions to read or preparing medical doctors to practice can be seen as good expressions of the love of Christ for all people. That can be an appropriate church mission.

The composition of the student body of a university as a whole may be less significant than some other factors in a student's development, because a student's experience may be influenced more by informal student subgroups or by clustering students in formal residential arrangements than by a university's student body as a whole.

Decades ago the studies of Theodore Newcomb and others[1] on the impact of colleges on students highlighted the importance of an institution's or institutional subgroup's student culture for educational outcomes. In many areas of student growth of interest to churches, the impact of students on their peers is significantly greater than the impact of faculty members on their students. Indeed, in some of these areas one can say that the principal influence of the board, faculty, and administration is in attracting to the campus or to campus sub-communities students of the kind needed to achieve the group's mission. The chain reaction among the students themselves takes over as the major factor in providing or not providing for desired student outcomes.[2]

In Newcomb's concept of "accentuation" referred to earlier, students with college goals join peers with similar interests, and their initial interests are "accentuated." If the students' goals have personal, social, and spiritual, as well as cognitive dimensions, their association with peers with similar goals can accentuate their growth in those areas.

Educating students at large is certainly a contribution churches can make to the larger society, as in churches' urgently needed contributions in schools in the Two-Thirds World, even when the schools had few students interested in church perspectives. Whether educating students at large should be a church priority in an American society which is already assuming its responsibility for sponsoring many other good schools is a matter for church discernment.[3] Historically, a decline in the proportion of church-interested students in a school sometimes contributed to a lowered interest in and support of the school by the sponsoring church, which indicated that educating students at large was not one of its top priorities. Over the long run, whether a church's effectiveness in its mission to interested students is attenuated by the presence of many students attending only for reasons of proximity, convenience, or academic program is an important question.

In a summary statement of his research on student outcomes, Alexander Astin says: "Perhaps the most compelling generalization from the myriad findings summarized in this chapter is the pervasive effect of the peer group on the individual student's development."[4] Having the right long-term faculty may be more critical than having an appropriate student body as a factor in the accomplishment of an institution's mission, but an inappropriate peer culture can blunt the effectiveness of a faculty in bringing about desired student outcomes, particularly in the areas of affective student growth of special interest to religious and other culturally distinctive groups.

In the past decade, "enrollment management" has been approached with greater intentionality than in earlier years, but the focus has typically been on numbers and on academic criteria.[5] A school with a church mission also needs to be concerned about prospects' contributions to and ability to profit from the aspects of the campus culture of special importance for the mission.

Appropriate Packaging

In today's academic world, enrollment managers and institutional admissions counselors are frequently under great pressure to gain as many applications ("apps") as possible. In some cases, their jobs depend on it.

Even in an Ivy League college where the number of first-year students to be admitted is set in advance, gaining more applications increases the "selectivity"—i.e., the ratio of those who apply to those admitted—and this is sometimes viewed as one of the indices of quality among elite institutions. The selectivity index increases with the percentage of applicants the institution turns away. The use of this index can lead image-makers to develop academic myths and symbols that may not be highly correlated with actual student outcomes.

Communicating to prospective students a college's educational goals and its image of the campus culture it is seeking to create may be an even greater challenge for religious and other distinctive groups than it is for selective institutions with limited enrollments and traditional academic missions. Many less selective institutions have mixed goals in their admissions policies: they frequently say they want the students their mission statements say they exist to serve, but they also want more students! Some admissions staff administrators in Christian colleges have, with the help of national advertising specialists, prepared multi-colored viewbooks that do not include any reference to the Christian emphases or church relationships of the school. In many instances, admissions counselors are under great pressure to be admissions salespeople. If an admissions staff person advises too many students to apply to other institutions in which their educational needs might be better met, and the institution loses the students, the admissions staff person may be replaced!

Of course there is a certain disincentive to egregious deception in image-making, since retention of first-year students (the percentage of first-year students that continue attending the institution beyond that first year) is sometimes also used as an index of quality. If, after their actual arrival on campus, too many first-year students come to believe that the reality they are experiencing does not correspond to the image they had before their arrival, the perceived disjunction between image and reality may be reflected in the lowering of an institution's retention rate. Withdrawals by first-year students who were planning to complete degrees and then discovered that the culture of the institution they entered was not what they anticipated can indicate a communication problem and "deceptive packaging."

Enrollment Growth

The conventional wisdom is that enrollment growth is economically and academically advantageous for colleges and universities. It is certainly true that having empty dormitory beds is economically disadvantageous, but that is sometimes a result of over-building rather than of under-enrollment. The fact that having unused facilities is economically disadvantageous does not mean that attracting and accommodating more students is advantageous.[6] An unexpected increase in enrollment in September that leads to overloading teachers and putting more students in dormitory rooms designed for fewer occupants can be financially advantageous in the short term. But in the longer term, the additional students will require additional contributed dollars, since student tuition does not cover educational costs.[7]

Faculty members welcome planned enrollment increases because they are accompanied with personnel additions to their departments and program additions to their curricula. Growth permits greater and greater faculty specialization within disciplines, which moves the college toward the research university model of academic excellence. It is less clear that greater and greater specialization within disciplines is correlated with better student outcomes in general education or in undergraduate education generally.

Having an institution that attracts the interest and applications of increasing numbers of students is almost universally regarded as an affirmation of the institution's public image, reflecting favorably on the institution's leaders. It is an intangible prestige factor quite apart from any gains in operating efficiency or academic excellence. But educational professionals need to separate prestige factors from actual financial and educational considerations.

Beyond any of these real or imagined advantages of growth are the widely held beliefs in the larger American society that "growth is good," "all organizations must grow to survive," "you need to work for market share," and "bigger is better." Every president of an institution can assume that the first questions alumni and other supporters who want to express their interest in the institution will ask will be, "How were the applications this year?" or "How was the enrollment last September?"

The conventional wisdom that enrollment growth is financially or academically advantageous needs further scrutiny. Some prominent institutions, from Haverford to Harvard to Berkeley, have gained in traditional excellence while limiting enrollments rather than expanding indefinitely. In a quantitative analysis of the data, Sandin has found that, above very low enrollments of less than 500, "we do not find evidence of a systematic effect of increased size in lowering costs of education per student."[8] A recent study of the actual relationship between growth and financial strength in a set of Christian colleges and universities has shown that institutions characterized by great enrollment growth in a given year were not characterized by gains in overall financial strength.[9] The available data do not support the conventional wisdom that enrollment growth almost always results in greater financial health.

When facilities are appropriately planned and designed, building expanded facilities for more students will not lead to lower costs. And, in most situations, increasing enrollments is not a long-term way of strengthening an institution's bottom line or increasing academic excellence. While most administrators would profess a commitment to guarding the heart and soul of their respective institutions, there are institutions that, by following the conventional model for enrollment growth, are unwittingly surrendering their distinctive missions in return for small to non-existent financial gains.

Broadening the Appeal and Enrollment Growth

Already in his 1972 Carnegie Commission work on Protestant colleges, Pace observed that academically elite colleges and distinctive religious colleges would "survive and, we hope, prosper." He was less optimistic about the group of Protestant colleges with "tepid environments," i.e., with neither national reputations for their academic programs nor strong support from churches.[10]

After a survey and his lifetime of visits to colleges and universities, Earl McGrath wrote:

> Institutions have misjudged the social climate if they believed that the weakening or abandonment of their religious traditions will *ipso facto* improve their drawing power with prospective students and donors.... The pressure of increased competition for patronage

has caused some colleges to submerge or obscure their religious goals. They assumed that by playing down their religious features they would attract both students and philanthropic support.[11]

McGrath then notes that, while attracting students from anywhere and with any goals may seem like a way of increasing enrollments in the short run, a study of denominationally affiliated colleges from 1965 to 1975 showed that those schools with clearly focused commitments grew faster than others. As cited earlier, more recent studies of colleges from 1980 to 1991 and from 1990 to 1999 confirmed McGrath's earlier findings: in the long run, colleges with clear religious commitments grew faster than others.

A Challenge for Church and School

A problem for a church and a religious college or university can originate in home congregations where young people are first baptized or confirmed as members. They may join these congregations without anyone recommending to them the kind of postsecondary educational experiences that might properly equip them to use their gifts as future members and prospective leaders, even when hard data demonstrate the difference higher educational experiences can make. Because the local pastor and youth group leaders need to relate to members in all kinds of educational institutions, these congregational leaders may not want to offend members or the parents of members who are in public institutions by speaking straightforwardly about the difference the church college or university experience can make. A church student may go to a high school guidance counselor, who may advise the student in the context of the values of the larger American culture, rather than those of the student's church. An admissions person from the student's church school may be seen as a salesperson and not fully trusted to give unbiased counsel.

The church, in its denominational and congregational forms, has to consider the meaning of baptism or confirmation and how it regards the education of its younger members. What is said in a baptism or confirmation class about the implications of membership? Is it understood by congregations and colleges that members going to their church colleges will actually get a chance to explore Christian beliefs and practices in a way that typically would be more difficult and less intentional if they went to a non-religious or public university? The congregation presumably provides a Sunday school for its children. Does the congregation then give tangible financial aid to young people who continue their interest in church perspectives and prepare for future participation and leadership in the church at its church colleges and universities? A church can ask its colleges and universities to do research studies and give suggestions on the best ways congregations can foster the education of their future members, but actually implementing actions that help young people while they are in their congregations is a responsibility for the congregations and denominations themselves.

The challenge for a church and for administrators of church-related schools is to develop communities of students who join with other students in benefiting from and furthering the missions of their schools.

Short-Term Tactics and Long-Term Strategies

Short-term pressures on admissions staffs can prevail if church and school leaders cannot assure that long-term considerations are given priority. Boards with responsibilities for the long-term mission-accomplishment of their institutions need to have data on the social, religious, and racial-ethnic, as well as the academic, characteristics of their entering students over decades and determine whether the trends they observe are those they want to see continued into the longer-term future.

Studies of college choice have shown that, while young people may decide on a particular college when they are juniors or seniors in high school, they typically develop assumptions about going to college and the kind of college they want to attend much earlier—in the late elementary grades and the early years of high school. Church college admissions efforts focused on students in their last years of high school may be approaching students whose decisions about attending church colleges have already been made. College admissions efforts relating to young people and their parents and friends in the late elementary grades will not show results in actual enrollment applications for years. College admissions officers under too much pressure for immediate results will not have much incentive to develop the kinds of strategies that may be of the greatest value to their churches or schools in the long term.

Practical Suggestions

In assembling an appropriate student peer community, a church or other group with a distinctive mission and its schools can take the following practical steps:

1. The board or other designated representatives of the church or other group with a distinctive mission will phrase their enrollment expectations clearly.

   The enrollment targets for segmented groups of students will be stated separately, and the degree to which the targets are met will be monitored annually. In the annual reporting, special attention will be given to longer-term trends in the service of the groups of students of primary interest.

   The enrollment expectations will be set and monitored by board members and other stakeholders with responsibilities for the longer-term mission-accomplishment of the institution—including persons and groups somewhat removed from the day-to-day operation of the institution.

   The goals will be realistic. Church representatives may need to consult with denominational, judicatory, and congregational youth leaders, as well as with enrollment professionals, concerning the enrollment goals and the ways in which they can best be phrased as measurable objectives.

   The goals will be shared with faculty members and other interested groups.

2. The board or other designated representatives somewhat removed from the day-to-day operation of the institution will provide for an "outside" review of the concurrence of admissions mailings and documents with the goals for the kinds of students to be served in mission statements and other board-approved, long-range planning documents.

   If the church or other sponsoring group is interested in an institution that differs at points from the prevailing American culture, this needs to be clearly expressed in admissions documents in such a way as (1) to attract students interested in the institution's distinctiveness and (2) to adequately inform students not interested in the institution's distinctiveness of the institution's primary mission and character. Religious institutions should model truth in advertising.

3. If, in working at long-term goals, admissions staff members are expected to spend a significant part of their time and budgets in communicating with young people in the late grades and their parents and church friends, the staffs will not be

evaluated only in terms of immediate results in the annual applications of older high school seniors and the fall enroll- ments of new college students. Instead, they will be reviewed in the context of the approved overall long-range plans and strate- gies of enrollment and admissions staffs.

Chapter 14 Endnotes

1   Theodore M. Newcomb et al., *Persistence and Change: Bennington College and Its Students after Twenty-five Years* (New York: John Wiley & Sons, 1967); Theodore M. Newcomb and Everett K. Wilson, eds. *College Peer Groups: Problems and Prospects for Research*, National Opinion Research Center Monographs in Social Research (Chicago: Aldine Publishing Company, 1966); Feldman and Newcomb, *The Impact of College on Students* (San Francisco: Jossey-Bass, 1969).

2   Newcomb and Wilson, eds. *College Peer Groups*, 15.

3   One church executive told me his denomination had fewer than fifty students at its denominational university of more than 2000 students. He said he had been encouraged to ask me as a consultant whether I thought his denomination's financial contribution to the university was a good investment of their church dollars. Was it the best way of working with their church's young people and investing in their denominational future? Was their university distinctive enough to be funded as a priority in the allocation of their church mission dollars? In question were not only the dollars flowing to the university from congregational offerings but also the contributions from church individuals because of the denomination's "accreditation" of the university as a church program.

4   Alexander W. Astin, *What Matters in College? Four Critical Years Revisited*, The Jossey-Bass Higher and Adult Education Series (San Francisco: Jossey-Bass, 1993), 363.

5   Martin Marty of the University of Chicago emphasized the importance of student market forces in "Secularization and the Academy" (*Sightings*, twice-weekly e-mail newsletter, Martin Marty Center, University of Chicago Divinity School, August 14, 2000). Marty asked, "What occasions secularization in societies and their institutions of higher learning? . . . The main agent, at least currently, the market." Marty looked at newspaper supplements in the back-to-school season in 2000 and found that, of twenty colleges and universities, only one put its religious face forward. He writes, "If they did not advertise how good they are at business, computers, management, finance, or technology, they would fail to lure prospects who would like to make good livings. . . . But if they put no liberal arts or religion faces forward, these institutions . . . have to be noted when scholars and prophets account for the forces of secularization."

6   In other terms, we can say that financial health is not a linear function of enrollment change.

7   From a project supported by the Mellon Foundation, Williams College economics professors Gordon Winston and David Zimmerman report, "Private schools have fairly inflexible charitable wealth from which to subsidize their students, so if they expand the number of students, they decrease the subsidy each of them gets . . . . So enrollment expansion risks a school's relative position in its access to student quality" ("Where Is Aggressive Price Competition Taking Higher Education?," *Change: The Magazine of Higher Learning* 32, no. 4, July/August 2000, 10–18). In other words, getting more students can be disadvantageous, rather than advantageous, for a school's financial situation if it wants to keep its student quality constant.

8   Robert Sandin, "Educational and General Expenditures per Student," *HEPS Profiles of Independent Higher Education* 1, no. 6 (Higher Education Planning Services, September 1991), 2. We should also recall Astin's findings on economics of scale cited in Chapter 11.

9   Meyer and Sikkink, "What Does It Profit A College to Add More Students? The Relationship between Enrollment Growth and Financial Strength," 97–113. This finding is supported by the more recent work of Samuel C. Wood, lecturer at Stanford University. See Goldie Blumenstyk, "Why For-Profit Colleges Are Like Health Clubs," *The Chronicle of Higher Education*, May 5, 2006.

10 Robert C. Pace, *Education and Evangelism: A Profile of Protestant Colleges*, ed. Clark Kerr, The Carnegie Commission on Higher Education (New York: McGraw-Hill, 1972), 104–5.

11 Earl J. McGrath, "Between Jerusalem and Athens: The Position of the Christian Institution," in *Diversity among Christian Colleges,* ed. Walter C. Hobbs and L. Richard Meeth (Arlington, VA: Studies in Higher Education, 1980), 73–78.

15

MISSIONS THAT GUIDE DECISION-MAKING

Studies of boards of trustees frequently say that the primary responsibility of a board is to represent the mandating society in keeping the long-term mission of its institution in sharp focus and then providing for the accomplishment of that mission.[1] These studies often do not outline the obstacles boards face when they try to take this task seriously. Boards face major challenges as they seek to carry out their responsibility for defining and implementing an institution's long-term mission.

Boards and Mission Statements

Mission statements have become popular in the business and educational worlds in recent decades. Some have inspired workers or given direction to enterprises in crisis. A recent survey of eighty-eight corporations about their mission statements, however, found that some "were an assemblage of trite phrases that impress neither senior managers nor low-level employees." In the words of the researcher, "The overall conclusion is that . . . the vast majority are not worth the paper that they are written on and should not be taken with any degree of seriousness."[2]

Writing statements of purpose for educational institutions is even harder than writing statements for business corporations, partly because the outputs of schools are harder to assess and quantify. Typical school mission statements are stated in such general terms as to give almost no guidance for day-to-day board, administration, or faculty decision-making. An institution that says its mission is to '"do good and oppose evil" can change its fundamental purposes radically while insisting that everything it is doing continues to be within the scope of its mission statement!

In practice, boards frequently ask their administrators to prepare the first drafts of their mission statements. The administrators form faculty committees to do the work. By the time the final draft reaches the board for approval, the text is a rather broad public relations statement that has arisen more from what the institution is doing at the time than from a vision of what the mandating society intended the institution to be. The board can propose minor editorial changes, but is hardly in a position at that stage in the process to carry out effectively its responsibility for focusing the long-term mission.

It is particularly important for boards of colleges or universities with distinctive missions and supported by groups with distinctive beliefs and practices to be clear on what their institutions are to be and do, and how they are to be different from other institutions. If an institution is sponsored by a church or other subgroup in the larger society, the board representing the sponsors will have to consider the expectations of the sponsoring group. If the institution is independent, its board will need to lead its external and internal constituents to a reasonable consensus on its institution's mission.

The Current Calls for Accountability

The principal general accrediting associations of higher education institutions in the United States, the six regional associations,[3] have for years accredited institutions with different missions. Their requirement has been that an institution state its mission clearly and that it then show that it is accomplishing the stated mission. For years, the conventional wisdom has been that organizations should have clear measurable objectives, that they should proceed to measure the degree to which they are meeting their objectives, and that they should then use the results of their measurements as feedback for making course corrections in their operations. It has been assumed that the principal objectives of the organizations could be stated clearly, and that it is feasible to measure the degree to which they are meeting their stated objectives.

Increasing ambivalence in North America about institutions in general and about higher education institutions in particular has led to a public demand for greater institutional accountability. Jeffrey Selingo says, "Higher education is under more pressure than ever to lower costs and be more accountable." He refers to the "contradictory demands" of students, parents, and policy makers.[4]

In 1992 the U.S. Congress proposed a radical change in accreditation procedures in an attempt to increase institutional accountability. Rather than to rely on traditional accreditation approaches, every state was to have a "State Postsecondary Review Entity" (SPRE). The proposals met with an outcry from educators and friends of education everywhere, and it was only after the 1994 election seemed to indicate that the public also wanted fewer rather than more regulations from Washington that the implementation of the proposed regulations was rescinded.

The ambivalence about American colleges and universities is reflected in the September 2006 final report of a Commission on the Future of Higher Education created by President George Bush's Secretary of Education, Margaret Spellings.[5] In a press release, Spellings says that "America has the finest system of higher education in the world." Her Commission says, "American higher education has been the envy of the world for years." At the same time, the Commission says that "U.S. higher education needs to improve in dramatic ways," and that there is "much that requires urgent reform." Educators have been concerned that the government's current focus is more on regulation than on increasing financial aid to give greater access to needy students. Educators are concerned about new kinds of record-keeping and reporting that can involve little useful information and increase institutional costs, as well as raise privacy issues.

The charter of Margaret Spelling's Commission stated that "the purpose of the Commission is to consider how best to improve our system of higher education to ensure that our graduates are well prepared to meet our future workforce needs and are able to participate fully in the changing economy." There are repeated references to "workforce needs." Educators have responded by saying that some institutions have missions that go beyond preparing workers for the American economy.

The Commission wanted the federal government to "provide incentives for states . . . to develop outcomes focused accountability systems" and "the creation of a . . . database . . . to weigh and rank comparative institutional performance." But an increased use of one-size-fits-all evaluations and ratings would certainly make life more difficult for colleges and universities that were not trying to be like everyone else. It would certainly reduce the diversity for which American higher education is known around the world.

The recent public concerns about accountability have highlighted what observers of educational institutions have known for years: that formal mission statements in front pages of catalogs and other publications that institutions use in relating to their publics are often so vague and unrealistic as to be of little use as bases for evaluation of performance.

Educators are currently working on ways of meeting the concern for greater accountability without introducing procedures that would require enormous expenditures of institutional time and expense without yielding much useful information. It is already clear, however, that greater accountability without reducing America's unique diversity of institutions will require clarity on what different institutions are to be accountable to be and do.[6]

Mission Diffusion and Mission Drift

One residential church college that I visited decades ago had a board that failed in its responsibility to keep its mission in focus. The school had a specialized professional major. Some professionals in its geographical region wanted postgraduate work in their field and twenty-seven prospective students were ready to enroll the next year. Projections were that the program could pay for itself. The faculty department and administration proposed going ahead. The board approved the proposal rather routinely. Then a new dean-elect who was to begin his work in the next school year visited the campus and began to ask questions. All students in this postgraduate program would be commuters. None would be taking the general education courses upon which the college's curriculum had been built. None would be at all-campus convocations. The new dean-elect asked how the new postgraduate program had anything to do with the reasons the church and principal constituencies had established the school in the first place. How was the new program a part of the school's mission? Only after the new dean-elect raised these questions was the proposal sent back to the administration and the board, and plans to initiate the new program were canceled.

Several decades ago, other schools I visited went into land speculation. Some ventures made money for the operating budget for several years. Then problems arose. Boards and committees got emotionally involved in issues that had nothing to do with education. In one case, where the school's name was used in promoting investments, widows and other trusting constituents bought in and then lost life savings. The president had to resign. In cases like these, boards have lost their focus on the primary missions of their schools.

More recently, many colleges with church-wide constituencies have initiated degree completion programs for their local communities as money-raisers—as "cash cows." A Princeton University researcher, Diane Winston, directed a major three-year project funded by the Lilly Endowment on the impact of adult B.A. degree programs on the institutional missions of faith-based colleges and universities. In one summary of her project's findings, she said:

> The result is a compelling portrait of the secularization process. Despite the best intentions of college administrators, adult BA degree programs facilitate secularizing trends. In general, they are not well integrated into the life of the college community. Often invisible, adult degree programs on many campuses are the core of a two-tiered system. Staffed by adjuncts, detached from the campus community, and undergirded by educational goals tailored to the business world, these programs are relatively unaffected by the institutional mission of their sponsoring schools. According to alumni of adult BA degree programs, little of the schools' religious sensibility is conveyed in classes, curriculum, or interactions.[7]

Chait, Holland, and Taylor affirm the conclusions of Chaffee's 1984 study, "Successful Strategic Management in Small Private Colleges," which they say "demonstrated that ... institutions are not well-served over the long term by strategies designed principally to cut costs, respond to the marketplace, and increase the flow of resources."[8]

Schools can have different missions. Certainly they can serve local communities while serving regional or national constituencies in special ways. But if they engage in efforts that are not within their priority missions, they need to know that they are doing this. By engaging in lower-priority missions they need to be aware that they may be putting their priority missions in jeopardy. And they should not develop or invoke mission statements that are so broad as to be useless for decision-making.

After twenty-five years of experience as a faculty member and administrator, George Keller published a work in 1983 that led the field in strategic planning.[9] Keller promoted strategic (as opposed to short-term, or tactical) planning. He proposed identifying distinctive and advantageous programs and positions of an institution in its field, emphasizing and enhancing those areas of strength, and making the most of those distinctive strengths in the market. And, in "A New Approach to Saving Small Colleges,"[10] Karen Gross, professor at New York Law School, observed that at least twenty-seven small, largely residential colleges had closed since 1997. She proposed that some small colleges would find it advantageous to focus on distinctive "educational social initiatives" as strategic goals.

In the short run, the easy way is to imitate what others are doing. Depending on the availability of funds, it is easiest to increase or decrease all program budgets from year to year by the same percentages, rather than to be making tough decisions, but good institutional strategic or long-term planning focuses on an institution's distinctive mission and uses the institution's resources to further that mission.

Getting Beyond Generalities

If we want to get beyond generalities in talking about distinctive missions, we need to talk about the specific missions of churches or other groups and their schools.

I am particularly familiar with Mennonites, who do have some distinctive beliefs and practices. They began around 1525 in the Reformation as a group of academics and clerics who came to believe that the Christian church needed to reflect more faithfully the vision they found in the Greek and Hebrew biblical texts they were discovering in the Renaissance spirit of their times. But most of the intellectual leaders among the early Mennonites were killed in the first few years. Their followers were dispersed. Only in relatively recent times have Mennonites in America returned to serious research and scholarship. They have the opportunity to learn from the past experiences of others. If they want to continue to have schools in the foreseeable future, they can learn from a review of those factors that have almost universally led to increasing mission drift and school-church distance in the past. If they want to have schools that are different, they will need to be clear on why they want to have these schools and how they want them to be different.

Christians interested in having schools that are different today will need to talk about authentic Christian commitments as they understand them—not just civic values that were held by state university faculty members almost universally a hundred years ago or by most educated, liberal North Americans today. Church schools are presumably to do more than just to reinforce popular values.[11]

Some Mennonite beliefs are fairly widely understood and accepted in academic circles today, as in such areas as peace, service, and environmental stewardship.[12] But they also have had and still have some important and distinctive "values" (to use a rather general term) that are not particularly popular in liberal North American circles just now. They observe that Jesus said his followers should love their enemies, which, for Jesus, precluded killing them. Mennonites have also seen the church as existing in local settings in the form of communities of commitment. They see the local communities as engaging in communal discernment, not just the decision of isolated individual candidates.[13] This emphasis on the importance of the community, which is at odds with the individualism of the contemporary American culture, is sometimes called "discriminatory" and "exclusivist"—just as some critics characterize a school's attempts to hire faculty members who support the school's distinctive mission. Mennonites are not quite in tune with the individualism of our times.[14]

Another Mennonite conviction, thoroughly rooted in the Anabaptist movement from the time of the Protestant Reformation, but now shared with many others in the Free Churches: inviting friends and neighbors to faith in Jesus Christ and membership in local communities of God's people. Again, while this core "value" is affirmed in some church circles, it is not particularly popular among educated liberal North Americans today, who tend to think that each of us should be "doing his or her own thing" and should not "force our beliefs on others." Certainly Mennonites have believed since the Reformation that people should not force their beliefs on others—that is one of the reasons so many were martyred by other religionists of their times—but they object strenuously to the individualism of our time when this is taken to mean that people should not speak of what they have seen and heard. In the Mennonite understanding, a society, democratic or otherwise, should not force religious conformity on its citizens, but, on the other hand, it does not thrive when citizens leave their moral and religious convictions at the church door.

Mennonites have also had a concern for the disadvantaged and victims of disasters around the world. This concern led to the incorporation of terms of study and service in the Two-Thirds World in the general education program of a Mennonite college forty years ago and the adoption of cross-cultural experiences as curricular components of the programs of other Mennonite schools. Many faculty members had had experience in service assignments overseas and came to the conviction that it was important that today's liberal arts college graduates have some time in study and service with the ninety-four percent of the peoples of the world outside the United States, and particularly among those of the Two-Thirds World. The church and the college thought this study and service should be a part of the general education program for all baccalaureate students, just as laboratory work might be a part of the natural science component of the general education program for all students. The idea was that students who are to be considered liberally educated need experiences they cannot get in libraries or classrooms. In the college with the longest experience with a core program of this kind, students typically spend a fourteen-week term in study and service in the Two-Thirds World in non-English-medium settings—in Haiti, Costa Rica, China, Ivory Coast, Nicaragua, Senegal, Cambodia, etc. Some other schools have had a few juniors studying abroad rather than having study and service abroad as a part of the standard general education program. Although some schools have long had students in Europe, that is different from having students in Two-Thirds World settings, which are much more representative of most of today's world.

The innovation was not popular forty years ago. Educators and foundations thought having undergraduates study abroad was "a funny idea," "not real education"—not really bad, perhaps, but like requiring students to have courses in playing chess. And the conventional wisdom of top experts in international education in those times was that only a few carefully selected North American college students could have good learning experiences in the Two-Thirds World. A college administrator and his colleagues with unusual gifts for getting foundation grants were unable to find any significant outside funding four decades ago to initiate the college's "Study-Service Term." The college's new program had to be fully supported with institutional funds.

Educators have changed in the past forty years. The world has changed. Now everyone is talking about global education that through actual experience and service learning deals with what more of the world is like.[15] Many universities now have vice provosts and associate deans of international education. In 2000, the Clinton administration identified a policy priority of increasing the number of American students studying abroad and getting more colleges and university to offer study-abroad programs. The Bush and Obama administrations have continued to support that interest. The numbers have increased significantly in recent years, but the latest data show that, even with the new support, only one percent of American undergraduates are studying abroad.[16]

If a Mennonite college or university wants today to assess the degree to which it is dealing with certain unpopular understandings that Mennonites would consider important, it needs to ask questions like these: Can it be shown that its college seniors are, in general, more ready to join and exercise leadership in the life of local Free Church communities in various denominations than they were as entering first-year students? Are the seniors just more vaguely tolerant, or are they more ready to share their understandings and experiences with their associates, to listen to and learn from the sharing of others, and to invite their friends to become involved in the Christian community than they were when they entered as first-year students? Have students gained enough of a first-hand understanding of and empathy for the situations of friends in the Two-Thirds World to make a difference in what they do with the rest of their lives?[17] In answering such questions, the board and its school have to be clear on the exact nature of their mission.

Believers of different traditions have distinctive beliefs and practices of different kinds. Adventist Christians and their schools have for years—and well before the current interest in the larger American society—emphasized nutritious and healthful living as an expression of the goodness for which God created humankind. Adventists emphasize the importance of weekly Sabbath worship and rest as an important part of the cycle of life in a fast-paced society. Pentecostal schools emphasize the work of the Spirit. Jewish rabbinical schools have different and distinctive beliefs and practices.

If a group with distinctive beliefs and practices wants to learn from the experience of others, and if it wants to pay for having schools at a time when there are many other good schools, it will need to be straightforward about its distinctive commitments, not just about values that happen to be popular at the time in the surrounding society. Environmental forces can almost inevitably lead to mission drift if institutions are not clear on their missions and if their missions are not implemented in actual structures and programs.

Need for Clarity

As we have seen, most mission statements are vague and most institutional plans do not deal with long-term goals. If a school is to take short-term steps that lead to goals desired in the long term, the school has to know what its long-term goals are and state them specifically enough to guide its tactical planning and day-to-day decision-making.

The missions of many institutions have changed over time. Some changes are due to exogenous environmental forces as the world has changed. Environmental factors have led to the dramatic and worldwide increase in higher educational enrollments in the past century. But the changes of some institutions in the past decade have been similar to those of other institutions two decades ago, and, again, to those of still other institutions four decades ago, even though the environments were different in those different decades. If institutions do not want just to follow the leaders, they will have to be ready to foster the development of counter-forces and unconventional ways of working that make it possible for them to reach their distinctive goals.

Board and Mission

A board's most important responsibility is to articulate its organization's mission and develop a long-term plan for implementing the mission. It cannot delegate this responsibility to the organization's employees.

The board will typically need to begin with a retreat of more than one day to begin work on its fiduciary responsibility for mission definition, clarification, and implementation. Before and after working in plenary workshop or break-out sessions, the board will typically need to ask a board subcommittee to prepare initial agenda arrangements and drafts of needed documents. A board of a college or university will then need to work later with administrators and faculty members in the editing of the documents that can project the direction of the institution. The board needs to oversee an extensive process of consultation with on-campus and off-campus groups (in which the initial drafts may well be critiqued and modified), but the board or an appointed executive board needs to take creative leadership in preparing initial drafts and in carrying the ultimate responsibility for the adoption of the needed statements.

Many boards are not taking their responsibility in goal- and strategy-setting seriously. In one school we visited, an in-house faculty-administration group drafted a planning document that was not specific about the kinds of students the school was to serve. Indeed, it implied that what the school wanted was just what many schools want: more academically gifted students and, in the end, more students of any kind. The board sent the document back for revision. Finding it also inadequate when it came back, the board sent it to the on-campus group a second time. With perseverance, the board finally—meetings later—got a document that was more appropriate and specific regarding the students the school was seeking to serve, but the process was so exhausting that the board ended up ignoring other parts of the document that should have had attention.

A typical large board of thirty-plus members will need to have a working group of not over a dozen members. The board can appoint an executive board or a "committee on the future of the college" that includes some faculty and administration representatives to consider long-term trends and to make proposals for its organization's mission and long-term (e.g., ten-to-twenty-year) future. The projections need to be reviewed and revised every several years, but they provide a needed framework for day-to-day decision-making.

Deciding why a school exists, whom it is to serve and how, and the kinds of people it must employ to achieve its mission, are not matters a board can delegate to others. Although boards can delegate many questions to specialists and should not micro-manage, they cannot abdicate responsibility for responding to fundamental questions of mission and long-term strategy. Boards have no more important responsibilities.

How Can a Board Be Specific?

How can a board and staff develop statements that are specific? What can we learn from failures and successes of many colleges and universities over the years?

The board or board committee and groups involving administrators and faculty senate members can best work initially in their brainstorming and group processes by themselves in executive sessions. Beginning by trying to draft a public relations document tends to lead to the vagueness and generality that have made many formal mission statements objects of ridicule in the past. Public relations statements have a place. An institution must communicate with its various publics. But if the public statement is called a "mission statement," there should be a different internal document clarifying the institution's mission in more technical "insider" language and referred to by a different name. There is a difference between a soap advertisement designed by the marketing department for the public and a chemical formula for the soap prepared by the production department for the factory. Those most directly involved in the leadership of a college or university need "chemical formulas" that can be useful for their day-by-day decision-making, not only "soap advertisements."

In the face of the myths of contemporary academia, a school may not wish to say publicly that it wants to attract more average-SAT students who have other gifts. Or it may or may not want to say publicly initially that it is more concerned about gifts in leadership or service-motivation than about traditional intelligence. Or a church may want to have a school that says it wants to become more elite in a traditional sense and attract more high-SAT students. In any case, leaders of the church and school need to be clear among themselves on the student clientele they wish to serve. The desired profile of students to be served may or may not be part of a public mission statement at the outset but it certainly needs to be realistic and a part of an internal document. It needs to be sufficiently specific to be useful in a periodic evaluation of the progress of the institution.

Sometimes an institution has an internal document called a "strategic plan." By whatever name, an internal document for an educational institution needs to begin with twenty-year or longer-term goals (or "ends") in key areas, not just three- or five-year goals. If it is called a strategic plan, it needs to deal with goals and strategy, not just tactics. Documents outlining specific next steps and shorter-term projections need to be based on internal documents reflecting the long-term mission and direction of the institution.

We have noted that one of the differences between business and educational organizations is in the difficulty of quantifying the outcomes of educational institutions. The real impact of a college on its students is intended to be revealed in its students' lives after graduation, not just in their characteristics at graduation. The loyalty of students, alumni, and churches to their institutions is based partly on reputations and images that change only slowly over time. When colleges and churches distance themselves from one another, it typically happens gradually over time—and both colleges and churches often have reasons to want to retain the support of their constituents and to say to their publics that nothing is really changing in their relationships. Serious educational planning that is in touch with reality has to begin by looking at trends of past decades and to ask whether the planners want to project more of the same or something different into the longer-term future.

Chait, Holland, and Taylor say that, in an orientation of new trustees, "the discussion should move beyond standard catalogue copy to stress the features that distinguish this college from others that may look quite similar to an outsider."[18] A strategic plan (or internal document with another name) will be most useful in guiding day-to-day decisions if it or a related document indicates clearly how the institution seeks to be different at a point in the future from what it is at present. It can be helpful if the document indicates what the institution does not intend to do as well as what it does want to do.

After extensive consultation with on-campus and off-campus groups, and the adoption of a draft mission statement, the board may be prepared to

list, without elaboration, perhaps four to eight areas for longer-term attention and then to oversee a process of consultation that will lead to formulation of a more detailed twenty-year strategic plan. This can be an extended
process. If a college or university is church-related, its long-range documents can be related explicitly to the mission and planning documents of
the church to which it is related. Faculty members can assemble frequently,
but since most boards do not have weekly or monthly meetings, the board
may designate a board committee or board representatives to participate
in faculty-staff discussions. The faculty and staff have essential information and perspectives to bring to the process, and their input is important.
The board or boards of a church representing a denomination or a tradition
speak on behalf of the school's mandating society in providing leadership in
the process.

The institution needs to work proactively as well as reactively. Internal
documents need to be reviewed and updated periodically. The twenty-year
goals need to be reviewed and updated at regular intervals—at least every
three years.

Documents for Outside Agencies

Boards need to be involved in the preparation or approval of formal documents going to outside agencies. Here, again, a change in traditional practices is needed if boards are to move from marginality and begin to assume
their proper role, beyond their initiative in the drafting, phrasing, and adoption of mission statements and strategic plans.

Self-studies prepared by institutions for general accrediting agencies
are usually expected to begin with chapters on the missions of the institutions. These chapters are not just internal documents used by administrators; they are semi-public statements submitted to outside visiting and
evaluation teams. Sometimes these chapters are drafted, at least initially, by
administrators on the basis of previously written mission statements and
internal strategic plans.

In any case, where an institutional board has a responsibility for the
long-term future of its institution, it should have a schedule and a procedure
for review and approval of public and semi-public self-studies and other
documents going to outside accrediting groups and to the public. The procedure may involve designating two or three trusted board members to review
the documents in the light of board interests and past actions. If necessary,

the designated board members can then bring any issues that need board attention to the whole board.

The Board Role in Keeping a Distinctive Mission Clear

The procedures we have outlined above are not typical ways of working in American academia. Most mission statements are drafted by faculty-staff committees and presented to their boards only for final ratification. Boards frequently are hardly aware of institutional purposes and commitments expressed in accreditation self-studies submitted by their institutions to outside agencies. Hence, when the accreditors make requirements for changes, the boards are not aware that the accreditors are sometimes simply requiring steps initially desired and proposed by the institution's administrators.[19]

Faculties and boards rarely refer to their public relations mission statements in their actual decision-making. Conventional procedures and mission statements may be adequate for schools that want to be typical American colleges or universities, but societal subgroups and schools that want to "march to the beat of a different drummer" will have to be ready to be explicit, at least in internal communications, about ways they intend to be different.[20]

Chapter 15 Endnotes

1   Earl J. McGrath lists having clear statements of purpose first in his proposals for Christian colleges. He states reasons for the importance of mission statements, but does not propose specific ways in which institutions may develop useful documents. (McGrath, "Between Jerusalem and Athens: The Position of the Christian Institution," in *Diversity among Christian Colleges,* ed. Walter C. Hobbs and L. Richard Meeth [Arlington, VA: Studies in Higher Education, 1980], 75–76.)

2   Study by Christopher K. Bart, professor at McMaster University, Hamilton, Ontario, reported in *The New York Times,* sec. 4, February 13, 2000.

3   The Southern Association of Colleges and Schools (SACS), the North Central Association of Colleges and Schools (NCA), the Western Association of Schools and Colleges (WASC), the Middle States Association of Colleges and Schools (MSA), the New England Association of Schools and Colleges (NEASC), and the Northwest Commission on Colleges and Universities (NWCCU).

4   "Colleges Face Contradictory Demands from Those Seeking Lower Costs and More Accountability" in *Today's News, The Chronicle of Higher Education,* November 3, 2006.

5   U.S. Department of Education, "A Test of Leadership: Charting the Future of U.S. Higher Education" (Washington, DC: 2006).

6   A review of accreditation approaches is in Jon F. Wergin, "Higher Education: Waking Up to the Importance of Accreditation," *Change: The Magazine of Higher Learning* 37, no. 3 (2005), 35–49.

7   Letter of November 1999 to project participants. A more detailed report was published by the Mission, Formation and Diversity Project as "The Mission, Formation and Diversity Survey Report" (Princeton, NJ: Center for the Study of Religion, 1999). Winston is currently in the Knight Chair in Media and Religion at the University of Southern California Annenberg School for Communication.

8   Richard P. Chait, Thomas P. Holland, and Barbara E. Taylor, *The Effective Board of Trustees,* American Council of Education/Oryx Series on Higher Education (Phoenix: The Oryx Press, 1993), 16–17.

9   George Keller, *Academic Strategy: The Management Revolution in American Higher Education* (Baltimore: Johns Hopkins University Press, 1983). This work has been influential: it sold out in six weeks, and has had six additional printings. After his death in 2007, a friend summarized his work: "Properly understood, George said, strategic planning meant finding the strength to say no to many things, even those that had formerly been a part of its identity. To adopt a 'strategy' was not merely a question of determining what the institution would do, but deciding what it would *not* do . . ." (Wilfred M. McClay, "George Keller: Intellectual Whirlwind," *The Chronicle of Higher Education,* November 23, 2007).

10 *The Chronicle of Higher Education,* July 22, 2005.

11 This is one of the principal themes of Budde and Wright, eds. *Conflicting Allegiances: The Church-Based University in a Liberal Democratic Society* (Grand Rapids: Brazos Press, 2004).

12 Some of these fields have been recognized as legitimate academic fields only relatively recently.

13 The Reformation forebears of the Mennonites combined the importance of communal discernment with an emphasis on respect for the free adult decisions and commitments of individuals who wanted to be members. They consciously sought to combine these emphases as they saw them combined in the pre-Constantinian Christian church. See Alan Kreider, *The Change of Conversion and the Origin of Christendom* (Eugene, OR: Wipf & Stock, 2007).

14 Not only Mennonites are concerned about the individualism of our contemporary American culture. There are calls on several sides for a more communitarian vision, not only in American church life but also in the larger society. See works from different perspectives by Robert N. Bellah et al., *Habits of the Heart: Individualism and Commitment in American Life* (Berkeley: University of California Press, 1985); Amitai Etzioni, *The Spirit of Community: The Reinvention of American Society*, Touchstone (New York: Simon & Schuster, 1994); and Robert D. Putnam, *Bowling Alone: The Collapse and Revival of American Community* (New York: Simon and Schuster, 2000).

15 Professionals sometimes refer to this trend today as "campus internationalization."

16 Holli Chmela, "Foreign Detour en Route to a College Degree," *The New York Times*, October 19, 2005, and private communication, Institute of International Education, April 13, 2009.

17 In comparing seniors with first-year students, an administrator must, of course, take into account changes that occur as other late adolescents mature in the larger population. Not all changes can be attributed to schools.

18 Chait, Holland, and Taylor, *The Effective Board of Trustees*, 121.

19 For example, administrators of a nursing department may want nursing faculty members to have lighter teaching loads than other faculty members. They can put this with recommendations for the future in a self-study that goes to the national association that accredits nursing schools. The accreditors can then pick this up and include the change as a requirement for continued full accreditation without negative "citations." The university administration and board then receive the accreditation report and are told that the change is a requirement set by the professional accrediting agency—when actually it was initially a proposal from the nursing department administrators.

20 The concern in this chapter has been with the board's role in initiating and overseeing the preparation of meaningful mission and long-range planning documents. But mission and planning documents need broad ownership and this involves wide participation in their processing. Plans should be communicated in public releases, as much as possible. The ultimate goal is to elicit broad support from faculty members and constituents.

16

Trustees that Hold in Trust the Long-Term Future

An institution's board has the ultimate responsibility of holding in trust for an institution's church or other mandating society[1] the institution's long-term mission, choosing its chief executive officer, and making other major decisions determining the long-term future of the institution. The board is uniquely responsible for monitoring the link between a school and its sponsors or partners.

Boards Could Be More Effective

It has become increasingly apparent that many boards of business and educational entities are not playing their roles effectively. In the prevailing American pattern of organizational structuring, boards are the "weakest link." John Carver cites Peter Drucker: "There is one thing all boards have in common, regardless of their legal position. *They do not function*. The decline of the board is a universal phenomenon of this century."[2] Richard Chait writes, "Is inept governance contagious? Has the germ that infected corporate America contaminated colleges and universities, too? For every Enron, Tyco, and WorldCom, we seem to have an academic equivalent."[3] More recently, however, *The Chronicle of Higher Education* reports more hopefully, "By most accounts, the glory days of rubber-stamp governing boards have passed."[4]

Unlike the situation in faculty recruitment, where there are few published proposals for practical alternatives to the kind of conventional team-building that has led to problems in the past, there are many published works on practical aspects of board functioning. Authors and foundations have focused on the problem. More recently, following the crises at Enron, WorldCom, Tyco, Global Crossing, Adelphia, AIG, and Bank of America, study commissions and the U. S. Congress have proposed changes in procedures of for-profit corporations that have changed and will change the practices of many of their boards.[5]

In the educational sector, under the leadership of Robert Gale, Richard Ingram, and Richard Legon, the Association of Governing Boards of Universities and Colleges has sponsored meetings and publications. The Lilly Endowment sponsored a project for strengthening the boards of directors of the theological schools sponsored by some churches and other groups with distinctive beliefs. With the help of a lead grant from the W. K. Kellogg Foundation, the Association of Governing Boards of Colleges and Universities and Independent Sector established the National Center for Nonprofit Boards in 1988; this center has been sponsoring studies and resources for strengthening lay boards.

Among church-related institutions and other institutions with distinctive missions, the problem has had two aspects: (1) a lack of general effectiveness in keeping the long-term goals of their church partners or other sponsors of their institutions in mind, and (2) difficulty in implementing good decisions in the face of internal and external pressures. Boards frequently ask how they can implement decisions effectively without "micro-managing."

Implementing Long-term Objectives

In the summer of 2000, one college's president resigned when it was discovered that the college's long-term endowment had fallen from $34 million to less than $13 million without the awareness or involvement of the board of trustees. The board included the president and president emeritus of two of the leading national higher educational associations in Washington and the respected vice president of a third national association and co-editor of a national higher educational journal. In public statements, the chair of the board said, "The blame has to lie directly with the trustees." The president under whose watch the endowment fell said, "If they [the board members] were careless at all, it was because they had such great confidence in me."

A news report said, "By stacking the board with hand-picked trustees who didn't question his decisions, . . . [the president] may have created a lapdog."[6]

In many institutions, boards function primarily as cheerleaders for the president. In some institutions, the president plays a major role in appointing board members. The board members are expected to make large financial contributions and to encourage others to do so. Or the president tries to enhance the prestige of the board by appointing national educational leaders who have other full-time responsibilities. The president has a rolling list of supporters and big donors; if there are board members whose support wavers, the president replaces them with stronger supporters from the list.

Typical boards of private institutions are large—they often have thirty or more members.[7] Getting more supporters involved as board members can increase their readiness to contribute and to encourage others to do so. It pays in the short run. Presidents in American institutions of higher education are much more likely to be seen as successful leaders if they are good fund-raisers. Having board members who are good cheerleaders helps.

But these typical boards are not designed for effective decision-making. Consider, for example, the matter of board size. While observing that local situations vary, a major Kellogg Foundation work prepared by an experienced leader in American institutions and currently sponsored and distributed by the National Center for Nonprofit Boards notes that "authorities dealing with a functional category of boards have . . . recommended that a college board should have from seven to twelve people."[8] Boards of most public higher education institutions responsible to taxpayers and to the larger public for long-term decisions typically have seven to twelve members. Very few independent colleges and universities have decision-making boards of only seven to twelve members!

Carver, author of several books and other publications on board governance, speaks pointedly to the question of board size: "The simple rule is to justify any number over seven. There is nothing magic about this number; however, as boards grow progressively beyond this size, they pay an increasingly higher price in awkwardness, discipline, and unfocused energy." Carver then lists specific weaknesses of large boards.[9]

In a project supported by the Lilly Endowment and the Office of Educational Research and Improvement of the U.S. Department of Education, Chait, Holland, and Taylor are equally clear. They note Taylor's survey showing that independent college boards have thirty-two members on average. They say this "limits trustees' participation and their sense of authority and accountability." Citing research, they say, "The larger the board, the less likely any one board member will feel a sense of individual responsibility."[10] With references to the work of Useem[11] and Lazerson,[12] Collis says, simply: "One obvious suggestion is to cut down the size of boards. . . . It is already recognized among the educational community that boards with thirty-plus trustees are simply unmanageable."[13]

Why do so many colleges and universities continue to have large boards? I have hinted at some of the reasons above. Most institutions tend to follow the leader and do what other institutions do—in this case, have large boards. (What is called "educational research" is often simply surveying what other institutions are doing. In the case of church colleges and universities, the fact that some past and current practices have typically contributed to unintended school-church dissociation does not seem to be taken seriously.[14]) Another reason for the current predominance of large boards may be that chief executive officers sometimes find short-term advantages in having boards that do not ask too many questions—and the boards save time and effort by leaving matters to the CEO. A third reason is that a larger board with good donors can be helpful for fund-raising in the short term.

A problem arises, however, when the board needs to find a new president or when someone needs to bring a longer-term perspective into other major decisions that will affect the future of the institution for decades to come.[15]

As mentioned in the previous chapter, one way a board can retain the advantages of a large board for fundraising purposes without the large board's disadvantages in decision-making is through the large board's choice and empowerment of a smaller executive board or the appointment of a standing "committee on the future of the college."

At present, many private boards are designed more for cheerleading than for effective decision-making.

Boards in Institutions with Distinctive Missions

The problem is particularly acute when a college or university has a distinctive mission—when it wants to be different from most other colleges and universities. Short-term institutional pressures for diffusing a school's focus can come into sharp conflict with long-term goals.

Consider a not-uncommon situation: The president of a church-related college is under pressure to get more contributed dollars. The faculty is unhappy because it seems that the president is not able to raise funds as well as his predecessor. The president's survival as president is at stake. To help broaden the institution's appeal, the president adds to the board wealthy donors and potential contributors who have little understanding of or commitment to the institution's special mission. This has little impact on church relationships initially, since the large board and the church continue to look to the president for his or her academic and spiritual leadership of the institution, and the president continues to provide this leadership.

But when the president resigns or retires, the board has to arrange for a search for a new president. The church wakes up to discover that the enlarged board is not adequately informed or concerned about the churchly mission of the institution. But the new board with its new uninformed and uncommitted members is now responsible for the search for the new president. It carries full legal authority for the other decisions that will determine the future of the institution. The board forms a search committee of faculty members, board representatives, and other constituents, and they nominate a new president, who has done well as a second-line administrator in a leading university and has demonstrated leadership and fundraising skills, but has had little experience or understanding of the new institution's church context. The board proceeds to inaugurate its new president. The church wakes up to another instance of church-school distancing and movement toward dissociation.

This situation with variations has been repeated often enough in the past that it can be seen as a fairly common scenario in the dynamics of dissociation. In each instance, no one inside or outside the institution has specifically intended it, but the process has ineluctably led over time to a distancing of school from church or the church movement that gave it birth.

A college or university that wants to go with the flow in the mainstream of American institutions can perhaps rely on the prevailing expectations of students, faculty members, parents, donors, and other constituents of American higher education institutions generally for direction in times of transition and major decision.[16] A college or university that wants to implement a distinctive mission needs to have a board with more distance from day-to-day campus pressures and interests if it wants to keep the mission and long-term objectives of the institution and the larger mandating society in focus and operational as it makes decisions affecting the long-term health and mission-accomplishment of its institution. A board of an institution that wants to be effective over the long term will have to work creatively, not just reactively.

The Board's Role

When we ask how boards could handle their fiduciary responsibilities better in the future than they often have in the past, we need to recognize that good people can disagree on the roles boards should play. And boards can have different roles in different contexts.

At one extreme, some writers, with all-too-little humor, have said a board has only two agenda items: (1) should we fire the president? and, (2) if not, how can we support our president? At the other extreme, there are boards—especially of local nonprofit neighborhood agencies that have no staff employees at all—whose members do whatever needs to be done. Most boards of private colleges and universities are closer to the former extreme than to the latter.

In the American context, where an organization is formally instituted and mandated by a society, the mandating society normally appoints a lay board, i.e., a board of nonprofessionals.[17] The fundamental purpose of the board is to represent the society at large in providing for the achievement of the mission mandated by the society. In the case of a college or university whose principal mandating society is a church, the fundamental fiduciary purpose of the board is to represent the church in providing for the achievement of the church's purposes in having the school.

Is the board of a school actually to give priority to the achievement of its mandating society's purposes in having the school or to the school's own interest as it competes with other schools? A survey has shown that "trustees of private colleges almost invariably perceive the board's essential role as being the guardian of the institution's long-term welfare."[18] A board chair of a college we visited said, "After only one or two meetings with the board, I began to think more about the immediate self-interest of the college as an institution than about the reason our constituents wanted to have the college in the first place." The perspective on the way the school is to be a part of the mandating society's mission can get lost when the board starts focusing on next year's budget and students. It is not that boards do not want to be effective representatives of their constituents. They may have good intentions, but can lose track of them in the press of immediate problems.

Neo-institutional organizational theorists observe that a board or president can do little about what faculty members do in the classroom. A faculty member in an academic discipline will be influenced more by what is happening among professionals in the discipline than by the board of the school. English professors in Indiana, for example, will be influenced more by what members of the Modern Language Association are doing in Massachusetts and California than by their presidents or provosts. A board needs to understand this.

The board's key role is different from that of the faculty. Where there is a reasonable consensus on the institution's mission, a board can play a key role in providing for the kind of professional faculty team that is gathered to implement the mission. It can keep the long-term mission in clear focus, choose top administrators that are committed to implementing the mission, and adopt policies that guide its implementation.

Textbooks on boards would all agree on these basic ideas. But when we get serious, we run into the same problem we encountered when we dealt with faculty recruitment. Everyone agrees in principle with the idea that a school needs some faculty members committed to its mission. But then few deal seriously with what it is going to take in today's academia if the ideal is to be realized in actual institutional practice. Foundation reports and textbooks would agree that boards must exercise leadership, but how can boards be leaders rather than followers in actual practice?

In Chapter 15, I said that a board needs to prepare the initial drafts of mission and strategic planning documents. It may do this by appointing a "committee on the future of the college," but it cannot just delegate to its institution's staff the initial drafting of documents so important for its long-term future. The board or its committee needs to keep asking, "Why does this college or university exist? What is its mission?" To deal with long-term direction and progress, boards or designated subcommittees need to initiate most of the items on their agendas instead of spending more than half of their meeting time processing reports and proposals from their staffs.[19]

At first blush this idea may seem reasonable. But how many boards actually function in these ways? How can the task of actually initiating most agenda items possibly be added to board meetings already full of staff reports and approvals of staff proposals? Most board agendas are already crowded.

Implementing the ideal is more than fine-tuning present structures and practices. Systemic change requires a kind of paradigm shift in faculty recruitment —from "selection" to "search." It requires an accompanying paradigm shift in board functioning as well.

Boards and Administrators

In American colleges and universities, the board usually appoints a president or other chief executive officer as its representative and administrator to oversee the implementation of its decisions between board meetings. In this model, the role of the board is differentiated from the complementary role of the organization's administration, for the longer-term existence, continuity, and direction of the organization.

We can cite an illustration from a not-quite-parallel setting: in the Federal government of the United States, the Congress may be as representative of the mandating U.S. society as the Supreme Court, but the Supreme Court makes decisions based on a perspective of greater distance from immediate organizational activity. The House of Representatives and the Senate may be overly influenced by short-term political interests. The Supreme Court has to ask how actions reflect basic commitments expressed in the Constitution and other longer-term understandings of fairness and justice on which the future of the American people as a nation depend.

In brief and over-simple terms, we can say that faculty members take primary responsibility for the quality of the education of their majors in terms of the traditional criteria for excellence in their respective disciplines; presidents and their administrative officers are especially engaged in responding to day-to-day and year-to-year market conditions; and boards are then the guardians and trustees of the long-term mission-fulfillment of their institutions.

If, for example, it appears that little attention is given in many institutions to the general and liberal education of undergraduates (as distinct from the more specialized preparation of students in their major fields), and if general education is a significant part of the mission of these institutions, it will often fall to their boards to take the special steps needed to see that the general education part of the mission gets adequate attention. The board will not administer the general education program. It will monitor the student-learning outcomes and the implementation of the program in the light of the institution's mission.

A board cannot be strong if it is intimidated by the fact that it is more distant from the workings of the enterprise than the staff is. It needs to see its distance from the day-to-day operations as a key element in its mandate and contribution to the strength of the organization.[20] The board role is particularly important at colleges and universities with distinctive long-term missions—institutions that cannot assume that simply following prevailing practices among American colleges and universities will assure their ability to achieve their special missions over the long term.

I have spent most of my professional life as an administrator and as a resource person in orienting institutional board members. I have found that administrators have a common tendency to believe that a board member who questions one of their administrative proposals is simply not close enough to the situation to understand. The administrator then wants the board member to spend more time on campus, read more campus publications, survey and interview more constituents. Even after that, it may turn out that the board member is still not as close to the institution as the administrator is! Administrators can ask board members to become so involved in gaining information, making development contacts that ought to be handled by salaried development staff workers, and other administrative tasks that the board members are not able to give adequate attention to longer-term questions that should be at the heart of the primary agenda of the board.

Dual-Board Possibilities

Most private colleges and universities have large, single-institution governing boards. But most American students are actually in dual-board institutions, since most public colleges and universities have dual-board systems and well over three-quarters of the American students in higher education are in public colleges and universities.

The whole point of a dual-board arrangement is that the overarching board—usually a statewide board in the public sector—is concerned with the long-term educational needs of its mandating society. The institutional boards can then devote themselves more fully to more immediate matters relating to their several institutions. The overarching board is to identify higher educational needs in its region or state and then (1) decide where institutions and programs should be established and maintained and (2) provide a context for decision-making in the light of longer-term, as opposed to immediate, educational objectives. The boards on each level are freer to fulfill their special responsibilities.

Philip Moots and Edward Gaffney suggest a "double-tiered governing structure which allows the retention of selected fundamental decisions by the sponsoring religious body and permits all other actions to be taken by the board of the college" as a way churches can take responsibility commensurate with their legal liabilities and avoid legal exposure to ascending liability suits.[21]

Educational organizations differ from business organizations in the ease with which stakeholders can assess success. There is an interesting parallel, however, in the adoption of multidivisional organizational forms by business organizations after World War I and the interest in multi-campus educational systems, especially in the public sector, after World War II. In perhaps the leading current text on organizations, Scott says:

> Chandler argues that . . . the M [multidivisional, "dual-board"]-form is superior to the U [unitary, "single-board"]-form because it frees selected officials from the tyranny of daily operational decisions and allows them to concentrate on positioning the organization in its environment.

Williamson highlights the differentiation "between the long-range policy decisions, to be handled by the general office, and the short-run operational decisions, to be determined at the divisional level."[22]

Few denominations have had churchwide boards in a position to engage in effective decision-making and decision-implementation regarding their colleges. In their 1966 Danforth-sponsored major study of church-related higher education, Pattillo and Mackenzie[23] commented on the weakness and marginality of most denominational boards, and on the resulting proliferation of institutions and the absence of reasonable long-range planning in most denominational systems. Parsonage's 1978 report comments on the need in these words:

> Some denominations . . . are expressing the need for system-wide planning among their colleges. . . . [This] group suggests that system-wide planning and strategy are essential if costly duplication of effort among the denomination's colleges is to be overcome, if equitable funding of the church's institutions is to occur, if a public policy position congenial to the survival of independent higher education is to be formulated and widely supported within the denomination, if there is to be a sense of common purpose and identity among the colleges of a denomination, and if there is to be some standard for determining which colleges deserve the continuing support of the church.[24]

Most church-related colleges sprang up as independent institutions on the American frontier. A part of the weakness of church-related higher education in the past century has been in its failure to bring longer-term perspectives into its decision-making structures and procedures.

I referred in Chapter 6 to the demise of the Committee on Higher Education of the Presbyterian Church U.S.A. and the termination of the Education Commission of the Southern Baptist Convention. Although some churches have associations of presidents or of institutions, these cannot take the place of boards or commissions representing the long-term interests of churches as churches. If individual presidents are under enormous pressure from every side for survival and short-term "success," an association of presidents will not necessarily lead to a focus on long-term objectives. It can exacerbate the emphasis on short-term interests.

Historian Philip Gleason of Notre Dame describes the demise of the Jesuit Educational Association:

> The reason was not that [the Jesuit presidents] felt no concern for the overall good of Jesuit higher education. No doubt they did, but they were much more concretely concerned about the good of the institutions for which they were immediately responsible. By 1970 they were able to throw off the oversight of the association, substituting for it an informal conference of Jesuit university presidents who consulted together but had no obligation whatever to coordinate their activities toward some suprainstitutional Jesuit educational goal.[25]

A church that wants to implement a special mission should seriously consider having a board or commission of dedicated and experienced church leaders willing and able to represent the long-term interest of the church as a church. The board should involve members who are able to articulate the church's interests and assure the church of their implementation. In practice, a denomination's general churchwide board will normally oversee an education board or commission with these educational responsibilities.

A Denominational Board's Members

Two criteria are important in the appointment of members to a churchwide education board or commission:

1. *The members and the board as a whole must have enough distance from the immediate day-to-day tasks of operating institutions to be able to keep long-term church goals in clear focus.* An institutional board can focus on longer-term institutional interests. But to represent church interests, the church's education board or commission cannot represent only an institutional interest or a collection of institutional interests.

2. *At the same time, the board must have enough members knowledgeable about higher education to be able to translate*

long-term church goals into the language of academic admin-istration. The general board of the denomination will not nor-mally function adequately as the education board, not only because of the meeting time needed for educational matters but also because the education board should include members gifted and experienced in academic leadership.

The functions of the education boards of different mandating groups will differ. A church may have one way of working with its universities and another way of working with its theological seminaries. Indeed, a church may relate to different colleges in different ways. The education board may have some governance reserve powers in its relationship with some insti-tutions, e.g., appointing or approving the appointment of an institutional president. The board might have a procedure involving visiting teams and stated criteria for accrediting certain institutions—and removing others from accreditation, as necessary—as institutions of the denomination.

In any case, the denominational board has a responsibility to represent its supporting constituency also in providing its constituency with informa-tion and advocacy for the programs and institutions that are implementing constituency interests. A church or group with a mission cannot just aban-don its institutions to self-promotion and support. An education board may promote some institutions in one way and as working toward some goals; it may promote other institutions in other ways commensurate with their roles in the larger constituency mission. But the education board must work with integrity. It cannot give institutions blank checks. A church education board cannot give church people and donors the impression that an institu-tion is giving priority to serving church interests and its churchly mission when it is not. It must, however, be ready to allocate resources and to pro-mote institutions the church needs to carry out its mission.

Appointing and Orienting Board Members

If, in the American lay board model, boards are to represent their mandat-ing societies authentically, and if a board is to be more than a cheerleading section for its chief executive, the executive should not be appointing his or her own board. At the same time, the executive and the administrative staff members are more likely to come into contact with prospects for board membership in the course of their regular constituency contacts. The input of the executive and administrators on board appointments is needed.

The appointment of board members can present a challenge. If the board is an effective small board, it needs to have the range of kinds of experience and expertise needed for effective decision-making. Boards whose members are appointed separately by many different groups without regard to the composition of the board as a whole tend to be weak.[26]

Related to board appointments is the question of the evaluation of the performance of board members and the reappointment of incumbents to new terms, where these are permitted and desired. The people in the best position to evaluate the functioning and effectiveness of a given board member are those who sit with the board member from meeting to meeting. But asking board members to decide that some of their number should be reappointed to additional terms and others should not is asking them to function out of character. We normally want board members to accept each other with their individual strengths and weaknesses and to complement one another in their functioning as a team without spending too much time in critiquing each others' performance.

How can the information from staff contacts with constituents, the voices of outside representatives of a mandating society, and the awareness board members themselves have of the kinds of commitment, experience, and expertise they need for effective functioning best be brought together in board appointments and reappointments? The most effective arrangement we have seen in actual practice has been having a board designate two or three of its members as a "Committee on the Board" or "Nominating Committee."[27] Members of this committee can get suggestions from the president and administrators with constituency contacts. (The committee and board are free to follow these suggestions or not to follow them.) The committee members are available for receiving confidential counsel from individual board members. Sometimes a committee member has been asked to interview each board member individually and confidentially. If outside church districts or other constituencies actually appoint their board representatives, the committee or its representatives can have sessions with the district or other leaders at times when they meet (or can be brought together) to have them bring the names of possible nominees, to discuss board needs, and to have them arrive at a set of candidates that will best meet their needs for representation and the board's needs for able members and a good range of kinds of expertise and experience in its membership.

A committee of this kind can also propose nominees for board officer positions at times when these are needed. The committee can consult confidentially with each board member to be sure each board member is heard at the time of the appointment and reappointment of board officers. Sensitive matters, such as those involving a need to have an appropriate schedule and process for replacing a chair when most board members feel this would facilitate the board's functioning, can be processed and presented to the people involved and to the board by this committee. The goal is getting the best possible representation of gifts and experience in the institutional board.

All of the above assumes that we are dealing with the kind of single board typical of most private institutions. In a dual-board system, the institutional boards or most of their members may be named by the overarching board. In getting the best possible representation of gifts and experience in the institutional board, the committee on the board of an institutional board can then work with the representatives of the overarching board that makes the actual appointments. Indeed, getting strong, small, and effective institutional boards is one of the advantages of a dual-board system.

Sometimes an institution with a traditional large board appointed or elected by outside groups has moved toward greater board effectiveness by appointing a smaller executive board and granting it decision-making authority in many areas of board responsibility. Some have called the large entity a "corporation" and then have had the corporation choose an executive that carried effective decision-making power. In either case, the large entity, the corporation, can name to the smaller decision-making executive board some of its own members and some outsiders whose gifts and expertise are needed. The executive board can have a still smaller two- or three-person "Committee on the Board" to assess its membership and leadership needs, nominate new and continuing members, lead board workshops, and provide for evaluation of its performance. The challenge in this arrangement is to have members of the larger bodies feel that they are sufficiently involved when they are aware that many major decisions will be made by the smaller groups. Having the traditional large board of thirty-plus members and the smaller executive board represents an attempt to have some of the advantages of involving more constituency representatives on a board and still having a smaller board able to fulfill its role in effective and responsible decision-making in its relationships with administrators.

I mentioned earlier another arrangement through which a large board can have large-board advantages and still have small-board effectiveness: the large board's appointment of a "committee on the future of the college" to provide the large board with leadership in handling major board responsibilities. The committee can study trends and make proposals for the formulation and long-term implementation of the school's mission.

The Nature Conservancy is a large international nonprofit organization. Following a series of critical articles in The *Washington Post*, it appointed an independent five-person "Governance Advisory Panel," one of whose members was Derek Bok, former president of Harvard University. In March 2004, the panel recommended changes in Nature Conservancy's thirty-person board, the formation of and delegation of ongoing oversight to a new executive committee of eleven members, and a "Governance Committee" with responsibilities similar to those of the committee on the board proposed here.

In the short term, many chief executive officers like to have cheerleaders, but having a compliant board that simply supports whatever the CEO may want to do is not necessarily in the interest of the CEO, to say nothing of the implications for the long-term mission of the institution. Providing for leadership groups of a size and shape appropriate for effective representation of an institution's mandating society and implementation of the institution's mission is a critical element in the systemic change proposed in these pages. This may not be so important for colleges wanting to be like other colleges, but it is critical for colleges and universities wanting to be distinctive.

Board Responsibilities

Most listings of board functions mention ten or twenty tasks, and these can be helpful as a checklist for a board in periodic evaluations of its work. In elaborating our understanding of the way boards of special-mission institutions can best view their functions, we will limit ourselves here to an overview of three principal board tasks:

1. *If a board's fundamental purpose is the achievement of the mission mandated by a society, the board's first task is to articulate the mission of its institution or institutions clearly and to provide for review and updating of the mission in changing times.* Sometimes board members are called "trustees"—they hold the institution or institutions in trust for the sponsoring people. Sometimes they are called "directors"—they give direction to the enterprise. In any case, they are responsible for the institution's fulfillment of its mission.

2. *Another key task of a board is employing a staff executive or executives to implement the mission on behalf of the board.* The

board may meet only three or four times a year if its members represent a broad geographical area. Board members act as a body, not just as individuals, and their major actions are normally taken when they are in session. To achieve the mission of their institution, they must appoint a staff executive or executives to be their "eyes, ears, hands, and feet" between their meetings. Having the right executive staff leader is important for the effectiveness of the board in most or all of its other functions. (See Chapter 17.)

3. *A board needs to take the ultimate responsibility for the major decisions bearing on the longer-term existence, direction, and mission-achievement of the institution.* The board is responsible to ask for information on long-term trends as background for its decision-making on actions bearing on the long-term future.

Many standard works on boards include helpful principles of board functioning. But some board member responsibilities are worth emphasizing. For example, almost all of the serious works on boards say that a board member should not try to force his or her institution's president to do what the board member as an individual may want—especially when the board member is trying to force the president to do something on which other board members disagree. The president is to get his or her direction from the actions of the board as a whole.

The principle sounds clear. But all of us who have served as consultants have encountered institutions where the board chair or the treasurer or another individual board member has intervened as an individual and tried to throw his or her weight around. The fact that certain rules of board functioning seem obvious and non-controversial does not mean they are not too often violated in practice.[28]

I consider having CEOs members of the boards to which they should, in principle, be accountable to be a frequently violated principle of good board functioning. (Unless specified otherwise, saying that they are members "ex officio" does not mean that they are not full members. The term actually speaks only to the way they have become members.)

Every board meeting should have at least a brief executive session, where the board meets without any staff employees present. Such executive sessions, without exception, should be followed immediately afterward by an executive session with the CEO present. The chair needs to be sure that the executive session without the CEO confines its agenda to matters involving the work of the CEO or staff. In the executive session, a board member may ask about a rumor. The meeting with the CEO alone immediately afterward gives the board the chance to ask questions of the CEO and to give the CEO the chance to respond to concerns or questions that may otherwise float around in the minds of board members for months after the meeting. The session with the CEO also gives the CEO the chance to discuss with the board in confidence some of his or her concerns.

Beyond the obvious rules of good board functioning, however, and particularly until the past decade or two, the standard works on boards sometimes provided a kind of conventional wisdom that was counterproductive. In my earlier years of work in orienting boards of educational institutions, I found some of the available materials and workshops themselves to be a problem. For example, I found that the traditional attempt to limit boards to policy making, while attempting to point in the right direction, often had the effect of inhibiting board members who were already unsure of their competence in educational matters from taking full responsibility for important matters they needed to address. Indeed, the choice of a president is not a policy matter—but it is certainly an important board responsibility. The choice of chief executive officer is a unique decision for a given time, not the development of policy generalizations that would apply in different times and places. Again, the construction of a large building in the middle of the campus might not be a policy issue, but it could affect the options of future administrations and boards for years to come. The primary question for a board to decide is not, "Is this policy?" The question is: "Is this decision important for the long-term survival, health, and mission-achievement of our institution?"[29]

Moreover, when publications on boards had the net effect of telling board members they should be reading more and more campus publications, visiting the campus more and more often, and, generally, learning more and more about their institutions, board members were sometimes afraid to exercise the kind of leadership only they could provide. They were intimidated. Sometimes they felt that they were not qualified to speak in board meetings because they did not know as much about the daily operations as staff members. Carver says, "Boards caught in the trap of being better staff than staff . . . cannot lead."[30]

Houle's 1989 work is refreshing. In a foundation-supported project, and with the support of the National Center for Nonprofit Boards, Houle, a former professor at the University of Chicago, provided practical counsel that moved beyond some of the conventional wisdom of his time. For example, on the very important question as to which decisions fall in the realm of the board's responsibility and which ones are for the CEO and staff, Houle writes:

> In recent years, determined efforts have been made to define the distinctive rights and duties of the two partners [board and staff] .... But this distinction ultimately proves unsatisfactory, both theoretically and practically. . . .
>
> As has already been noted, many authorities on boards have enunciated a single, fundamental rule by which to define the function of the board as contrasted to the function of the executive. Most frequently they say, often with an air of profundity, that the board should determine policy and the executive should carry it out. Brian O'Connell has responded succinctly "This is just not so" and has called that distinction "the worse illusion ever perpetrated in the nonprofit field."[31]

Houle's work concerns nonprofit boards generally,[32] but it contains many useful principles of good functioning relevant for educational boards.

In 1993 Chait, Holland, and Taylor used interviews and performance indicators to conduct an empirical study of actual board behaviors to identify characteristics of strong and weak boards.[33] They list six dimensions of board competence, and they focus on college boards. But to the degree that they study existing boards, which are in many ways very similar to one another in American private higher education institutions, their findings largely assume that boards will operate in the framework of present structures and practices. The methodology of their project could hardly have been expected to lead to projecting a vision for substantial change.[34] Chait et al. can be helpful for those who want to see the future as a projection of the structures and practices of better institutions of the past and present. For church colleges and other institutions that want to be distinctive and envision a future somewhat different from the past, this earlier work of Chait, Holland, and Taylor gives less practical help.

In a more recent work, Chait, Ryan, and Taylor say that boards should engage more fully in "generative" work—in more creative work on goals— in addition to their work of finding plans for reaching goals and using their resources in the pursuit of their missions.[35] They give helpful suggestions for tools for "generative" work.

John Carver's publications have proposed change.[36] Of the authors of the available writings on boards, Carver seems to see most clearly and specifically the extent of the systemic change that is needed. Carver goes beyond accepting current structures and asking what might be done to effect minor improvements. In the face of serious weaknesses in present boards, particularly those of institutions wanting to be distinctive, Carver moves beyond descriptions of the ways boards are to projecting what could be. Instead of just reflecting on abstract possibilities, Carver provides very practical illustrations from institutions that have adopted his "Policy Governance" model.

Carver says that public or nonprofit groups that have distinctive values and that want schools with missions that reflect those values will have to have boards that can effectively implement their missions. Those boards will need to be initiators and leaders. Carver sees that this will require more than fine-tuning of present ways of working.

Carver proposes practical guidelines for implementing his model. For example, how can a board develop its own agenda? How can it find time to develop documents that show board initiative and leadership? What are typical boards doing that is unnecessarily time-consuming and distracting? Carver gives specifics and examples from his years of work with organizations.

As I refer to Carver's stimulating publications, I must note that Carver's use of the term "policy" throughout his work and in his references to his "Policy Governance" model is unconventional and potentially misleading. Carver uses the term "policy" to denote overarching organizational "values and perspectives."[37] For example, he begins his listing of what he calls "policies" with "Ends," i.e., components of an institution's mission. He says he is not using the term "policies" to refer to "procedures, as in personnel 'policies.'"[38] Carver's usage is so different from our normal usage as to require special attention. The first definition for "policy" in a recent dictionary of the English language is "a definite course of action adopted for the sake of expediency, facility, etc."[39] Carver's usage is simply different. Overarching "values and perspectives" are not the same as "a definite course of action." But when we get past differences on these usages, and although it may not be initially evident from Carver's use of terms, both Carver's emphasis on policy governance and the focus of Chait et al. on "generative" board work actually share our emphasis throughout these pages on board initiative on those matters of greatest importance for the long-term health and mission-accomplishment of the board's organization.

Board members and presidents can refer to Carver and Chait, Ryan, and Taylor for examples of the kinds of agenda items that a board of a church-related institution can deal with in the board-initiated parts of their meetings—i.e., the parts not devoted to staff reporting. Some items:

- Drafting, updating, and reviewing mission and twenty-year strategic planning statements in the light of the missions of the school's supporting constituents.
- Developing ways of determining to what degree its mission and strategic planning goals have been met in the past three to twenty years and are being met currently. What are the trend lines? How can the board gain information on what is important, not just what is easy to quantify?[40] For example, how can the board determine whether student learning is better or worse than a few years ago? If this is related to its mission, how can it get quantitative and qualitative evidence for change in the spiritual development of its students?
- Reviewing and reflecting on data and evidence provided by its agreed-on evaluation procedures.
- Asking how its institution could better achieve aspects of its mission in the future. Are changes indicated, and, if so, which?

These are all items bearing on the long-range mission-fulfillment of the institution. The key questions are these: is it in the long-term interest of the sponsors of this college or university to have this institution and, if so, why? What can the sponsors and the institution do to better accomplish the mission?

A church board with responsibility for several institutions could gain professional help and assist the boards of its schools to develop procedures for working at these questions and develop procedures of its own for working with the institutional evaluations.

Although the published works to which we have referred above contain valuable information in the various areas discussed so far, none of these resources deal adequately with the way institutional forces work. In 1993, Chait et al. emphasized the board's need to understand and work within the culture of academia, but, as we have seen, that is hardly encouraging a board of an organization with a distinctive mandate to be different from others in its organizational field. When Houle and Carver say that boards should lead in representing what their mandating societies want, they provide in principle for colleges and universities that are different from most colleges and universities—but, as we have seen elsewhere, a simple rational bureaucracy understanding in which a board represents what the people want and gives orders down the line to its CEO and staff hierarchy for implementing the will of the people is inadequate. It is particularly inadequate as an understanding of boards of schools with special missions.

It is not only faculties and administrators who are subject to environmental forces and tend to want to be like their colleagues in other colleges and universities. The constituents ("the people") the boards are supposed to represent also assume that everyone knows what a "good" American college or university is like, and they frequently would like to see their schools becoming better as measured by the usual short-term indices of success. A board is not supposed to govern by conducting Gallup Polls among constituents and then implementing the top-of-the-head wants and wishes of its people. A board has to reflect on the long-term goals of its constituents and help them understand how their goals can be attained. Sometimes short-term sacrifices may be needed to attain long-term goals. Particularly in the case of an institution that wants to be distinctive over the long term, the board must help its constituents understand what it takes to get from here to there. Board leadership must be leadership of the constituents the board represents, not just of its institution's staff and faculty.[41]

Evaluating Educational Institutions

Many members of boards of colleges and universities have been members of boards of other nonprofits or of commercial firms. Some principles of board functioning apply to boards of many kinds. But in some ways boards of educational institutions are different—and especially those of institutions with distinctive missions. Board members of institutions with special missions need to be aware of the differences.

Measuring the performance of educational institutions is more difficult than measuring outcomes of some other organizations. It is hard to set quantifiable goals—what Carver calls "Ends policies." A manufacturing firm can plan to produce so many widgets per year. A bank can project expected profits in dollars. The primary "product" of a hospital may be somewhat harder to measure, but it can report on patients served in specific ways, as well as some morbidity and mortality outcomes measures. A manufacturer may have products identified as "flawed" or "dangerous" and a hospital may have to readmit a patient who is not recovering, but almost no colleges have had to recall alumni as "production defects"![42]

Peter Ewell, a leading American educator, says, "Ensuring academic quality is a fiduciary responsibility; it is as much part of our role as board members as ensuring that the institution has sufficient resources and is spending them wisely."[43]

In goal-setting, a board can ask a college or university to end its year in the black. It can follow enrollments. But a college does not exist to maximize financial profits or enrollments. The most important product of most schools is student learning—especially learning that affects students' lives five and ten years after college—and that is notoriously hard to quantify. A researcher can measure input variables, such as numbers of volumes in the library, Ph.D.s on the faculty, etc., but the correlation of these variables with actual student learning is not high. Serious researchers know that the most popular rankings, the *U.S. News & World Report* ratings, tend to measure reputations and inputs, not actual learning.

I had an interesting conversation with a member of the board of trustees of a university in California a few years ago. A fruit grower, he told me that he had a printout on the net return on his previous day's production on his desk by 8:00 a.m. the next morning. His computers used the previous day's prices for his oranges and grapes, and his people entered his labor, refrigeration, depreciation, fuel, and other costs into the calculation. He said he could do the same thing for the production of his university, and he offered his services. I said I appreciated his readiness to serve and thought he might have something to contribute to the business office, but said I had to ask him how he would measure the difference between (1) what the university students knew and could do at the end of the previous day and (2) what they knew and could do at the beginning of the day.

Chapter 6 refers to one of very few really solid measures of an educational outcome that can be used over decades, the institution-by-institution data on the baccalaureate origins of earned doctorates. What percentage of the four-year graduates of each institution later earned doctorates (Ph.D.s, M.D.s, etc.) in a given ten-year period? These are hard data—a graduate either earned a doctorate in a given year or not—but the problem is that producing doctoral-level scholars is not the only, or even the primary, mission of many colleges with special missions.[44]

In recent decades, accrediting associations have increasingly required that its institutions present assessment plans and data in their institutional self-studies reports. These are examined and evaluated in accreditation visits to the institutions. Most institutions rely heavily on surveys in which students evaluate themselves.[45] Assessment of outcomes is not a very exact science, but a college or university board can review the assessment reports that are available and have been used in accreditation self-studies and attempt to phrase strategic plans and student-learning goals in terms appropriate to the institution.

In recent years, some colleges have participated in the National Survey of Student Engagement (NSSE or "Nessie"),[46] an evaluation of some process variables (e.g., student-faculty contact) that researchers believe to be related to actual student learning outcomes. Since its initial administration in 2000, almost two million students from 1,300 colleges have participated in the survey. Because most colleges have not been willing to have scores of individual institutions made public, comparisons among individual institutions have been more difficult, but colleges can get their own results and some group averages. A board can ask that its institution participate in the national assessments, compare its outcomes with some national norm groups, and work on areas of possible improvement. Private colleges and universities may be encouraged by the fact that their institutions as a whole have done very well in the NSSE findings.

Since 2000, assessment tools and longitudinal data more specifically focused on non-cognitive outcomes (e.g., personal and spiritual growth) have been collected and analyzed in the Comprehensive Assessment Project of the Council for Christian Colleges & Universities. The project was begun as a "Collaborative Assessment Project" in 1994 and partially funded for its first seven years by the Fund for the Improvement of Postsecondary Education of the U.S. Department of Education.

The Collegiate Learning Assessment (CLA) Project has developed a performance-based assessment model for directly measuring student freshman-to-senior learning. The instrument has been used by over 400 colleges and universities since 2002. In 2007–2008, 41,700 students participated.[47] Richard Ekman and Stephen Pelletier report on their experience with the CLA and assessing student learning in a recent article.[48]

Some general works on boards say that board members should get their information through the CEO and then hold the CEO accountable. In an educational institution, this approach could mean that board members should not be talking with faculty members or students. What can we say about this?

- A board should get good information from its CEO and staff on a regular basis. Principal findings from assessments should be reported to the board. Staff members should be informed on what students and faculty members are thinking, and should be staying in touch with church and other constituents as a part of their regular public relations work, and these data should be reported to the board by the CEO.[49]

- On a practical level, it is hard to imagine a college or university in which some board members do not have close personal relationships with some faculty members or students. The board member inevitably receives some information from the campus. Most observers would not say that a loyal board member with a son or daughter on campus would have to resign from the board. Of course the board member would have to hold in confidence all confidential information he or she received in board meetings.

- Provision must be made at the outset for a very clear and important exception to the general rule that the board gets its information from the CEO. At regular times, such as in an annual or otherwise scheduled meeting with deans or faculty department chairs (or other faculty groups) and at the times of the periodic reviews of the work of the CEO, there are formal arrangements for board member contacts apart from the CEO with such stakeholders as representatives of elected faculty committees, representative students, and a sample of outside representatives of supporting constituents. At times of periodic reviews, an announcement may say that a board member will meet with individuals from these groups who request a meeting. An educational institution and its leaders cannot be evaluated solely in terms of quantitative data on its "production." Some interviews and other qualitative evaluations are needed.

In October 2008, leaders of several national higher education associations and foundations agreed to form a new alliance "to promote the measurement and improvement of student learning at colleges."[50]

If a board wants to know whether its institution is doing what it has set out to do, it has to decide whether it will measure what is easy to measure, or what is important.

Evaluating Board Functioning

How does a board know if it is doing its own job? Students have quizzes and exams that give them feedback on their progress. Faculty members have evaluations and tenure reviews. Effective boards have periodic reviews of their chief executive officers. But how do boards know if they themselves are doing what they are supposed to be doing?

Many boards do not make serious attempts at evaluating their functioning. Most of those that do, evaluate themselves. But these self-evaluations have limitations. Chait, Holland, and Taylor headed a foundation-supported project of the Center for Higher Education Governance and Leadership at Maryland. One of their three major findings was: "Self-assessments by boards of trustees are of questionable validity as accurate and objective measures of actual board performance and competence" (2).[51]

Elsewhere Chait et al. make these observations:

> Attempts to measure effectiveness through trustee self-evaluations were not as successful. . . . (See Chapter 2 for a further explanation of the flaws seemingly inherent to self-evaluations.) (5). . . .Trustees self-evaluations have limitations and potential blind spots and an objective, accurate appraisal of the board's performance are not one and the same. (38). . . . Ashford (1989) concluded that self-assessments of any kind are almost universally inaccurate for several reasons. . . . (39)[52]

Board self-evaluation is better than no evaluation, but self-evaluation is not adequate. Boards interested in the serious evaluation of their performance will need to utilize outside resources. Most college and university boards do not do this—but the weakness of most present boards has been a problem. A board that wants to do better will have to be ready to "cut some new grooves."

A denominational board or outside agency could make available an experienced "resource person for board functioning" who might be willing to assume this role for a number of institutions—as an "auditor" of board functioning. Or an institutional board itself might ask a trusted and experienced resource person to assume this role.

- At the outset of the evaluation assignment, the resource person might discuss pros and cons of several models of board functioning with the board and arrive at agreement on the kind of model the board wants to project. All boards will presumably want to choose the presidents/CEOs of their institutions. Some will be ready to assume initiative in developing their institutional mission statements and strategic plans, as we have advocated. Others will want to monitor the work of their CEOs and staff as they prepare documents of these kinds, with the understanding that the boards will approve the final drafts. Will the boards work primarily in monitoring the work of staff people, or will the boards take initiative on certain matters important for the longer-term health and mission-accomplishment of the institutions? If the latter, which kinds of matters?

- The resource person might be a silent participant in a series of meetings as an outside auditor of board performance.
- At the end of the term of observation, the resource person will report to the board or boards and make suggestions for possible changes.

The resource person might work with a checklist of items for observation, including items that might be added by the board itself at the outset. The resource person will ask about the degree to which the board was representing the church or other mandating society, not just concerns representing internal interests of the organization. The key question should be: Was the board's work during the time of the review optimal for its implementation of the mission of its institution?

Given the widespread awareness that past studies and foundation projects have documented board weaknesses and have shown the promise in change in this area of American organizational governance, foundations might well be ready to support creative proposals from denominations or institutions for preparing "auditors" as resource persons for this kind of board evaluation and development in higher education.

The awareness in the past decade that college and university boards can and should be strengthened is promising for the future.

Chapter 16 Endnotes

1   Examples of "mandating societies" would include citizens of the State of Ohio (for Ohio State University and the other universities in the system), members of a Roman Catholic order, a Protestant denomination, Jewish sponsors of a rabbinical school, or Christians in larger circles of Evangelicals, or "Ecumenicals" generally.

2   John Carver, *Boards That Make a Difference: A New Design for Leadership in Nonprofit and Public Organizations*, 2nd ed., The Jossey-Bass Nonprofit and Public Management Series (San Francisco: Jossey-Bass Inc., 1997), 7. The reference is to P. F. Drucker, *Management: Tasks, Responsibilities, Practices* (New York: HarperCollins, 1974), 628.

3   Richard P. Chait, "When Trustees Blunder," *The Chronicle of Higher Education*, February 17, 2006. After reviewing a May 2006 report of the Office of Federal Housing Enterprise Oversight, which highlights the weakness of some corporate boards, Morgenson says, "The Enron verdicts were, at best, the end of the beginning of this dispiriting corporate crime wave. . . . There is obviously much work to be done . . . before we can be sure that other Enrons will not happen" (Gretchen Morgenson, "Are Enrons Bustin' Out All Over?," *The New York Times*, May 28, 2006).

    Some long-overdue changes are being made. For example, in the March 17, 2006, *New York Times,* sec. C, Claudia H. Deutsch reports that "Fewer Corporate Chiefs [CEOs] Are Also Serving as Chairmen [of their boards]." We wonder how a board can properly oversee the work of its CEO when the CEO is chairing the board?

4   "13 Reasons Colleges Are in This Mess," *The Chronicle of Higher Education*, March 13, 2009. (Author not identified.)

5   The Sarbanes-Oxley Act of 2002 applied to for-profit organizations, but in 2005 the Senate Finance Committee and its chair, Senator Charles Grassley, considered a draft of a White Paper with provisions that would apply to nonprofit boards, including those of educational institutions. The front-page scandals at American University in 2005 have led to proposals for the removal of the president from full board member-ship and for performance evaluations of trustees.

6   John L. Pulley, "Eyes Wide Shut: How Eckerd's 52 Trustees Failed to See Two-Thirds of its Endowment Disappear," *The Chronicle of Higher Education*, August 18, 2000.

7   The board of the college referred to above had fifty-two members and met only twice a year. The board chair said, "If you have a 52-member board and you don't have that frequent committee-meeting habit, you have the danger of any given member assum-ing that somebody else is doing the job." He noted that only "about 60 percent of [the college's] trustees typically attended the board's semi-annual meetings" (Pulley, "Eyes Wide Shut," August 18, 2000).

8   Cyril O. Houle, *Governing Boards: Their Nature and Nurture* (San Francisco: Jossey-Bass, 1989), 65.

9   Carver, *Boards That Make a Difference*, 223.

10   Richard P. Chait, Thomas P. Holland, and Barbara E. Taylor, *The Effective Board of Trustees,* American Council of Education/Oryx Series on Higher Education (Phoenix: The Oryx Press, 1993).

11   M. Useem, "What Tyco Tells Us," *The Wall Street Journal*, June 5, 2002.

12   M. Lazerson, "Who Owns Higher Education: The Changing Face of Governance," *Change: The Magazine of Higher Learning* 29 (1997), 10–15.

13 William G. Tierney, *Competing Conceptions of Academic Governance: Negotiating the Perfect Storm* (Baltimore: Johns Hopkins University Press, 2004), 64.

14 One observer with a sense of humor has said that organizations in an institutional field are like the herd of Gadarene swine of Matthew 8 rushing down the steep bank into the sea: one pig tells the next, "Just keep your head down and keep moving!"

15 Chait, Holland, and Taylor make this point in these words: "Presidents may be able to reign supreme over a disengaged board. . . . But when the president leaves a board like this one, the trustees frequently falter—just when the need for leadership is greatest. . . . From a CEO's perspective, a passive board sometimes seems quite desirable. . . . Many presidents attempt to lull their boards into complacency and compliance. In the short run, presidents may welcome the latitude they gain. . . . In fact, though, there are advantages over the longer term to a president who works to develop a better informed and more strategically focused board" (*The Effective Board of Trustees*, 116). Richard P. Chait was formerly at the University of Maryland and is currently at Harvard; Thomas P. Holland is at Georgia; and Barbara E. Taylor was formerly with the Association of Governing Boards of Universities and Colleges and is now with the Academic Search Consultation Service.

16 In the language of organizational theorists, the forces of "mimetic isomorphism" take over.

17 There are, of course, self-perpetuating boards not formally representing external constituencies and whose members appoint their successors. In some cases, the chief executives appoint new board members—in effect, CEOs appoint those to whom they are accountable.

18 Chait, Holland, and Taylor, *The Effective Board of Trustees*, 7.

19 If the board is a typical large board, expecting most of the board's agenda to be generated by the board itself is usually unrealistic. One can then anticipate that the board will designate a smaller group (e.g., an executive board or committee on the future of the college) to carry significant responsibilities, and the smaller group will then be the group that will initiate most of its agenda.

20 That Supreme Court justices are not also members of the executive branch of the American government and that there is a certain "separation of powers" are usually seen as strengths of the American form of government, not as weaknesses. There are tensions between branches, but the tensions are built-in stresses that arise because of differences in roles. They are a part of the "checks and balances" design.

21 Phillip R. Moots and Edward McGlynn Gaffney, *Church and Campus: Legal Issues in Religiously Affiliated Higher Education* (Notre Dame: University of Notre Dame Press, 1979), 9.

22 The citations are from Richard W. Scott, *Organizations: Rational, Natural, and Open Systems*, 5th ed. (Upper Saddle River, NJ: Prentice Hall, 2003), 275–76.

23 Pattillo and Mackenzie, *Church-Sponsored Higher Education in the United States: Report of the Danforth Commission* (Washington, DC: American Council on Education, 1966), 276–277.

24 Robert Rue Parsonage, ed. *Church Related Higher Education: Perceptions and Perspectives* (Valley Forge, PA: Judson Press, 1978), 288–89.

25 Philip Gleason, "The American Background of *Ex corde Ecclesiae*: A Historical Perspective," in *Catholic Universities in Church and Society: A Dialogue on Ex corde*

Ecclesiae, ed. John P. Langan (Washington, DC: Georgetown University Press, 1993), 8.

26 One weak university board with which I worked comprised over forty bishops and denominational leaders, each representing a district within its geographical region.

27 Carver, who leans generally against having personnel, executive, program, and finance committees on a board, does see a "nomination committee" as "a proper governance committee and . . . the only board committee that may need to be described and empowered in the bylaws." See Carver, *Boards That Make a Difference: A New Design for Leadership in Nonprofit and Public Organizations*, 155.

28 The media gave national publicity to a violation of the above-mentioned principle of board functioning several years ago. On September 18, 2000, a college board's chair asked publicly for the resignation of the president of his institution of 18,000 students when neither the other four board members nor the president of the faculty senate supported his view. (Erik Lords, "In Continuing Feud, Community-College Board Member Calls for President's Job," *Today's News, The Chronicle of Higher Education,* September 21, 2000.) Violations are not unique to educational boards. A front-page article in the May 2, 2005, *New York Times* reports, "Without the knowledge of his [Corporation for Public Broadcasting] board, the chairman, Kenneth Y. Tomlinson, contracted last year with an outside consultant to keep track of the guests' political leanings on one program, 'Now With Bill Moyers.'" Tomlinson is no longer chair.

29 Widmer and Houchin cite B.E. Taylor, R.P. Chait, and T.P. Holland ("The New Work of the Nonprofit Board," *Harvard Business Review* 94, no. 5 [1996]: 36-46): "Taylor, Chair, and Holland question the dictum that policy is always the board's domain and that implementation is always the staff's. They see board and management working together in many areas of both policy and implementation . . . . Differentiating policy from implementation is not the answer" (Candace Widmer and Susan Houchin, *The Art of Trusteeship: The Nonprofit Board Member's Guide to Effective Governance*, The Jossey-Bass Nonprofit and Public Management Series [San Francisco: Jossey-Bass, Inc., 2000], xvi).

30 Carver, *Boards That Make a Difference*, 22.

31 Houle, *Governing Boards: Their Nature and Nurture*, 88. Houle's reference is to Brian O'Connell, *The Board Member's Book* (New York: Foundation Center, 1985), 44.

32 It is limited to the discussion of tripartite systems (i.e., systems in which board, executive, and staff are distinguished from one another), but higher education institutions are normally tripartite systems.

33 Chait, Holland, and Taylor, *The Effective Board of Trustees.*

34 Among the recommended competencies of boards, for example, we see that "the board understands and takes into account the culture and norms of the organization it governs," "the board adapts to the distinctive characteristics and culture of the college's environment," and "the board relies on the institution's mission, values, and traditions as a guide for decisions." These recommendations have more of a tone of accommodation to existing ways of doing things than of strong and innovative leadership.

35 Richard P. Chait, William P. Ryan, and Barbara E. Taylor, *Governance as Leadership: Reframing the Work of Nonprofit Boards* (Hoboken, NJ: John Wiley & Sons, Inc., 2005).

36 In his bibliography in *Boards That Make a Difference*, Carver lists sixty-eight of his own publications and many other works on boards and board functioning.

37 Carver, *Boards That Make a Difference*, 24.

38 Ibid., 25.

39 *Random House Webster's Unabridged Dictionary*, 2nd ed. (New York: Random House, 2001), 1497.

40 An introduction to the relationship between values and metrics by a respected leader in American higher education is in Peter T. Ewell, "Power in Numbers: The Values in Our Metrics," *Change: The Magazine of Higher Learning* 37, no. 4 (2005): 10–23. Board members can review findings from some qualitative methodologies appropriate to the missions of their institutions (e.g., interviews, writing samples), as well as quantitative instruments.

41 We can note the parallel in the American political system. Our principal national decisions are not made through referenda or national town meetings. Americans pay legislators and executives to look into issues more carefully than is possible for most citizens, and then to articulate possibilities for the future and lead the nation in the direction of longer-term goals. When legislators and executives pander to a people's immediate wants and wishes and fail to lead, everyone loses.

42 On a very few occasions institutions have recalled the diplomas of perpetrators of particularly egregious crimes, but these can be considered "exceptions that prove the rule."

43 Peter T. Ewell, *Making the Grade: How Boards Can Enhance Academic Quality* (Washington, DC: Association of Governing Boards, 2006). Derek Bok, a former president of Harvard University, has an excellent article on "The Critical Role of Trustees in Enhancing Student Learning" in *The Chronicle of Higher Education,* December 16, 2005. He discusses the role of trustees vis-à-vis that of the faculty.

44 An interesting finding in these studies of the 1980s was that an unusual number of scientists and other academics came from small private colleges, even though preparing doctoral-level professionals was not among the primary missions of many of these institutions. With respect to diversity, it should also be noted that liberal arts colleges are sending a higher percentage of women on to get Ph.D.s than are doctoral universities. (Robin Wilson, "A Hothouse for Female Scientists," *The Chronicle of Higher Education*, May 5, 2006.)

    A few years ago there was an attempt to correlate the raw data also with test scores of entering students at the institutions studied to find "value-added" data. This needs further study.

45 The Higher Education Research Institute at UCLA has a Cooperative Institutional Research Program Freshman Survey and a College Student Survey for seniors that some institutions use for longitudinal student self-evaluation data that can be compared with those of peer institutions.

46 A program launched in 2000 by the Pew Charitable Trusts and sponsored by the Center for Postsecondary Research, Indiana University School of Education, 201 North Rose Avenue, Bloomington, IN 47405–1006. Alexander C. McCormick is project director.

47 Information can be obtained at *www.cae.org/cla*. The philosophy underlying recent attempts to measure cognitive outcomes directly can be found in Stephen P. Klein

and others, "An Approach to Measuring Cognitive Outcomes across Higher Education Institutions," *Research in Higher Education* 46, no. 3 (2005): 251-276.

48 Richard Ekman and Stephen Pelletier, "Assessing Student Learning: A Work in Progress," *Change: The Magazine of Higher Learning* 40, no. 4 (2008): 14–19.

49 One particularly effective president I observed presented arguments against, as well as for, each proposal he brought to the board.

50 "New National Alliance Plans to Promote Measurement of Student Learning," *News Blog, The Chronicle of Higher Education,* October 13, 2008, http://chronicle.com/ article/New-National-Alliance-Plans/41786/.

51 Numbers in parentheses are page numbers in the work by Chait et al.

52 Chait, Holland, and Taylor, *The Effective Board of Trustees*, 2, 5, 38–39. The reference to Ashford is to S. Ashford, "Self-assessments in Organizations," in *Research in Organizational Behavior* 11 (1989): 133–74.

17

PRESIDENTS WHO IMPLEMENT THE LONG-TERM MISSION

If it is important for an institution with a distinctive mission to have at least a core of faculty members committed to the mission, it is certainly even more important that the president and chief administrative officers, who take the leadership in developing and implementing procedures for searches for faculty and staff members, be committed to the institution's mission.

The President and the Mission

Institutional histories almost invariably refer to the influence of strong presidents, often presidents with long periods of service. Strong presidents can lead institutions away from distinctive emphases and toward popular values in their times. Or they can focus on the distinctive missions of their schools and provide innovative leadership for their faculties and constituents in doing what other schools are not doing.

The problem is that presidents are typically under enormous pressures to get top student applicants and to raise funds. In the Ivy League it is a matter of increasing the institution's selectivity, getting big gifts, and attracting leading scholars. In some other institutions, everyone cheers when the president leads the administrative team in increasing enrollments. Getting the students by September and the dollars by June are seen as marks of success. In formal evaluations and in less formal ways, presidents are rewarded by faculty members, students, boards, and constituents for meeting short-term goals.

As we have noted, the average American college or university president serves less than seven years, but steps set in motion by a given president often have implications for the long-term mission fulfillment of the president's institution that are visible only decades later.

In American governance arrangements, the lay board is supposed to represent the longer-term interests of the mandating society.[1] The board has the ultimate responsibility for appointing and monitoring the work of the president. The board needs a strong president. If the president is a weak leader, the board may find that its decisions are simply not effectively implemented. But a strong president without support from somewhere for work on long-term goals can easily give priority to work toward short-term goals that seem to have everyone's support. When the president is a strong leader, the board may need to be a strong board if it is to provide a context in which its president has a support base for articulating and implementing long-term perspectives in its decision-making.

If the school is a church college or university, having a strong president and staff committed to the long-term mission accomplishment of the church and its school is especially important. If the church and school invoke the name of Jesus Christ in calling themselves Christian, they will have to remind themselves that Jesus Christ himself was not a success by some short-term criteria. With a strong board, a strong president and staff team can be a tremendous resource to a church as it seeks to meet new challenges and to achieve long-term objectives.

Chapter 4 observed that the "liberal arts college" and the "research university" are well established institutions of the larger American society. Individual colleges and universities exist in organizational fields. Contemporary organizational theorists identify three principal ways that schools in these organizational fields relate to their environments:

1. Through the influence of the societal institutions in the organizational field with which they are identified. For a liberal arts college, that means that there are general understandings on roles and expectations held by staff members of other liberal arts colleges, by members of the professional and trade

organizations of their faculty and staff members, and by their students, parents of their students, donors, and society at large.

2. Through the formal governance arrangements in which representatives of the societies to which they are accountable make major decisions (e.g., boards, presidents).

3. Through market forces (e.g., the availability of personnel, students, and dollars, and the need to attract resources).

If a college or university is affiliated with a church and if a core of the school's staff members and students participate in the life, culture, and mission of the church, the influence of the church's culture will be a significant environmental influence on the school quite apart from formal governance arrangements and market forces. If, however, those responsible for the school's leadership have neglected to provide for this core of staff members and students, and if this core is missing, there is little those responsible for the governance of the school can do to implement a distinctive school mission. As Chapter 13 indicated, a school that wants to be distinctive must have at least a core of faculty and other staff members committed to the school's mission. The role of the president and the president's administrative officers is crucial partly because these officers can take leadership in implementing faculty and staff recruitment policies and procedures that further the school's achievement of its mission.

The president's role is also critical in the second and third of the above-mentioned ways in which the school relates to its environment. In American governance arrangements, the lay board is to represent the mandating society and the board appoints a president to function on its behalf in implementing its actions and in monitoring the work of the school between board sessions. The administrative officers formulate proposals for carrying out the mission of the institution in the context of changing market and other environmental forces. The environmental forces can be challenging. Responding to them requires imagination and creativity, as well as steadiness and trustworthiness.

Among all the characteristics of desirable academic leadership which can be listed, I find a combination of two particularly important:

- Vision. Initiative in suggesting and proposing possibilities for the future.

- Ability to listen sensitively and non-defensively when others test and comment—and even propose alternatives to the leader's ideas—as they all consider steps forward.

A strong board in a symbiotic relationship with a strong president and staff team can be an invaluable resource to a church as it seeks to achieve its objectives and meet new challenges.

Presidential Searches

Some of the considerations mentioned earlier in connection with faculty searches are even more important in presidential searches.

From the outset, the process should be projected as a search, not a selection.[2] Candidates who apply in response to an advertisement of a vacancy should be given equal consideration, but the process must not be viewed as a selection from a list of candidates who apply. The strongest prospect in a search may be an administrator who has a good job, who is doing well, and who does not want to jeopardize relationships with his or her present associates by publicly declaring interest in a change. A search committee or its representatives have to take the initiative if contacts are to be made with such prospects.

There is very frequently a tension between the interest of faculty members and other major constituents in having a chance to visit with several leading prospects, on the one hand, and the unwillingness of some of the strongest prospects to engage in a public "political" and competitive process involving a number of candidates, on the other. Strong prospects with good jobs are frequently willing to "go public" and accept affirmative or negative responses from board and campus people if they are presented as single candidates of choice, but some withdraw their names from consideration if they are expected to campaign publicly in a larger field.

In the case of a church-related institution, the search committee needs to be carefully formed in such a way as to have the confidence of church people, the boards, faculty members, and other important constituents. In the light of the fact that some church and campus people have the impression that searches should be completely open and participatory, from the outset the boards and search committee should weigh the alternatives and air the ground rules for the search with the faculty and other interested groups. Everyone needs to understand in advance that an open competition involving public appearances by several final candidates may mean that some of the strongest prospects may be unavailable, and, on the other hand, that a process in which a search committee works in confidence and presents a single candidate at a time may feel like "secrecy" and "intrigue" to some constituents who have not reflected seriously on the alternatives. Being clear from the outset on the pros and cons and on the process to be actually followed in a given search can help to minimize criticism of the process in the later stages of the search and can maximize the possibility that the institution will secure the strong leadership it needs.

The way a church views its schools' presidents can be seen partly in the way the school leaders are authenticated. Installation services can convey the impression to participants and viewers that the candidate is being authenticated ("ordained," in some traditions) as a church person in the context of the larger church within which he or she will find his life and mission—or just traditionally inaugurated as an educational leader in the circle of his or her institutional peers.

Enlarging the Pool

Selingo summarizes a 2006 conference in these words: "Unless campus leaders do more to identify and nurture new talent, higher education will face a leadership crisis in the coming decades as the baby-boom generation of college administrators retires and the pool of potential replacements shrinks."[3]

Americans generally have ambivalent feelings about their leaders in politics and culture, as well as in education. Americans say they want strong leaders, but their trust in leaders in many spheres of public life has plummeted in recent years. The President Nixon hearings, the impeachment of President Clinton, the Iraq War, the scandals in the Roman Catholic Church, the indictments of CEOs of leading corporations, and the current financial crisis have exacerbated trends in public opinion that were developing before the late 1990s.

When I was in institutional academic administration decades ago, faculty members tended to say, "We are not sure why Dean Meyer did such-and-such, but he probably knows something we don't know—he probably knows what he is doing!" Few academic vice presidents and deans are enjoying that kind of benefit of the doubt these days.[4] One consequence is that today's administrators feel that they must, out of fear of attacks from special interest groups and perhaps even legal liability, "play it close to the book." They are tempted to be cautious and, in the end, to exercise less creative leadership. Some abuses of power are no doubt avoided, but, in the long run, we end up with an overdependence on quantitative metrics that can be documented rather than important qualitative considerations. We end up with fewer gifted candidates who want to be administrators. And everyone loses when educational institutions do not have the benefits of strong and creative leadership.

In the cultures of research universities, faculty members often view teaching as a necessary evil and "administration" as a bad word. Career paths through research to full professorship are clear. Rewards for taking time for good teaching are typically less evident, and paths beyond departmental chairing to institutional administration are still less clear.

Studies of faculty roles and rewards show that, in spite of the culture of academia, some faculty members actually (sometimes secretly) find more fulfillment in their teaching than in their research. And some find the kind of administration that builds teams and helps staff members be what they can be to be exciting and rewarding. How can those interested in and showing promise for administrative work be identified? How can they prepare for roles in administration? In particular, how can the pool of vice presidential and presidential candidates be enlarged?

Sociologist Wittberg, in wrestling with these questions,[5] reports a lack of informal mentoring, of formal training, and of a "theology . . . that values administration." She concludes:

> It is no longer possible simply to place underqualified members into administrative positions there, and then mentor or educate them afterward. This implies that:
>
> - The administrative and board needs of sponsored institutions need to be anticipated years ahead of time and members encouraged to undertake the extensive training necessary to meet them.
> - Theologians within each denomination might be encouraged to develop . . . a theology [of institutions].

The North Central Association of Colleges and Secondary Schools used to sponsor month-long workshops for leaders of institutional self-studies and others interested in larger educational issues, as well as for presidents- and vice-presidents-elect. Institutional and denominational administrators could identify younger faculty members and administrators and financially support their participation in workshops of these kinds.

With Lilly Endowment support, the Council of Independent Colleges (CIC)[6] is currently sponsoring a "Presidential Vocation and Institutional Mission" seminar-based program "designed to help prospective college and university presidents clarify their own sense of personal vocation, and to weigh it in the context of the missions of institutions they lead and might lead in the future."

The American Council on Education and the CIC sponsor short workshops for department chairs. Forward-looking educational leaders can see if regional and national associations and university departments of higher education are offering workshops to help candidates who show promise for work in administration explore their interests. A goal for a board working in a long-term perspective would be to enlarge the pool of good prospects for future leadership.

Planning Processes and Performance Reviews

One way in which the leadership of presidents and other chief administrators can be enhanced is through regular and routine planning processes, including performance reviews scheduled for perhaps every three or four years. Chapter 16 refers to such reviews as a responsibility of a board.

In a church school, a small committee appointed by the board or boards can interview faculty members, representative church leaders, and other constituents and then propose course corrections and other projections for the future. The past cannot be changed. The focus is on learning from the experience of the past in order to make timely course corrections— or changes of personnel, in the unusual circumstances where this is indicated—as an institution prepares for the future.

The processes to be followed should be articulated before a new president or other administrator begins the executive's first term of service. Announcements at the time of actual reviews should make it clear that the routine reviews are matters of regular policy—that they are not implemented only when there are suspected problems in the work of the administrator or the institution.

Where the administrator's continued service is planned, a review can help an administrator make course corrections before problems become serious. Almost any president worthy of the name must make some decisions that are unpopular with someone. A review can strengthen the hand of a board and its president. When an individual or a small special-interest group criticizes an administrator for taking an action they dislike, the board and president can respond with solid data on the opinions of the large majority of those it surveyed at the time of the last performance review.

The greatest dangers in performance reviews are that inexperienced and ill-prepared committees have sometimes followed procedures that have done more harm than good. They have sometimes pulled the plant up by its roots to see whether it was growing. In some instances, for example, they have tried to gain information by using top-of-the-head responses to written questionnaires rather than structured personal or telephone interviews in which they could pursue reasons for responses. In some cases, committees have even used anonymous questionnaires in which respondents have voiced what looked like the same criticism but for opposite reasons. In one situation, for example, two respondents checking "unwise use of time" included one respondent who meant the president was spending too much time in fund-raising with constituents off campus, and another who meant that the president was not spending enough time in raising funds off campus. Both criticisms were then chalked up as marks against the president!

Some review and planning committees proceeding without adequate orientation have included undigested survey data in their reporting, rather than their own considered conclusions and recommendations. In one situation, for example, a committee's draft report said that a faculty member felt that the president was spending too much time involving himself in faculty members' personal lives. The committee was asked to check into that criticism further and to bring its own assessment. It turned out that the criticism was voiced by only one faculty member—one who was unhappy about having been disciplined for sexual harassment!

An administrator implementing actions of a board or otherwise handling administrative tasks responsibly will from time to time make some people unhappy. The board-appointed committee conducting a review must not report "Gallup Poll" data to the board. It cannot criticize its administrator for doing what the board asked the administrator to do in implementing unpopular board decisions if it wants its administrator to exercise effective leadership on its behalf!

Most administrators already have heavy day-to-day responsibilities. In their performance reviews, boards of church schools will be especially interested in the degree to which their presidents and other chief administrative officers are able to withstand pressures for short-term rewards and implement effectively policies and practices that can lead to good church-school relationships over the long term.

Chapter 17 Endnotes

1 The focus here is on nonprofit boards. Corporate for-profit boards are supposed to be representing the interests of stockholders. Some of the weaknesses in for-profit boards are to be found in the nonprofit sector as well.

2 This is also one of the main themes of Marchese and Lawrence, *The Search Committee Handbook: A Guide to Recruiting Administrators.*

3 Jeffrey Selingo, "Colleges Must Plan Better to Attract and Keep Key Personnel, Panel Speakers Say," *Today's News, The Chronicle of Higher Education,* July 13, 2006. See also David Mead-Fox, "Tackling the Leadership Scarcity," *The Chronicle of Higher Education,* April 14, 2009, http://chronicle.com/article/Tackling-the-Leadership-Sca/44809/.

4 "'Search and destroy' is how the late Harvard sociologist David Riesman characterized our employment of administrators" (Marchese and Lawrence, *The Search Committee Handbook: A Guide to Recruiting Administrators*, 9). Marchese et al. also speak of the "recent sharp decline in the size of applicant pools for administrative posts. . . . In 1987, search committees placed ads and watched confidently as 100 to 200 applications arrived in the mail. Today, the same ads might bring 20 to 40 applications" (ix).

5 Patricia Wittberg, *From Piety to Professionalism—And Back? Transformations of Organized Religious Virtuosity* (Lanham, MD: Lexington Books, 2006), 232–33, 278.

6 One Dupont Circle, NW, Suite 320, Washington, DC 20036–1142.

18

Churches That Want Schools with a Difference

A school needs constituencies that want it to exist and are ready to give it tangible support. Somebody has to want the school to exist. If a school with a distinctive mission is to survive and thrive, it will need to have supporters and prospective students who want to have a school with that mission now and in the foreseeable future.

A College and Its Environments

A college or university relates to its environments in several ways: through market forces, through the participation of its staff members in professional cultures in its institutional environment, and through formal governance arrangements.

If a church with a distinctive culture has founded or is a significant part of the environment of a college or university, the church's culture can influence the school quite apart from formal governance arrangements and market forces. The influence of the church's culture can, however, change over time. Indeed, as we have seen, the typical story of institutions historically has been one of increasing institutional independence and gradual dissociation, with an increasing vagueness and lack of specificity in church identifiers. Some churches that have existed in cultural enclaves historically are finding that their members are now increasingly at home in the

American mainstream. Their young people may be spending more time watching TV than they spend in school. They are no longer living in the sub-cultures of their parents.

For churches that see their contributions as starting schools and then releasing them to merge with the cultural streams in the larger society, dis-sociation will be seen as a realization of their visions for their institutions. But some church and school leaders see their schools as having more dis-tinctive missions and church relationships that they want to continue into the foreseeable longer-term future. In these situations, formal relationships, such as those discussed later in this chapter, can be important.

Whether their church-school relationships are formal or informal, church and school leaders need to be sure they are clear and that they pro-vide for the implementation of their intentions for the longer term.

Colleges That Create Their Own Constituencies

Some colleges, like Wheaton (Illinois), Westmont, and Gordon have no formal ties with denominations but have, instead, identified themselves with Christian sub-populations in the larger American society.

As we have seen, the earliest American universities began in a time when it was assumed that the state and the larger society were generally Christian—indeed, Protestant. Some of them were begun as institutions with ties to spe-cific churches. As their ties with the churches of their origins loosened and they became more independent, they could still assume that they were a part of the general Protestant Christian society of their times. People assumed that an American institution could be Christian and Protestant without being very specific about what that meant and without being related to a particular church, since the whole society was dominated by Protestant Christians.

The story of these leading American universities has been told many times.[1] With the growing awareness and recognition of the pluralism of the American society, especially in the post-World War II years, the continued dominance of the Christendom of earlier times could no longer be assumed. The reliance of many mainline institutions on the Protestant establishment of their earlier years became a factor in their secularization.

However, other independent institutions have identified themselves as generally Christian, but have been closely related to Evangelical Protestant American subcultures. Some of them have moved from formal denomina-tional relationships to independence only relatively recently. Although strong conservative Protestant sub-populations exist in America, there are also strong pressures toward conformity to prevailing standards of academic excellence and to acculturation in the larger American environment.

Institutions that are not related to specific denominations have sometimes tried to maintain a Christian identity by defining themselves in terms of written creedal statements denominating what they believe to be foundational Christian beliefs. They seek to maintain a clear identity in the face of acculturation forces by recruiting faculty members and administrators who agree with their beliefs and by creating or denominating their own circles of supporters. They create "interdenominational denominations," so to speak. Some have created strong supporting constituencies. Sometimes these organizations have depended heavily on the existence of regional Evangelical Protestant "establishment subcultures," as one Baptist researcher has described them.[2] Sometimes these schools were founded by charismatic leaders and have been led by popular administrators.

In recent decades, denominational categories as identifiers for prospective students or donors have become less useful than they were earlier. Denominationalism has declined. Colleges and universities cannot count on denominational support to the degree that they once did. Members are increasingly mobile and ready to move from one denominational family to another. And consultants in marketing increasingly emphasize "branding"—which may involve identifying a school or a church body in terms of characteristics that can be understood in the market rather than in terms of traditional denominational categories.

A prospective student used to attend a college because it was the closest Methodist or Presbyterian college. Now that prospective student is more likely to attend a college near his or her home because it has a recognized social work program, a reputation for an emphasis on environmental science, or a curriculum in peace and conflict studies.

One can view these trends as good or bad. On one hand, the need to develop loyalties and relationships apart from traditional and official denominational channels can pose a challenge for churches and schools. On the other, the opportunity to express the special character and distinctive mission of a school or church in terms that are understood on the wider contemporary scene is an opportunity to clarify and focus the organization's mission both for the benefit of those inside the organization and of those without.

To maintain distinctive missions and cultures, independent colleges of these latter types, like other institutions, still need to meet new challenges over the long term in the face of the forces toward academic and societal conformity. We are living in times when formerly homogeneous environments are becoming increasingly pluralistic. American public and private colleges and universities are becoming more alike in the diversity of their sources of financial support and in serving students representative of the American society at large. When we examine trends in some colleges and universities that seem very conservative and traditional, we sometimes observe longer-term movement away from their distinctive characteristics and in the direction of conformity to the larger culture.

Formal Church-School Relationships as a Variable

In the 1970s, Robert Pace of the University of California at Los Angeles, perhaps the leading researcher on campus climates at that time, studied the correlation of Protestant college climate with specific dimensions of church relatedness. He published his empirical findings in a book on Protestant colleges in the Carnegie Commission on Higher Education series. He wrote: "One finds that the more firmly and zealously a college is related to a church the more clearly it emerges as a distinctive college environment."[3]

In a project at Stanford, Wade Cole studied tribal, historically African American, and "mainstream" colleges. He found that formal sponsorship made a curricular difference. Native American tribal colleges had ten times as many ethnocentric courses. Compared with mainstream colleges, privately controlled African American colleges offered fifteen percent more Afrocentric courses, while publicly controlled African American colleges offered seventy-three fewer courses of that kind.[4]

In a three-year study of 179 colleges that classified themselves as "Christian," Walter Hobbs and Richard Meeth reported major program differences between "colleges-of-the-denomination," on the one hand, and colleges that are more loosely denominationally-affiliated or not affiliated with a denomination, on the other. Hobbs and Meeth found that ". . . the nature of their church connection makes a difference in the substantive emphases they pursue."[5]

The degree to which formal relationships of the kind Pace and Hobbs and Meeth studied help colleges engage in distinctive missions over longer periods of time merits further study.

Clarity in Responsibility

Some denominations have specific sponsorship relationships with schools. Churches that lend their names to schools need to have structures that assure that they can be responsible for actions carried out in their name.

Churches are confronted with an increasing number of legal challenges. Assigning responsibilities to institutional administrators and board members without adequate mechanisms for continuing church accountability can make a church legally vulnerable to ascending liability litigation.

With the erosion of the doctrine of "charitable immunity," the lawsuit that has, more than any other, brought religious denominations to the awareness of their legal liability is Barr v. United Methodist Church, the 1979 "Pacific Homes" case. The church-related retirement homes in California made unwise contracts they could not fulfill with retirees. Residents lived longer than their actuarial estimates had projected. The case was aired on CBS' "Sixty Minutes" and was a nightmare for the church. "Damages sought by the plaintiffs exceeded $260 million, and the legal expenses incurred by various boards and agencies of the United Methodist Church . . . reached $900,000 in less than two years of litigation."[6] Edward Gaffney notes that the petition to the United States Supreme Court for a writ of a certiorari stated: "This is the first time in history that a major international religious denomination has been held to be suable as an 'unincorporated association.'" He continues: "Other denominations could be liable for the contracts . . . of thousands of schools, hospitals, homes, colleges, and agencies where the relationship is akin to that of Pacific Homes."[7]

Another case in which a religious body was held responsible occurred in Texas. When the Jesuits let a high school say it was a Jesuit school, "individual trustees and administrators were joined as defendants in several religious bodies which were alleged . . . to have joined together . . . in committing . . . acts that led to the financial collapse of the school."[8]

If a significant church relationship is intended, both church and school will want to know what that relationship is. Minimally, for example, church articles of incorporation and bylaws should outline the desired arrangements clearly.

Moots and Gaffney write:

It is also true that, like nuclear deterrents, existing legal powers may not readily be used. Even if the related religious body holds the legal ability [and responsibility] to compel a certain course of action by the college, there are powerful forces, both formal and informal, which may qualify or negate that power. The influence of an accrediting agency or governmental body, the views of faculty, students, or a class of influential donors, the probability of adverse publicity in the local community or within a certain constituency, threat of AAUP censure, the cost and delay of lawsuits, and a multitude of other constantly changing factors may preclude the exercise of actual legal power held by a sponsoring religious body.[9]

As they say, you can't use an axe when you need a surgeon's knife. You really don't want to kill a mosquito on a friend with a baseball bat.

Moots and Gaffney note that "the often-used requirement that a certain number of directors or principal officers be members of a particular religious body provides no continuing legal control at all, in and of itself. So long as the directors or officers meet the membership requirement, they can make any decisions they wish."[10]

The concern here is not just hypothetical. Some churches sponsoring colleges and universities thought informal understandings were adequate, but then in the past two decades they have sometimes realized that their institutions were able to take unanticipated actions, including dissociation and independence from their churches. Churches have been faced with expensive and unexpected lawsuits in recent years—sometimes in an attempt to retain relationships with schools they founded, and sometimes because they found themselves liable for institutional actions for which they had no ways of assuming responsibility. Clarity in documents outlining intended and realistic church-school relationships is important.

Past Patterns of Abdication of Responsibility

Dittmar observes that the "sole impetus" for work on a church affiliation document at Waynesburg came from college rather than church leaders. He writes:

> . . . Scholars who have studied the secularization of church-related colleges maintain that such mainline denominations, during the twentieth century, became increasingly less concerned with maintaining strong ties with their 'church-related' colleges for a variety of reasons including an increasing inability to provide fiscal support and a diminishing view of the college as an important mission of the Church.[11]

Historically, churches have often tended to abdicate their responsibilities and to ask the presidents of their institutions—often loyal church leaders—to fend for themselves. The administrators have an essential role, but it cannot be coalesced with the role of keeping the long-term goals of the enterprise in focus and assuring their implementation. Many churches have tried to cut expenses by asking administrators to combine roles that are not easily combined—such as asking presidents to think in terms of the long-term goals of the church while they are simultaneously supposed to be advancing the short-term interests and serving the short-term needs of their institutions.[12]

The president of one college I visited pleaded with the leaders of his denomination for an advisory committee of churchwide leaders who could help him and his institution keep church interests and needs in sharp focus. He was told that the denomination had very tight budgets and could not give him an advisory committee. The president was serious. He took counsel widely and by himself formed an institutionally based advisory committee of top denominational leaders. But what was the church saying when it would not take responsibility for speaking for itself?

I have noted that some denominations have assumed that associations of presidents could handle the churches' interests. But if presidents have a special responsibility for focusing on the short-term interests of their institutions, although associations of these officers can help focus trans-institutional interests, they can also, on the other hand, tend to increase the focus on short-term interests.

If a church sees having colleges or universities as a priority way of working with its future members and leaders and as an important way of sponsoring "intellectual workshops" of academics to help it meet the challenges of changing times, it will have to designate a church board, commission, committee, or agency with the resources it needs to articulate and implement its interests and goals. Doing this has a cost. Not doing this also has a cost. It has frequently meant that the church was spreading its resources through a proliferation of institutions and programs, or that it did not have the colleges and universities it needed when it needed them. Long-term church perspectives got lost.

Contributions: An Expression of a Church's Stake

Supporting churches have often been interested in finding ways of reducing their operating contributions to their schools. They have sometimes looked with envy at the large and highly competent fund-raising staffs of their schools and felt that it did not make any sense for their modestly staffed denominational offices to be sharing the hard-earned products of their church fund-raising with their already more affluent schools. Churches have frequently encouraged their school administrators to seek all the outside funds they could get. Initially it meant that the church benefited from having a church institution for which it needed to supply little financial support. But then, as the formal financial support from the regular church sources decreased over time, the closeness of school to church also decreased and the school and church found themselves, sometimes belatedly, on the well-worn path toward unintended dissociation.

Financial support is not as important as faculty commitment and some other factors for a church wanting to sponsor a school. A church can be influential in the life of a school, at least for a time, if the personnel and structures of relationship provide for an important church role. A church can almost leverage something with nothing, financially speaking. But financial disengagement has historically, along with other factors, contributed to the distancing of schools from their churches.

The Canadian denominational university cited in Chapter 10 as an instance of dissociation sought financial disengagement, finally, in order to get increased governmental support. The news item that appeared in the media said that it "may follow the example of other U.S. and Canadian church-related colleges and drop its church affiliation in order to qualify for greater increased government aid."[13]

Reporting Support from Individual Church Members

A problem has frequently arisen from the current practice among many development officers not to report as church contributions the financial contributions that come directly from church members who are also alumni or friends. Churches that provide offering-plate support for their schools are expressing their corporate support in a significant and tangible way, but contributions from church individuals can also be an expression of church support.

In some denominations, the preferred pattern is that church schools receive little funding through church offices, but very substantial sums from many deeply committed members who are giving to the schools as part of the work of the church. Some denominations encourage their members to give in this way. There are tax advantages in some states. When the church members are alumni, for example, are the members giving (1) as alumni first and Christian church members second, or are they giving (2) primarily as church members with a special awareness of the mission and contribution of the school because they are also alumni?

How should financial contributions from individual church members who are also alumni or friends be counted? At a college I once visited, the president told me, "We don't need the church. We have thirty donors and can operate without the church." I asked to see the list of the thirty donors. They were from different parts of the country. We looked at them one by one. Every one was a committed and an active member of the supporting church! Those we knew would certainly not have been giving to their college as they were if they were not seeing this as giving to their church's work. Although they could have been giving more through their congregations, most were probably already giving as much through their congregations as they thought they could without skewing their congregational budgets.

College and university contributions can be categorized in various ways as segmented approaches are made to various constituents—e.g., some donors may merit more personal approaches than others—but institutions and churches need to recognize church-inspired dollar flows regardless of their routing.

Denominations differ. Where a church group sees itself as having countercultural institutions as parts of a larger countercultural church mission, and where it encourages its members to give directly to its institutions as a part of their church giving, the church can well ask in turn that its institutions record the church affiliations of its individual donors in its computer databases and report the total church support it is receiving from church individuals and groups. Both church and institutions can then monitor longer-term trends in the total support that church people are giving to the institutions, as well as the part of that support that is flowing through offering plates and formal church channels.

I referred earlier to a budget crisis in 1993 and a time of re-structuring in the Presbyterian Church U.S.A. In recent years, college and university education has not been seen as one of the Presbyterian Church's priority denominational missions. Its colleges and universities have been asked to seek their own support. But the institutions have been free to use the name of the denomination in their attempts to maximize their contributions from individual church donors, and their members have responded. Presbyterian Church members may be giving more to their colleges and universities than to any other causes outside their local congregations! From one point of view, the net effect of the Presbyterian Church's actions has been to allow institutions, from many of which it is distancing itself, to make special appeals for church funds while the funding going to efforts and programs the denomination has designated as having priority are forced into serious cutbacks. The Presbyterian Church may be giving mixed signals to its members concerning their giving: that their institutions can appeal for funds as Presbyterian Church institutions but, at the same time, that these institutions are not engaged in missions the Presbyterian Church considers as having priority in the work of the church.

Why are many mainline Protestant churches suffering serious membership losses and denominational budget shortages? The major study to date of the Presbyterian Church U.S.A. concludes that the Presbyterian Church has failed to capture the interest and imagination of its young people with a distinctive vision of the relevance of its beliefs and practices for the future.[14] Could stronger relationships with higher education institutions that represent a more distinctive vision help the Presbyterian Church and some other mainline churches regain the interest and involvement of their young people in the life and work of their churches?

We have very recently observed some evidences of renewed and increased interest of some churches in their higher education institutions and their role in the future of the church.

Stewardship in the Use of Church Resources

Church donors, especially those with experience in business and the administration of large organizations, are interested in the degree to which the church's personnel and financial resources are used with a sense of stewardship in achieving church and school educational objectives.

Great numbers of American church colleges were founded in the nineteenth century. College communities on the frontier were relatively isolated from one another, and the patterns of autonomy and independence they initiated have continued to contribute to the structuring of church efforts in higher education until today.

One post-Christendom understanding of the church says that it should model in its own corporate life the order of God's intention for the larger society. It is to show as well as talk about how God intends human beings and groups to live and work together. Churches should do this in structuring their higher educational efforts, in discerning how many and what kinds of colleges and graduate/professional schools they need and then arranging for their relationships with needed institutions.

Some denominations have too many schools. Parsonage, Pattillo, and Mackenzie, the authors of the two major foundation-supported studies of American church-related higher education in the past half century, have all noted the contribution of patterns that have led to proliferation of efforts and to the weakness of the church's work in higher education.[15] The words of Pattillo and Mackenzie are still relevant:

> Some way must be found to control whimsical and unplanned founding of new institutions within denominations. We say this even though several of the newer colleges are highly significant ventures. Can anyone justify the operation of four Presbyterian colleges in Iowa, five United Presbyterian institutions in Missouri, nine Methodist colleges in North Carolina (including two brand-new ones), and three Roman Catholic colleges for women in the city of Milwaukee? Much of the damage was done in the nineteenth century, but such unplanned establishment of colleges is still going on in some churches.

We also may recall Philip Gleason's statement that "'proliferation' and 'duplication of effort'" have "militated against academic excellence in Catholic higher education."[16]

An important factor in a church's having strong church institutions is its ability to focus its resources on the missions of these institutions. The schools of some churches complain about a lack of support when the real problem is that the churches have more schools than they need or can reasonably support as church institutions. Some colleges and universities have complained about a lack of student applicants when the real problem has been that they have overbuilt. Sometimes short-term interests lie behind the founding of unneeded new programs and institutions and the pressures on existing institutions to expand. Some institutions have simply spent all of the funds they were able to acquire on expanding their programs and facilities without regard to the needs and missions of their churches.

In the public sector, university educators and state legislators have formed statewide boards of regents to provide for an alternative to line-item budgeting and control by legislators inexperienced in educational administration, on the one hand, and the proliferation of efforts and unbridled competition of public institutions, on the other. Taxpayers and legislatures have insisted on coordination in the public sector. The directors of both of the major foundation studies on American church-related higher education of the past half-century have observed that the church, too, must reexamine traditional and outdated patterns from the North American frontier, and adopt patterns that provide for the wise and effective use of church resources in meeting today's educational needs.[17]

If churches are to assess their needs, articulate their goals, and implement their decisions effectively, they cannot turn all responsibility for church education over to institutional administrators or associations of institutional administrators. The churches that see having educational institutions as part of their church missions will need to have their own boards or committees able to discern their church needs and implement their decisions. As discussed earlier, dual-board systems provide a very concrete way some denominations have taken responsibility for the use of their personnel and financial resources in implementing their church and school missions. This is a kind of practical counterpart to the statewide boards of regents common in the public sector. Savings through supporting a few strong schools rather than having a proliferation of initiatives and too many weak schools in places where they are not needed will not show up anywhere in a balance sheet, but they may be in the interest of a denomination and of its schools. In some cases they can be one of the very tangible long-term benefits to both the church and its schools of the work of an effective denominational agency.

The Study of Theological Education 1989–1995, a project of the Evangelical Lutheran Church in America, was a model of church initiative and leadership in educational planning. The project showed remarkable vision and leadership in its attempt to consolidate the work of its eight seminaries into a smaller number of "clusters" and to provide for having a few good programs rather than to have every seminary offering weak programs in every field. The Lutheran leaders in this effort avoided the temptation to propose a quick fix that would have resulted in little real change. They structured their moves toward their long-term goals in the form of steps to be taken over many years.[18]

Finally, where a denomination sees schools it founded as no longer central in its churchly mission and as now essentially independent, and where it now wants these institutions to gain their financial support from the society at large, rather than from church sources, the denomination may well require that the institutions refrain from any use of the denomination's name in their fund-raising efforts. One good reason for doing so is to avoid ascending liability for actions for which it exercises no governance responsibility, as well as to encourage its members to give to present church mission priorities rather than to institutions that should now be getting support from the society at large. Disengagement from worthy social institutions in which the church has pioneered can and should be done deliberately and with integrity.

Investment, not Charity

In the late 1990s, there was a bidding war between the major U.S. political parties over their support for education. Current budget deficits at the federal and state levels are now leading to cutbacks, but education is still seen by many as a key to leadership in the world of the future.

Churches with special missions should do realistic qualitative and quantitative assessments of possible returns on their investments in colleges and universities. Societal cost-benefit studies of the recent past can contribute ideas and formats for church studies. Churches need to consider the kinds of person- and thought-leadership they will need for their life and mission in the future and consider the types of investments that will best provide for those kinds of needed leadership.

Families do not put groceries or piano lessons for their children in their budgets as "benevolences."[19] Churches need to include education in their budgets, not as benevolences—"being charitable to someone else"—but as investments in their own corporate future roles and missions.

Peter Steinfels sees Catholic colleges and universities as crucial for the church's future in his recent bestseller, *A People Adrift: The Crisis of the Roman Catholic Church in America.*[20]

In the "Conclusions and Recommendations" of their study of church-related higher education, Pattillo and Mackenzie write:

> We think the time has come for most churches to reconsider their obligations to church-sponsored colleges and universities and to increase their appropriations substantially.[21]

A church and school with a distinctive mission can best leverage their assets by investing some of those assets in the preparation of leaders and members for the future.

Schools and the "Think-Tank" Mission

Many churches and church schools have not given the "think-tank" mission the attention and priority it should have. It is not just one mission option among many—it is a key element in healthy church-school relationships.

It is important for both church and school that a church school faculty and administration should be capable of and responsible for contributing significantly to denominational leadership as the church faces the challenges of the present and the future.

Although an educational organization is influenced by its environment, the influence does not need to flow only one way. An organization can help to create its environment.[22] Serving as a church think tank is one way of doing so.

Both churches and schools have responsibilities for passing learning and useful traditions of the past to future generations. But they both also must have feedback mechanisms and ways of implementing needed change in changing times. Church schools can serve as "eyes" and "ears" for their churches as they face the future together. State colleges and universities have responsibilities for serving the needs of the people of the states on which their future and the future of their fellow citizens depend. Similarly, church colleges and universities need to serve the churches upon whose health and support they depend.

In the face of school-church conflicts in recent years, some observers have said that the schools involved were too close to their churches to be academically free. One might approach the question from the opposite side by observing that perhaps the schools and churches had, over the years, allowed too great a distance to grow up between them and failed to see what was happening and to consider ways in which they could have been more mutually helpful before it was too late.

Manning Pattillo and Donald Mackenzie included a strongly worded recommendation in their 1966 Danforth Commission report. It is at least as relevant today as when it was first written:

> It is time for the colleges to turn their attention to the churches that have nurtured them and not merely regard the churches as sources of students and money. The grave problems faced by the churches have already been outlined. To reverse or redirect or adapt to a change in world view as profound as that through which we are passing cannot be simple. . . .
>
> In our judgment the faculties of church-related colleges are in the most favorable position to provide intellectual leadership in the study of the issues facing the church and the hammering out of proposals for action. College faculties include historians, philosophers,

sociologists, literary critics, political scientists, economists—scholars whose business it is to be sensitive to ideas and to understand
the meaning of the world around us. They are in touch with secular
thought, but at their best they care about the church and its future.

We urge the faculties of church-affiliated institutions to view
themselves as scholarly task forces for assessing the status of the
Christian Church in the changed and changing world.[23]

As with arranging for a new kind of faculty recruiting for teaching, providing for the "church think-tank" role of a school has implications for school
staffing. If a president and some key faculty members and administrators
are expected to be denominational resource persons and leaders as well as
academics, this expectation will need to be stated clearly in the job descriptions used in their recruitment. The interest and potential of various candidates for church as well as school roles will have to be significant criteria in
personnel searches.

Faculty members in various disciplines engage in contract work and outside consulting. Sometimes they and their students can engage in activities
of these kinds in connection with their regular teaching and research assignments. Indeed, such activities often contribute to lively teaching and significant research. Sometimes the ability to attract outside funding for research
weighs in tenure decisions. Sometimes students are especially interested in
sociological surveys or historical studies that are of interest to others, more
than in preparing papers that will only be put on the shelf or in archives. In
any case, activities that require extra time need to be included realistically
in overall staff time planning. If an important outside research or consulting
assignment takes extra time, arrangements need to be made to lighten the
staff members' loads at other points.

In one institution, the expectation that the president would be a denominational spokesperson in interchurch contacts led to the appointment of
a vice president to pick up part of the president's load. The outside representation contributed to the president's teaching and administrative work,
but it also required clock hours that needed to be counted and allocated
realistically.

Where a staff member's participation in denominational leadership is included within the staff person's job description, it should certainly be included, along with other assignments, in promotion and tenure
evaluations.

The way in which school faculties can be a think-tank resource for their churches depends not only on school arrangements, but also on the vision of the churches in eliciting the contributions of their school people. Scholars can be viewed like prophets in that their findings and observations ("prophecies") need to be tested. Those engaged in farther-out thinking and visioning are sometimes wrong or unhelpful. Neither church nor school should want the church to simply take whatever a scholar or team of scholars says without reflection and discernment. The processing and possible rejection of some findings does not need to involve personalities. It involves roles. Working at the edges of what is known is a part of the role of scholars; testing their observations is included in the roles of others in the church and society. Churches need the contributions of their scholars even when their specific contributions are affirmed only part of the time.

Most denominations have dual agency and ecclesial structures and the tendency has been for these to become increasingly distant from and unrelated to one another.[24] This trend is reasonable for denominations and institutions that want intentionally to move in the direction of dissociation. It is not necessarily a reasonable outcome for countercultural churches that want to have countercultural Christian institutions. Churches that want to utilize all their resources in facing the challenges of changing times should have institutional leaders and staff people who view contributions to and involvements in their churches as within their assignments.

Good church schools can play a vital role in helping a church stay on the cutting edge in the churchly mission in which both have significant parts and a long-term interest.

Covenants

Some denominations have moved toward formalizing their understandings with their colleges and universities by preparing formal agreements or "covenants" with their institutions. The significance of covenants in specific denominational settings depends on the nature of the particular items included in the agreements.

An annotated listing of typical items taken from current covenants (of "X Church") is as follows:

The college agrees to:

1. *Identify itself as related to the X Church in official documents.*
    This identification is significant if the meaning of relationship with the X Church is clear and the criteria for relationship

are understood. For example, at some point in the covenant there should be a specific reference to the way the college will relate to denominational boards or agencies.

2. *Be regionally accredited.*

A church and college need to know whether the church is responsible to evaluate the college's academic quality or whether the church accepts the word of the regional accreditation agencies for the evaluation of the academic part of its institution's program, however defined.

3. A. *Consider X members as it recruits students, faculty, staff, administrators, and trustees.*

If this item means only that searches would not discriminate against X members, this would be a very weak expectation. If this provision is intended to have greater significance, the expectations would need to be outlined clearly. Is or is not religious preference a factor in hiring?

or

B. *Have an institution in which a large majority of the faculty are Christians or members of a church.*

If no more than this would be said, one could assume that the faculty members might be of any American Christian denominations and might or might not share in any distinctive aspects of the particular mission of the X Church and its schools. A covenant provision on faculty recruitment ought to relate specifically to the institution's mission.[25]

4. *Include study of religion or other comprehensive perspectives within the required core curriculum.*

Would this be required of all students, regardless of their religious orientation and preference? Could this create problems? Some covenants include a curricular expectation; some do not. Some public and independent universities also have strong departments of religion and curricular offerings. However, they do not usually have curricular requirements in religion.

5. *Seek to provide an atmosphere conducive to religious life and growth.*

Many independent and some public institutions speak of "educating the whole person." Princeton University, which considers itself a secular university, nevertheless seeks to provide an atmosphere conducive to religious life and growth through its Department of Religion, its university-sponsored chapel and religious life program, and its Program of Jewish Studies and Center for Jewish Life. Would X Church be expecting more than this? If so, what?

6. *Provide intellectual stimulus to the X Church through research, publication, and by providing leaders, library resources, and a setting for some church activities and events.*

   As we have observed, this resource has frequently not been as significant a contribution of church schools in many denominations as it could be. Including it in more covenants could help. The Vatican has emphasized this mission of Roman Catholic colleges and universities.

7. *Through its president or his/her appointed representative, actively participate in the denomination's association of colleges and universities.*

   Expecting an institution to find an administrative appointee at some level to have this relationship with administrators of other denominational institutions would seem to be a minimal commitment. Depending on the particular phrasing and elaboration of this commitment, the provision might or might not have great significance for the life of the institution.

The church agrees to:

1. *Communicate to church governing bodies, congregations, and members an understanding of the college as an X Church-related college that provides students with an experience of living in a Christian community and a setting that provides for growth of the whole person: physically, spiritually, and intellectually.*

   Whether this commitment on the part of X Church has integrity depends on whether the church has ways of assuring that what it is affirming is correct. For example, what would it mean to say that an entering student would find an experience of living in a Christian community? Studies of the decades up to the 1990s tended to show that most students in most colleges and universities become less committed to religious beliefs and practices in the course of their undergraduate years.[26] More recent studies now report small increases in the value students attached to religion, but to religious values the students construct on their own, apart from traditional denominations.[27] Are there indications that students would typically experience a different kind of spiritual growth at X Church-related college? Does its X Church relationship make an actual difference in student outcomes?

2. *Work with college representatives in the recruitment of students for enrollment in the college.*

   Is the church able to make a difference at the student prospect and parent level in the choices of its young people? Is there clarity on the projected programming and on who will be budgeting for how much time and financing in the church's part of this effort?

3. *Encourage financial support for the college through congregational offerings, and through giving by individual church members to capital funds campaigns and deferred giving plans.*

   Church X needs to review carefully the present giving patterns of its congregations and members in the light of its discernment of all of its church priorities if it is to make this commitment with integrity. If a certain church effort is to be given more support, should another effort be given less? Or is the church really asking members to give more proportionately to all programs? Is this realistic? What have been the trends? What guidance is X Church seeking to give its members concerning the stewardship of their dollars?

Additional items that could be included in covenants are mentioned in the chapter on "Intervening in the System" later in this book.

With respect to the items above, X Church can appropriately ask questions such as the following: What is the margin of difference for a student attending this college as compared with the same student attending another college not related to X Church? How great an investment of dollars by X Church congregations and members is warranted by the evidence on the margin of difference?

The principal advantage of a covenant arrangement is that it can clarify specifically what the parties may expect of each other. If read carefully, a covenant can also imply what the parties may not expect of each other. A covenant is a basis for a significant relationship only if the covenant provisions are specific enough to be useful in guiding actual decision-making, if they provide for a relationship that has integrity and real meaning and significance for the parties, and if they provide a basis for periodic evaluation.

The principal disadvantage of an ad-hoc covenant approach to a formal relationship is that a covenant may focus the attention of the parties on what is to be gained in the short term rather than on elements in their longer-term relationship. As we have observed, one of the major occasions for unintended church-school dissociation over the long term is that both parties are subject to powerful short-term environmental forces. An ad hoc covenant can be changed rather easily by either party. It lasts only as long as both parties want it. But a covenant does not have to be an ad hoc covenant; it can be rooted in formal governance relationships.

Churches with long histories in American higher education have frequently been very reluctant to state that some of their historically church-related colleges and universities are no longer church-related in any meaningful sense. The churches are proud of the institutions they founded years ago. The churches are hesitant to recognize that times have changed and that some of their institutions may no longer want to be church-related. In any case, if churches and schools have covenants that are to be meaningful, the churches will need to have clear means of evaluating the observance of covenant provisions and removing with integrity the church "accreditation" of schools that are no longer interested in meaningful covenant agreements.

Apart from its value at a given moment in the lives of church and school, a covenant approach that is undertaken with integrity can also serve as an excellent means of transition as a church seeks to move toward more intentional long-term relationships with its colleges, universities, and seminaries, on the one hand, or toward the more intentional distancing from or secularization of those institutions, on the other.

A School That Is Part of a Church's Mission

Some churches that see their colleges and seminaries as integral parts of their churches' missions view the core communities of interested students and faculty members in their schools as "gatherings" or "congregatings" of God's people (in that sense, churchly), even though such communities in their schools would not be typical local congregations. The gatherings could be seen as having specific tasks and missions within the more holistic mission of the larger denominations in which they participate.

In a book reporting on their three-year study, Hobbs and Meeth make a major point of the differences in the academic programs and other characteristics between "colleges-of-a-denomination" and colleges that are "church-related."[28] There is a difference between a school that is viewed as an integral part of a larger church and an independent school that contracts or covenants with a church body. An overseas mission society of especially interested religious individuals is different from a mission board that is an integral part of a denomination's life and mission. There is a difference between a denominational mission board and a faith mission that might make ad hoc contracts or covenants with interested individuals. The mission board is an integral part of its denomination and related to holistic bodies (i.e., a denomination's general board) that represent the denomination. Similarly, there is a difference between an independent school and a school that is viewed as part of a church and its mission.

School and church people sometimes use a Pauline image[29] to refer to a church school as an arm of the church. Church schools viewed in this way as arms would not make covenants with church bodies as though they were equals. The relationship is not symmetrical. A body can exist without an arm; an arm of a body cannot exist without the rest of the body.

The advantages in a church-school relationship in which a core community at a school are seen as part of a church's mission are evident. The relationship can be stated clearly. A school that sees itself as distinctive can have a long-term rootage in a distinctive people with a history and a future and be less dependent on charismatic leadership that may be here today and gone tomorrow. It may be in a better position to withstand institutional and short-term environmental forces in the fulfillment of its longer-term mission. At their best, school and church can help one another respond in innovative and creative ways to the challenges of changing times.

The disadvantages of this model of church-school relationship are also evident. There are countless instances in the history of higher education when churches have interfered with good education at schools they have sponsored. Instances of these kinds have continued to the present.

In my view, the critical factor in determining whether or not it is advantageous for a school to be part of a church's mission is the nature of the church that sponsors the school.

The Character of the Church in the Relationship

Although we are living in a post-Christendom time, some churches still exhibit establishment characteristics of earlier times. Jesus Christ, whose name they carry, did not use the force of the governmental authorities of his time to force his beliefs on those with whom he came in contact. He gave people freedom for authentic decision and he accepted their decisions, even when it was clear to him that their decisions were not in their own or others' interest. He saw the possibility of using extraordinary powers to wield authority over others or to turn stones into bread to gain their support as temptations of the devil. Even when, in his last hours, he mentioned the thought of calling upon "legions of angels"[30] for what many would call legitimate self-defense, he did not do so.

Many of those who carry Jesus' name in our times nonetheless have difficulty allowing people to make authentic decisions of their own. Most mainline churches come from establishment traditions. Many conservative Christians have been quite ready to join evangelical or fundamentalist coalitions to enhance their political power over others. Some of our contemporaries continue to live in the world of Dostoevsky's Grand Inquisitor in wanting to force their ways on others because "the others don't or can't really understand what is for their own good." Many justify killing or even raining bombs on others they accuse of engaging in violent acts. Some kill others with whom they disagree in wars in the name of religion.

It is not hard to imagine that religious people with these orientations might cause problems when they sponsor schools and try to use them to impose their beliefs and practices on others. In these situations, the problem is not just with the relationship between church and school. The problem is much more fundamental—with the church itself.

Before advocating a close relationship between church and school, church and school leaders need to ask how the church in question understands being "Christian." How should the church give people the opportunity they need for authentic commitment? How does the church deal with pluralism, dissent, and conflict? Christians who have not gotten beyond the Crusades in their understanding of the Cross will do well, especially in our times, to reflect further on God's self-revelation in the One whose name they bear. We can all recognize differences among Christians on these questions and talk with one another seriously about the shape the church should take today.

School-Church Relationships in the Larger Picture

The development of clear school-church relationships is a part of the development of a more adequate institutionalization of "church college" or "church university" in the life of the church and in the larger society. If we want to move from where we are to where we would like to be, as we view missions for schools and churches in our times and models for church-school relationships, we need to be realistic in our assessment of the situations in which our different churches and schools find themselves at present and then advocate those models for lively, mutually health-giving relationships that are both appropriate to our present situations and that move us, however deliberately, toward our longer-term goals.

Chapter 18 Endnotes

1   George M. Marsden, "The Soul of the American University: A Historical Overview," in *The Secularization of the Academy*, ed. George M. Marsden and Bradley J. Longfield (New York: Oxford University Press, 1992), 9–45. Douglas Sloan, *Faith and Knowledge: Mainline Protestantism and American Higher Education* (Louisville , KY: Westminster John Knox Press, 1994).

2   Nancy Ammerman, "Living Together, Living Apart: Particularity and Pluralism in Christian Higher Education," Baylor University Sesquicentennial Symposium, October 1995.

3   Robert C. Pace, *Education and Evangelism: A Profile of Protestant Colleges*, ed. Clark Kerr, The Carnegie Commission on Higher Education (New York: McGraw-Hill, 1972), 37.

4   Wade M. Cole, "Accrediting Culture: An Analysis of Tribal and Historically Black College Curricula," *Sociology of Education* 79, no. 4 (2006): 355–387.

5   Walter C. Hobbs and Richard L. Meeth, *Diversity Among Christian Colleges* (Arlington, VA: Studies in Higher Education, 1980), 12, 18. Hobbs and Meeth were professors of higher education at the State University of New York at Buffalo. Their findings are supported in Earl McGrath's concluding chapter of their report. Donna Schaper, formerly area minister for the United Church of Christ in western Massachusetts and observer of the campus scene for years, emphasizes the difference between "organized religion" and a less-clear "spirituality" (Donna Schaper, "Me-First 'Spirituality' Is a Sorry Substitute for Organized Religion on Campuses," *The Chronicle of Higher Education*, August 18, 2000). William H. Willimon has said, "There are those college administrators and older academic intellectuals that still long for a kind of 'Let's all join hands around peace and love,' but that really is passé. Part of the joy of being religious is the particularities of our faith" (Beth McMurtrie, "Pluralism and Prayer under One Roof," *The Chronicle of Higher Education*, December 3, 1999).

6   Moots and Gaffney, *Church and Campus: Legal Issues in Religiously Affiliated Higher Education* (Notre Dame: University of Notre Dame Press, 1979), 11. At that time, Philip Moots and Edward Gaffney were director and associate director of the Center for Constitutional Studies at the University of Notre Dame.

7   Edward McGlynn Gaffney Jr. and Philip C. Sorensen, *Ascending Liability in Religious and Other Nonprofit Organizations*, Mercer Studies in Law and Religion (Macon, GA: Mercer University Press, 1984), 6, 13.

8   Moots and Gaffney, *Church and Campus*, 11.

9   Ibid., 6–7.

10   Ibid., 8.

11   James K. Dittmar, "Against All Odds: An Investigation into the Transformation of Waynesburg College," *Christian Higher Education* 8, no. 2 (2009): 85–114.

12   Within their institutions, some very small colleges have tried to save money by combining their development and business offices and found that that has not worked well. Development officers are supposed to share enthusiasm for their institutions and to expand their resources; business officers are responsible for being less exuberant about what might be and realistic about what can be done within the available resources. Both roles are important, but they are different. In a baseball park, a

ball team might try to combine the roles of first and second basemen, but the savings would come at the cost of more grounders becoming base hits!

13 The news item added, "Only 11 percent of the students are [affiliated with the denomination], so the transition to nonsectarian status should not be difficult."

14 Dean R. Hoge, Benton Johnson, and Donald A. Luidens, *Vanishing Boundaries: The Religion of Mainline Protestant Baby Boomers* (Louisville: Westminster John Knox Press, 1995).

15 Robert Rue Parsonage, ed. *Church Related Higher Education: Perceptions and Perspectives* (Valley Forge: Judson Press, 1978), 288–9; Manning M. Pattillo Jr. and Donald M. Mackenzie, *Church-Sponsored Higher Education in the United States: Report of the Danforth Commission* (Washington, DC: American Council on Education, 1966), 206–7.

16 Philip Gleason, "The American Background of *Ex corde Ecclesiae*: A Historical Perspective," in *Catholic Universities in Church and Society: A Dialogue on Ex corde Ecclesiae*, ed. John P. Langan (Washington, DC: Georgetown University Press, 1993), 5.

17 Pattillo and Mackenzie, *Church-Sponsored Higher Education in the United States: Report of the Danforth Commission*, 206–8; Parsonage, ed. *Church Related Higher Education*, 288–89.

18 "Faithful Leaders for a Changing World: Theological Education for Mission in the ELCA" (Chicago: Evangelical Lutheran Church in America, 1995), 40, and Phyllis Anderson, "ELCA Study of Theological Education 1989–1995: A Narrative Analysis of the Process" (Chicago: Evangelical Lutheran Church in America, 1998). The project director, Phyllis Anderson, is currently president of Pacific Lutheran Theological Seminary.

19 I am reminded of the poster of a tricycle in the middle of a sidewalk with the caption: "Of course children get in your way—but where are you going?"

20 (New York: Simon & Schuster Paperbacks, 2004).

21 Pattillo and Mackenzie, *Church-Sponsored Higher Education in the United States: Report of the Danforth Commission*, 207.

22 Scott, *Organizations: Rational, Natural, and Open Systems*, 146.

23 Pattillo and Mackenzie, *Church-Sponsored Higher Education in the United States: Report of the Danforth Commission* , 212–13.

24 "Contrary to how denominations usually are treated, they are not in general unitary organizations. Rather, they are essentially constituted by dual, parallel structures: a religious authority structure and an agency structure." Mark Chaves later qualifies this assertion: "Not all contemporary denominations are characterized by dual structure. . . . As organizations. . . unitary denominations are qualitatively different from dual-structured denominations" (Mark Chaves, "Denominations as Dual Structures: An Organizational Analysis," *Sociology of Religion* 54, no. 2 (1993): 147, 166).

25 The Council for Christian Colleges & Universities, for example, is a Christian association of institutions with employment policies as follows: "Member campuses have a continuing institutional policy and practice . . . to hire as full-time faculty members and administrators (non-hourly staff) only persons who profess faith in Jesus Christ" (321 8th Street NE, Washington, DC 20002).

26 Pascarella and Terenzini, *How College Affects Students: Findings and Insights from Twenty Years of Research*, 303.

27 Pascarella and Terenzini, *How College Affects Students: A Third Decade of Research* , 284–5.

28 Hobbs and Meeth, *Diversity Among Christian Colleges.*

29 Rom. 12:4–8; 1 Cor. 12:12–31.

30 Matt. 26:53.

19

INTERVENING IN THE SYSTEM

The goal of this book has been to move beyond history and analysis to suggesting actions that are practical and specific.

Actions

A summary listing of some actions that can be implemented by schools and churches wanting to have warm school-church relationships in the longer-term future is as follows:

1. *Implementing a "strategic faculty recruitment" alternative.*
   For the long run, developing a serious alternative to traditional faculty recruitment may be the most important single action in this list.
   The actual implementation of the alternative involves:
   - Creating a position and appointing a creative staff person or persons to work under the academic vice president and with the departments in the implementation of the alternative and
   - Raising designated endowment funding for the alternative as an investment in the long-term development of the institution.
2. *Board initiative in preparing, processing, adopting, and implementing twenty-year goals.*
   Traditional "public relations" mission statements have been vague. Documents that can serve to guide day-to-day

decision-making need to indicate (1) the relationships between church mission and school mission, (2) projections for the profile of students to be served, (3) arrangements for church financial support, and (4) school staffing for its think-tank service to the church. A board-appointed committee (e.g., a committee on the future of the college) and the board should provide leadership in preparing the initial drafts of long-term mission and planning documents. The board should then oversee a process of wide consultation with administrators, faculty members, and constituents that will lead to final statements for adoption.

In order to avoid vagueness, candid internal documents should be drafted before public relations documents for wider distribution are developed. What changes from present practices and trends are projected? How does this institution propose to be different from other institutions?

The documents should represent long-term projections of intentions twenty years into the future, and the twenty-year projections should then be reviewed and updated every one to three years in the light of progress.

After the initial adoption of documents, the board should spend at least half of each meeting in board-initiated agenda, including assessment of progress in attaining long-term objectives and preparation for mid-course changes in the light of experience. (See item 5 below.)

3. *Providing for effective church educational boards or commissions.* A denomination, conference, or middle-level judicatory that wants to relate to young people through its schools will need to play its part in its church-school relationships by having an appropriately staffed board or commission that can (1) articulate the church's interests and (2) establish and maintain relationships among its schools that further the church's missions in its educational work. The board or commission will need to have experienced educators in its professional staff. Included in the board's or commission's responsibilities is communicating with the church on the place of its schools, projecting realistically church financial support, and providing for stewardship in the use of church resources. A church educational board can help institutional boards function effectively.

4. *Changing from traditional "cheerleader" institutional boards to executive boards designed for effective decision-making.*
   Recent scandals have called attention to the need for change in traditional board structures. As observers have said for years, and as commissions responding to scandals have said more recently, a board or executive board needs to be structured with the size and composition needed for effective functioning. Board members may be legally liable. Boards should be structured in such a way as to enable their members to assume with integrity the responsibility they carry.

5. *Board or executive board reviewing, adopting, and implementing procedures for evaluating the work of its institution or institutions from year to year and over longer periods of time.*
   A board needs to take responsibility for its school's principal "product": student learning. How can a board and its faculty or faculties know how and what their students are actually learning? In the areas of research and service, how can a church-related board evaluate the contribution of its institution to the life and thought of its church, as well as its contribution to the larger society? How can it monitor trends?

   As its role is differentiated from the complementary role of the organization's administration, the board has a special responsibility for the longer-term existence, continuity, and direction of the organization. In the light of this responsibility, the board should review twenty-year data, as much as possible, and ask two questions: (1) Do we want the trend of the next twenty years to be like that of the past twenty? (2) If not, what do we need to do that is different?

   The evaluation of trends in a school's performance may require qualitative, as well as quantitative, methodologies, e.g., arrangements for first-hand interviews with students, recent alumni, and faculty members, as well as surveys.

6. *Nominating promising prospects and supporting their attendance at workshops to enlarge the pool of candidates for future faculty leadership and administrative assignments.*

7. *Providing for regular (e.g., three- or four-year) reviews of the work of its chief executive officer—its president—or officers, followed by timely course corrections.*

The review needs to be conducted in the context of the progress of the institution as a whole. Boards need to have and support executive officers who can effectively implement board actions.

8. *Board appointment of an effective "committee on the board" (sometimes referred to as "Governance Committee," "Personnel Committee," "Nominating and Orienting Committee," etc.).*
   The responsibility of nominating new board members and officers and considering the reappointment of continuing board members and officers in private consultation with each board member is particularly important. Two or three members of a board can function as an effective "committee on the board."

9. *Regular (e.g., every six years) use of an auditor for an evaluation of the functioning of the board.*
   A board that oversees the work of its faculty and administration should model good procedures in evaluating its own work. The use of an outside auditor of board functioning can avoid some of the problems traditionally experienced and inherent in board self-evaluation.

These proposals are not of equal importance. In the long term, having a way of developing faculty teams committed to the distinctive and countercultural missions of their schools may be the most important. On the other hand, even though it may not be the optimal arrangement, a school may work reasonably well with a large "cheerleading" board if it has a strong executive board, executive committee, or committee on the future of the college that leads the board in making important decisions. Having a student body with enough young people who are especially interested in the mission of the school may be helpful (and it may help a church with limited financial resources not to be using its scarce resources for the education of a sample of the American population at large), but this is not as important as having a faculty committed to the school's distinctive mission.

The proposals listed above are specific enough to serve as a checklist for churches and schools wanting to have strong church-school relationships over time. For example, a school will either have an "associate dean for strategic faculty recruitment," or it won't. A board or executive board will either be spending more than half of its meetings on board-initiated—rather than staff-initiated—agenda, or it won't. The board will work on and receive regular information on assessments of key objectives, such as student learning, or it won't. The board will have a board audit of its own functioning from time to time, or it won't. Individuals and groups within a church or other supporting constituency will either be maintaining or increasing their dollar financial support over time, or they won't. Trends of interest can be followed from year to year and over longer periods of time.

Systemic Change

The key elements in long-term church-school relationships are mutually reinforcing parts of a system. How can such systems be changed? As in family systems, an institutionalized organizational system is composed of interacting elements. Change can be initiated at different points. Change in one element can affect the equilibrium of the whole and can lead over time to change in other elements of the system.

In a church-related college, change can be initiated by a president who becomes aware of some of the dynamics of longer-term trends and who is willing to use some of his or her capital to intervene in spite of powerful pressures to work for short-term "success" from faculty members, constituents, students, and even, in some cases, the board. Or change can be triggered initially by a faculty researcher. A faculty historian or political scientist can highlight some recent trends at an institution,[1] or a sociologist or organizational theorist may call attention to the institutional dynamics involved and the way a university would need to make some changes if it did not want to simply succumb to almost universal institutional forces. Faculty scholars doing think-tank work for a church and its longer-term future may also turn their attention to the role of the school in the church's future and to initiatives that might enhance that role.

Church leaders might reflect on a cycle in which they are caught—e.g., that a church was reducing church financial support for a school that did not seem to be very different from other schools, while the school was simultaneously distancing itself from its church and relying increasingly on support from other constituencies because it was getting less and less support from the church. A church leader might take the lead in encouraging appropriate financial support for its schools, even though the schools were less distinctive than they could be. At the same time, the leader might invite their schools to play a greater role in furthering the life and mission of their church in the world.

Although boards have special responsibilities for the long-term mission fulfillment of their schools, it is hard for them to fill this role effectively.

Boards have only a few meetings each year. Board members are usually unpaid. They have other full-time jobs. Often they do not have data on longer-term trends. As in the case of other elements in a system, they cannot effect change alone, but they can take steps that initiate change. A board member has the advantage of distance and perspective. A board can ask for and insist on receiving needed data and information. A board member can ask hard questions: "Does the emperor really have any clothes on?" (In one board meeting I attended, the president said, "I believe we are wearing a bikini!")

Although accreditation processes usually tend to influence insecure institutions toward conforming to prevailing professional practices, rather than toward innovation or developing distinctive practices, I am aware of situations in which self-studies created an awareness of unintended and unwanted "mission drift" or in which possibilities for helpful change were suggested by visiting accreditation teams.

While change can be initiated at various points in a system, various participants in the system do usually have different ways in which they normally work most effectively. A board can play a major role in defining a school's mission and recruiting its key professional leaders. It can implement policies that, over time, influence the composition of the faculty and student body. It can monitor the interactions of the school with its environment and can initiate some needed course corrections. A president has a different role and different possibilities for effecting change. Faculty researchers and senate members have still different opportunities for making a difference. Since generations of students come with different interests and expectations, trying to relate to their changing needs can also stimulate change. Different participants in the system can utilize the opportunities afforded by their roles.

Clarifying Intentions

Churches should live in the present and future, not the past. In their present efforts and listings, churches should quit using the category "historically church-related" for their institutions. Some churches have been proud of having given birth to institutions that have become independent and, in some cases, academically excellent. Churches should be grateful for good non-church-related and public education. They need not do what others are ready and willing to do.

When a school founded by a church "goes secular," the church can send it forth with a blessing, even though the blessing may be tinged with some regrets. Maybe the departure has been caused partly by church actions that, by hindsight, are regrettable. Maybe the church failed to give adequate moral and financial support to its school or schools. If a church lists schools as church-related when the relationship is only historical, it opens itself to facing ascending liability suits, misleading publics, and sometimes facing other serious consequences of its refusal to accept reality.

Some churches have had close relationships with their colleges and universities to the present and are interested in new ways of working that will help them have good relationships in changing times. They are aware of past trends in the direction of dissociation and of present forces pushing them toward conformity. They want to learn from the experiences of others and chart new paths as they look to the future.

Some churches that decided several decades ago that higher education was not one of their priorities are now rethinking that decision. Some have a vestigial committee and staff person or persons in higher education and now would like to relate more helpfully to schools with which they were historically related and are still on their denominational lists as in some sense church-related. What can church-based educational leaders in these denominations do? When a church representative no longer has much of an influence on what the schools nominally related to the church are doing, what role can the church person play? Can the church representative be an agent of change in a system of that kind? Where can the church person begin?

In brainstorming interview sessions, we have received suggestions and gained some insights from denominational leaders in higher education who are interested in mutually health-giving relationships for the future.

- A church educational leader can initiate contacts with presidents and student affairs officers at church campuses and offer to use church media and events to inform prospective students of innovative and distinctive programs at these schools. Some schools might be sufficiently interested to help fund these church-initiated marketing and advocacy efforts.
- The church can offer scholarships to its members who want to attend the schools it is promoting.
- In cooperation with the administrators of the interested schools, the church can facilitate and encourage the formation of church student groups on these campuses. Some campus groups might be part of a national student organization that

provides for intercollegiate contacts and activities. In its student recruitment initiatives, the church might highlight the
possibilities at the campuses that had lively student peer
groups. Even if they are a small minority within a larger student body, a clustering of students with some shared church
interests and commitments on a campus can be a way of initiating some changes. Significant movements can be initiated by
relatively small minority groups.

- Some campuses might provide for small faculty groups of the
  kind funded at many campuses by the Lilly Endowment beginning in 1995 as "The Rhodes Regional Consultations on the
  Future of the Church-Related College."

In all of these activities, the church representatives have to work with integrity.
They cannot promote what doesn't exist. Some of the colleges and universities
on their "church-related" lists might be interested in cooperative efforts. Some
might not. If it is not related to a college in more immediate ways, a church must
assure itself, through procedures for reporting and campus visits—a kind of
church "accreditation"—that the schools it is promoting as cooperating with the
church are really working effectively in the cooperative efforts being promoted.
Churches should not engage in deceptive advertising.

A church can have good schools that deal with some areas of learning,
character development, and spiritual growth that cannot be dealt with adequately in the public sector. It can recognize this without denigrating public
education for what public schools can contribute and are contributing to the
society at large.

A church that has distanced itself from its schools in the past and now
wants to renew its higher educational relationships with young people can
ask schools with which it has had historical relationships whether they
want to be church-related in the present and foreseeable future—and by
whatever covenant provisions both see as reflecting reality and possibilities
for the future. The church must be ready to accept affirmative or negative
responses to initiatives of this kind. The church can then list and promote
as meaningfully "church-related" those institutions welcoming their church
relationships and those it sees as actually helping the church engage in the
church's mission in the world.

Renewing relationships that have become attenuated over time may
require faith and trust on the part of both church and school. The church may

be asked to support a school that does not yet fully embody their common vision. The school may be asked to trust a church that has not always been adequately supportive in the past and that as yet only partially realizes what the church could really be.

Chapter 19 Endnote

1   For example, Douglas Jacobsen, a political scientist, has commented on some trends
    at his institution in Richard T. Hughes and William B. Adrian, eds. *Models for Christian
    Higher Education: Strategies for Survival and Success in the Twenty-First Century*
    (Grand Rapids: Wm. B. Eerdmans, 1997), 341–2. Other faculty members comment on
    developments at their own institutions in this volume.

What Are the Prospects?

I do not believe the future is determined by the past. However, I believe we can best move forward in the future if we begin by facing realistically the available information on past trends and current experience.

New and renewed religious movements are springing up in our time. If the past is an indication, some of them will found schools. Over time, some of the new schools will eventually become accredited colleges and universities. And some new and formerly religious institutions will move toward dissociation and join the ranks of the thousands of independent or public higher education institutions in our society.

If some older or newer religious groups want to break away from the dissociation path and have healthy school-church relationships over longer periods of time, they will have to learn from the past and be prepared to make systemic changes in their ways of working in the future. They will have to be realistic both about the challenges, as well as the advantages, of the way colleges and universities are currently institutionalized in our society and about the environmental forces under which postsecondary institutions operate.

A religious group that is serious about a long-term relationship with interested young people and academics will have to see this as a significant mission and provide for leaders who understand the dynamics of school-church relationships. Short-term measures can, in the long term, result in the school's loss of its distinctive mission, "niche," and raison d'être.

A typical manufacturing firm needs to provide for research and development, as well as for an assembly line, if it wants to be prepared for longer-term future. An educational effort that wants to be different needs to provide for research on the experience of the past and for developing ways of working that meet the challenges of the future.

There continues to be a place for distinctive church colleges and universities. May this volume help church and school people who want to have good colleges and universities realize their intentions!

REFERENCES

Anderson, Phyllis. "ELCA Study of Theological Education 1989–1995: A Narrative Analysis of the Process." Chicago: Evangelical Lutheran Church in America, 1998.

Andringa, Robert C. "The State of Christian Higher Education: Thriving." Washington, DC: Council for Christian Colleges & Universities, 2003.

Astin, Alexander W. *Four Critical Years: Effects of College on Beliefs, Attitudes, and Knowledge.* San Francisco: Jossey-Bass, 1977.

_____. *What Matters in College? Four Critical Years Revisited.* The Jossey-Bass Higher and Adult Education Series. San Francisco: Jossey-Bass, 1993.

Barge, Scott. "Renegotiating the Goshen College—Mennonite Church Relationship: Harold S. Bender and Faculty Development at Goshen College, 1931–1944." *Mennonite Quarterly Review* 81, no. 4 (2007): 549–576.

Bellah, Robert N., et al. *Habits of the Heart: Individualism and Commitment in American Life.* Berkeley: University of California Press, 1985.

Benne, Robert. *Quality with Soul.* Grand Rapids: Eerdmans, 2001.

Berger, Peter L. "Protestantism and the Quest for Certainty." *The Christian Century* 115, no. 23 (1998): 782–791.

Berkhof, H. *Christ and the Powers.* Translated by John Howard Yoder. Scottdale, PA: Herald Press, 1962.

Blumenstyk, Goldie. "Why For-Profit Colleges Are Like Health Clubs." *The Chronicle of Higher Education*, May 5, 2006.

Bollag, Burton. "Scholars Kept Out." *The Chronicle of Higher Education*, June 15, 2007.

Budde, Michael L., and John Wright, eds. *Conflicting Allegiances: The Church-Based University in a Liberal Democratic Society.* Grand Rapids: Brazos Press, 2004.

Burtchaell, James Tunstead. "The Alienation of Christian Higher Education in America: Diagnosis and Prognosis." In *Schooling Christians: "Holy Experiments" in American Education*, edited by Stanley Hauerwas and John H. Westerhoff, 129–83. Grand Rapids: Wm. B. Eerdmans, 1992.

_____. *The Dying of the Light: The Disengagement of Colleges and Universities from Their Christian Churches.* Grand Rapids: Wm. B. Eerdmans, 1998.

_____. "Out of the Heartburn of the Church." *The Journal of College and University Law* 25, no. 4 (1999): 656–95.

Carnevale, Anthony P., and Richard A. Fry. "Crossing the Great Divide: Can We Achieve Equity When Generation Y Goes to College?" Princeton, NJ: Educational Testing Service, 2000.

Carver, John. *Boards That Make a Difference: A New Design for Leadership in Nonprofit and Public Organizations.* 2nd ed. The Jossey-Bass Nonprofit and Public Management Series. San Francisco: Jossey-Bass Inc., 1997.

Cavanaugh, William T. "Sailing Under True Colors: Academic Freedom and the Ecclesially Based University." In *Conflicting Allegiances: The Church-Based University in a Liberal Democratic Society*, edited by Michael L. Budde and John Wright, 31–52. Grand Rapids: Brazos Press, 2004.

Chait, Richard P., Thomas P. Holland, and Barbara E. Taylor. *The Effective Board of Trustees*. American Council of Education/Oryx Series on Higher Education. Phoenix: The Oryx Press, 1993.

Chait, Richard P. "When Trustees Blunder." *The Chronicle of Higher Education*, February 17, 2006.

Chait, Richard P., William P. Ryan, and Barbara E. Taylor. *Governance as Leadership: Reframing the Work of Nonprofit Boards*. Hoboken, NJ: John Wiley & Sons, Inc., 2005.

Chaves, Mark. "Denominations as Dual Structures: An Organizational Analysis." *Sociology of Religion* 54, no. 2 (1993): 147, 166.

_____. "Intraorganizational Power and Internal Secularization in Protestant Denominations." *American Journal of Sociology* 99, no. 1 (1993): 1–48.

Cherry, Conrad, Amanda Porterfield, and Betty A. Deberg. *Religion on Campus*. Chapel Hill, NC: University of North Carolina Press, 2003.

Chmela, Holli. "Foreign Detour en Route to a College Degree," *New York Times,* October 19, 2005.

Clark, Burton R. "Collegial Entrepreneurialism in Proactive Universities." *Change: The Magazine of Higher Learning, 32,* no. 1 (2000): 10–19.

Cole, Wade M. "Accrediting Culture: An Analysis of Tribal and Historically Black College Curricula." *Sociology of Education* 79, no. 4 (2006): 355–88.

Cothen, Grady C. *What Happened to the Southern Baptist Convention? A Memoir of the Controversy.* Macon, GA: Smyth & Helwys Publishing, 1993.

Cuninggim, Merrimon. *Uneasy Partners: The College and the Church.* Nashville: Abingdon Press, 1994.

_____. "Varieties of Church-Relatedness in Higher Education." In *Church Related Higher Education*, edited by Robert Rue Parsonage, 15–132. Valley Forge, PA: Judson Press, 1978.

Diekema, Anthony J. *Academic Freedom and Christian Scholarship.* Grand Rapids: Wm. B. Eerdmans, 2000.

Dittmar, James K. "Against All Odds: An Investigation into the Transformation of Waynesburg College." *Christian Higher Education* 8, no. 2 (2009): 85–114.

Ekman, Richard, and Stephen Pelletier, "Assessing Student Learning: A Work in Progress." *Change: The Magazine of Higher Learning* 40, no. 4 (2008): 14–19.

Etzioni, Amitai. *The Spirit of Community: The Reinvention of American Society*. Touchstone. New York: Simon & Schuster, 1994.

Ewell, Peter T. "Power in Numbers: The Values in Our Metrics." *Change: The Magazine of Higher Learning* 37, no. 4 (2005): 10–23.

Feldman, Kenneth A., and Theodore M. Newcomb. *The Impact of College on Students.* San Francisco: Jossey-Bass, 1969.

Finder, Alan. "Baptist Colleges Scale Back Ties to their Church." *New York Times*, July 22, 2006.

Foster, Richard J., and James Bryan Smith, eds. *Devotional Classics: Selected Readings for Individuals and Groups.* San Francisco: HarperCollins Publishers, 1993.

Gaffney, Jr., Edward McGlynn, and Philip C. Sorensen. *Ascending Liability in Religious and Other Nonprofit Organizations, Mercer Studies in Law and Religion.* Macon, GA: Mercer University Press, 1984.

Gleason, Philip. "The American Background of *Ex corde Ecclesiae*: A Historical Perspective." In *Catholic Universities in Church and Society: A Dialogue on* Ex corde Ecclesiae, edited by John P. Langan, S.J. Washington, DC: Georgetown University Press, 1993, 8.

Goldsen, Rose K., et al. *What College Students Think*. Princeton, NJ: D. Van Nostrand Company, 1960.

Gose, Ben. "A New Survey of 'Good Practices' Could Be an Alternative to Rankings: Colleges Seek Their Own Measures of Quality, But Will Institutions Make the Data Public?" *The Chronicle of Higher Education*, October 22, 1999.

Gray, Michael Loyd. "To: All Search Committees; From: A Stymied Job Seeker." *The Chronicle of Higher Education*, July 2, 1999.

Hauerwas, Stanley. *After Christendom?* Nashville: Abingdon, 1991.

Hauerwas, Stanley, and John H. Westerhoff, eds. *Schooling Christians: "Holy Experiments" in American Education*. Grand Rapids: Wm. B. Eerdmans, 1992.

Hauerwas, Stanley, and William H. Willimon. *Resident Aliens*. Nashville: Abingdon, 1990.

Heft, James L., and Fred P. Pestello. "Hiring Practices in Catholic Colleges and Universities." *Current Issues in Catholic Higher Education* 20, no. 1 (1999): 89–97.

Hobbs, Walter C., and Richard L. Meeth. *Diversity Among Christian Colleges*. Arlington, VA: Studies in Higher Education, 1980.

Hofstadter, Richard. "The Development of Higher Education in America." In *The Development and Scope of Higher Education in the United States*, edited by Richard Hofstadter and C. DeWitt Hardy, 3. New York: Columbia University Press, 1952.

Hoge, Dean R., Benton Johnson, and Donald A. Luidens. *Vanishing Boundaries: The Religion of Mainline Protestant Baby Boomers*. Louisville: Westminster John Knox Press, 1995.

Houle, Cyril O. *Governing Boards: Their Nature and Nurture*. San Francisco: Jossey-Bass, 1989.

Hughes, Richard T., and William B. Adrian, eds. *Models for Christian Higher Education: Strategies for Survival and Success in the Twenty-First Century*. Grand Rapids: Wm. B. Eerdmans, 1997.

Humphreys, Debra. *General Education and American Commitments: A National Report on Diversity Courses and Requirements*. Washington, DC: Association of American Colleges and Universities, 1997.

Jencks, Christopher, and David Riesman. *The Academic Revolution*. Garden City, NY: Doubleday, 1968.

Keller, George. *Academic Strategy: The Management Revolution in American Higher Education*. Baltimore: Johns Hopkins University Press, 1983.

Kennedy, James C., and Caroline J. Simon. *Can Hope Endure? A Historical Case Study in Christian Higher Education*. Grand Rapids: Wm. B. Eerdmans, 2005.

Klein, Stephen P., et al. "An Approach to Measuring Cognitive Outcomes across Higher Education Institutions." *Research in Higher Education* 46, no. 3 (2005): 251.

Kreider, Alan. *The Change of Conversion and the Origin of Christendom*. Eugene, OR: Wipf & Stock, 2007.

Langen, John P., ed. *Catholic University in Church and Society: A Dialogue on* Ex corde Ecclesiae. Washington, DC: Georgetown University Press, 1993.

Larson, Gerald James. "Contra Pluralism." *Soundings* 73, no. 2–3 (1990): 303–326.

Levine, Arthur. "The Campus Divided, and Divided Again," *New York Times*, June 11, 2000.

Litfin, Duane. *Conceiving the Christian College.* Grand Rapids: Wm. B. Eerdmans, 2004.

Lodwick, Hannah. "Largest Baptist Universities Face Watershed Leadership Changes." *Associated Baptist Press*, December 15, 2005, http://www.abpnews.com/index. php?option=com_content&task=view&id=842&Itemid=118.

Lucido, Jerome A., and Morton Owen Schapiro. "Joe, Mauricio, and the Public Trust." *Inside Higher Ed*, February 13, 2009, http://www.insidehighered.com/ views/2009/02/13/lucido.

Lyon, Larry, and Michael Beaty, "Integration, Secularization, and the Two-Spheres View at Religious Colleges." *Christian Scholar's Review* 29, no. 1 (1999).

Magner, Denise K. "The Imminent Surge in Retirements: Colleges Face a Generational Shift as Professors Hired for the Baby Boom Enter Their 60's." *The Chronicle of Higher Education*, March 17, 2000.

Mahoney, Kathleen, John Schmalzbauer, and James Youniss. "Revitalizing Religion in the Academy: Summary of the Evaluation of Lilly Endowment's Initiative on Religion & Higher Education." Indianapolis, IN: Lilly Endowment, 2000.

Marchese, Theodore J., and Jane Fiori Lawrence. *The Search Committee Handbook: A Guide to Recruiting Administrators.* 2nd rev. ed. Sterling, VA: Stylus Publishing, LLC, 2006.

Marsden, George M. "The Soul of the American University: A Historical Overview." In *The Secularization of the Academy*, edited by George M. Marsden and Bradley J. Longfield, 9–45. New York: Oxford University Press, 1992.

_____. *The Soul of the American University: From Protestant Establishment to Established Nonbelief.* New York: Oxford University Press, 1994.

Marsden, George M., and Bradley Longfield, eds. *The Secularization of the Academy.* New York: Oxford University Press, 1992.

Martin, Warren Bryan. *Conformity: Standards and Change in Higher Education.* Edited by Joseph Axelrod and Mervin B. Freedman. The Jossey-Bass Series in Higher Education. San Francisco: Jossey-Bass, 1969.

McClay, Wilfred M. "George Keller: Intellectual Whirlwind." *The Chronicle of Higher Education*, November 23, 2007.

McGrath, Earl J. "Between Jerusalem and Athens: The Position of the Christian Institution." In *Diversity among Christian Colleges*, edited by Walter C. Hobbs and L. Richard Meeth, 70–83. Arlington, VA: Studies in Higher Education, 1980.

McMurtrie, Beth. "Pluralism and Prayer under One Roof." *The Chronicle of Higher Education*, December 3, 1999.

Mead-Fox, David. "Tackling the Leadership Scarcity." *The Chronicle of Higher Education*, April 15, 2009.

Mead, Loren B. *The Once and Future Church.* New York: The Alban Institute, 1991.

Meyer, Albert J., and David H. Sikkink. "What Does It Profit A College to Add More Students? The Relationship between Enrollment Growth and Financial Strength." *Christian Higher Education* 3 no. 2 (2004): 97–113.

Meyer, John W., and Brian Rowan, "Institutionalized Organizations: Formal Structure as Myth and Ceremony." *American Journal of Sociology* 83, no. 2 (1977): 340–63.

Monsma, Stephen V. *When Sacred and Secular Mix: Religious Nonprofit Organizations and Public Money*. Edited by Allen D. Hertzke Religious Forces in the Modern Political World. Lanham, MD: Rowman & Littlefield Publishers, Inc., 1996.

Monsma, Stephen V., and J. Christopher Soper, eds. *Equal Treatment of Religion in a Pluralistic Society.* Grand Rapids, MI: Wm B. Eerdmans, 1998.

Moots, Philip R., and Edward McGlynn Gaffney Jr. *Church and Campus: Legal Issues in Religiously Affiliated Higher Education*. Notre Dame: University of Notre Dame Press, 1979.

Morgenson, Gretchen. "Are Enrons Bustin' Out All Over?" *New York Times*, May 28, 2006.

Newcomb, Theodore M., et al. *Persistence and Change: Bennington College and Its Students after Twenty-five Years*. New York: John Wiley & Sons, 1967.

Newcomb, Theodore M., and Everett K. Wilson, eds. *College Peer Groups: Problems and Prospects for Research*. National Opinion Research Center Monographs in Social Research. Chicago: Aldine Publishing Company, 1966.

O'Neil, Robert M. "The Ward Churchill Case." *Change: The Magazine of Higher Learning* 38, no. 5 (2006): 37.

Orfield, Gary. "Affirmative Action Works—But Judges and Policy Makers Need to Hear That Verdict." *The Chronicle of Higher Education*, December 10, 1999.

Pace, C. Robert. *Education and Evangelism: A Profile of Protestant Colleges*. Edited by Clark Kerr. The Carnegie Commission on Higher Education. New York: McGraw-Hill, 1972.

Palmer, Parker J. "Truth Is Personal: A Deeply Christian Education." *The Christian Century* 98, no. 33 (1981): 1051-55.

Palmer, Parker J., Barbara G. Wheeler, and James W. Fowler. *Caring for the Commonweal: Education for Religious and Public Life.* Macon, GA: Mercer University Press, 1990.

Parsonage, Robert Rue, ed. *Church Related Higher Education: Perceptions and Perspectives*. Valley Forge: Judson Press, 1978.

Pascarella, Ernest T., and Patrick T. Terenzini. *How College Affects Students: Findings and Insights from Twenty Years of Research*. Edited by Kenneth A. Feldman. The Jossey-Bass Higher and Adult Education Series. San Francisco: Jossey-Bass, 1991.

_____. *How College Affects Students: A Third Decade of Research*. Higher and Adult Education Series. San Francisco: Jossey-Bass, 2005.

Pattillo, Jr., Manning M. and Donald M. Mackenzie. *Church-Sponsored Higher Education in the United States: Report of the Danforth Commission*. Washington, DC: American Council on Education, 1966.

_____. *Eight Hundred Colleges Face The Future: A Preliminary Report of the Danforth Commission on Church Colleges and Universities.* Saint Louis: The Danforth Foundation, 1965.

Pulley, John L. "Eyes Wide Shut: How Eckerd's'52 Trustees Failed to See Two-Thirds of Its Endowment Disappear." *The Chronicle of Higher Education*, August 18, 2000.

_____. "Public Universities' Ambitious Campaigns Vex Many Small Private Institutions." *The Chronicle of Higher Education*, December 3, 1999.

Putnam, Robert D. *Bowling Alone: The Collapse and Revival of American Community*. New York: Simon and Schuster, 2000.

Raffel, Stanley. "Some Effects of Columbia College on its Students." New York: Columbia University, 1965.

Reisberg, Leo. "Independent Report in 1997 Assailed Substance of 'U.S. News' College Rankings." *Today's News, The Chronicle of Higher Education*, August 28, 2000.

Riesman, David. "The Academic Procession." In Riesman, *Constraint and Variety in American Education*, 25–65. Lincoln: University of Nebraska Press, 1956.

Riley, Naomi Schaefer. *God on the Quad: How Religious Colleges and the Missionary Generation Are Changing America.* New York: St. Martin's Press, 2005.

Samuelson, Robert J. "The Worthless Ivy League?" *Newsweek*, November 1, 1999, 45.

Sandin, Robert T. "A Taxonomy of Religiously Affiliated Higher Education." In Robert T. Sandin, *Autonomy and Faith: Religious Preference in Employment Decisions in Religiously Affiliated Higher Education.* Atlanta: Omega Publications, 1990.

Schaper, Donna. "Me-First 'Spirituality' Is a Sorry Substitute for Organized Religion on Campuses." *The Chronicle of Higher Education*, August 18, 2000.

Schlabach, Theron F. "Goshen College and Its Church Relations: History and Reflections." In *Models for Christian Higher Education: Strategies for Success in the Twenty-First Century*, edited by Richard T. Hughes and William B. Adrian, 200–221. Grand Rapids: Wm. B. Eerdmans, 1997.

Schmidt, Peter. "Promoting Students' Moral Development Is Devilishly Tricky, Studies Suggest." *Today's News*, *The Chronicle of Higher Education,* April 14, 2009.

_____. "Q & A: Researcher Describes Mixed Educational Benefits of Campus Diversity." *The Chronicle of Higher Education*, February 17, 2009.

Schwartz, John. "U.S. Is Urged to Lift Ban on Foreign Scholars." *New York Times*, March 18, 2009.

Scott, W. Richard. *Organizations: Rational, Natural, and Open Systems*. 5th ed. Upper Saddle River, NJ: Prentice Hall, 2003.

Sider, Ronald J. *The Scandal of the Evangelical Conscience: Why Are Christians Living Just like the Rest of the World?* Grand Rapids: Baker Books, 2005.

Sikkink, David. "Conservative Protestants, Schooling, and Democracy." In *Evangelicals and Democracy in America; Volume 1: Religion and Society*, edited by Steven Brint and Jean Reith Schroedel. New York: Russell Sage Foundation, forthcoming.

Sloan, Douglas. *Faith and Knowledge: Mainline Protestantism and American Higher Education*. Louisville, KY: Westminster John Knox Press, 1994.

Smith, Christian. *The Secular Revolution: Power, Interests, and Conflict in the Secularization of American Public Life.* Berkeley: University of California Press, 2003.

Smith, Daryl G., et al. *Diversity Works: The Emerging Picture of How Students Benefit*. Washington, DC: Association of American Colleges and Universities, 1997.

Steinfels, Peter. *A People Adrift: The Crisis of the Roman Catholic Church in America*. New York: Simon & Schuster, 2004.

Stoltzfus, Victor. *Church-Affiliated Higher Education: Exploratory Case Studies.* Goshen, IN: Pinchpenny Press, 1992.

Thomas, Cal, and Ed Dobson. *Blinded by Might: Can the Religious Right Save America?* Grand Rapids: Zondervan Publishing House, 1999.

Trainor, Stephen L. "A Delicate Balance: The Catholic College in America." *Change: The Magazine of Higher Learning*, March/April 2006, 14–21.

Turner, Caroline Sotello Viernes. *Diversifying the Faculty: A Guidebook for Search Committees*. Washington, DC: Association of American Colleges and Universities, 2002.

U.S. Department of Education. "A Test of Leadership: Charting the Future of U.S. Higher Education." Washington, DC: 2006.

Wergin, Jon F. "Higher Education: Waking Up to the Importance of Accreditation." *Change: The Magazine of Higher Learning* 37, no. 3, May/June 2005: 35–49.

Widmer, Candace, and Susan Houchin. *The Art of Trusteeship: The Nonprofit Board Member's Guide to Effective Governance*. The Jossey-Bass Nonprofit and Public Management Series. San Francisco: Jossey-Bass, Inc., 2000.

Wilson, Robin. "A Hothouse for Female Scientists." *The Chronicle of Higher Education*, May 5, 2006.

Wink, Walter. *Engaging the Powers: Discernment and Resistance in a World of Domination*. Minneapolis, MN: Fortress Press, 1992.

Winston, Gordon C., and David J. Zimmerman, "Where Is Aggressive Price Competition Taking Higher Education?" *Change: The Magazine of Higher Learning* 32, no. 4, July/August 2000: 10–18.

Wittberg, Patricia. *From Piety to Professionalism—And Back? Transformations of Organized Religious Virtuosity*. Lanham, MD: Lexington Books, 2006.

Wolterstorff, Nicholas. "The Schools We Deserve." In *Schooling Christians: "Holy Experiments" in American Education.* eds. Stanley Hauerwas and John H. Westerhoff, 3–28. Grand Rapids: Wm. B. Eerdmans, 1992.

Wuthnow, Robert. *The Struggle for America's Soul: Evangelicals, Liberals, and Secularism.* Grand Rapids: Wm. B. Eerdmans, 1989.

Yoder, John H. *The Legacy of Michael Sattler*. Edited by Cornelius J. Dyck. Classics of the Radical Reformation. Scottdale, PA: Herald Press, 1973.

Zammuto, Raymond F. "Are the Liberal Arts an Endangered Species?" *Journal of Higher Education* 55, no. 2 (1984): 184–211.

The Author

Albert J. Meyer has been a physicist, an academic administrator, and a student of American and Christian higher education. He served for many years as chief executive officer of the Mennonite Board of Education and as an educational coordinator with the Committee on Liberal Arts Education of the North Central Association of Colleges and Secondary Schools. He has been a long-time member and was, at one time, chair of the Executives for Church-Related Higher Education group, whose members represent most of the denominational and church-affiliated institutions in the United States.

Reared in northern Ohio, Meyer did his undergraduate studies at Goshen College and his doctoral work at Princeton University. He had research leaves at the universities in Basel, Switzerland; Paris, France; Berkeley, California; and Princeton, New Jersey. He served for three years in assignments for the Mennonite Central Committee in Central Europe and made shorter visits to service units elsewhere in Europe, Africa, the Subcontinent, and China. He and his wife, Mary Ellen, have five married children. They live in Goshen, Indiana.